IMAGES
of America

HIGHTSTOWN AND EAST WINDSOR

Acknowledgments

Current and former residents have been more than generous and helpful to us as we collected images, compiled anecdotes, and composed captions for this publication. Particular thanks is due to those who opened their personal and family records and photograph albums as well as to those who assisted us in identifying individuals, buildings, and locations.

Donors' assistance has been acknowledged in parentheses following the applicable captions.

We are particularly indebted to Richard S. Hutchinson of the Hightstown-East Windsor Historical Society for his unselfish assistance and constructive suggestions. He has provided guidance in locating archival records and has served as an invaluable reference in verifying historical data.

Cover photograph: THOMAS & TAYLOR (*c.* 1904). The older man in the doorway is probably Mr. Thomas. By 1906 James A. Taylor had bought out Thomas' interest in the general tin and stove business, which also included plumbing and slate roofing. Taylor, who married Annie E. Cox in 1906, was born on an East Windsor farm where Lockheed-Martin is located today. (Vinton and Maribelle Taylor)

IMAGES
of America

HIGHTSTOWN AND EAST WINDSOR

Peggy S. and Frank J. Brennan, Jr.

ARCADIA
PUBLISHING

ISBN 978-0-7385-7233-8

Published by Arcadia Publishing
Charleston, South Carolina

Printed in the United States of America

Library of Congress Catalog Card Number: 2009932644

For all general information contact Arcadia Publishing at:
Telephone 843-853-2070
Fax 843-853-0044
E-mail sales@arcadiapublishing.com
For customer service and orders:
Toll-Free 1-888-313-2665

Visit us on the Internet at www.arcadiapublishing.com

We dedicate this book to all those who lived, worked, and studied in Hightstown and East Windsor from the towns' beginnings, contributed to their unique heritage, and made these communities what they are today. Specifically, the book is dedicated to the authors' four sons: Kevin Raymond, Francis Joseph III, Patrick Spahr, and Timothy Mills.

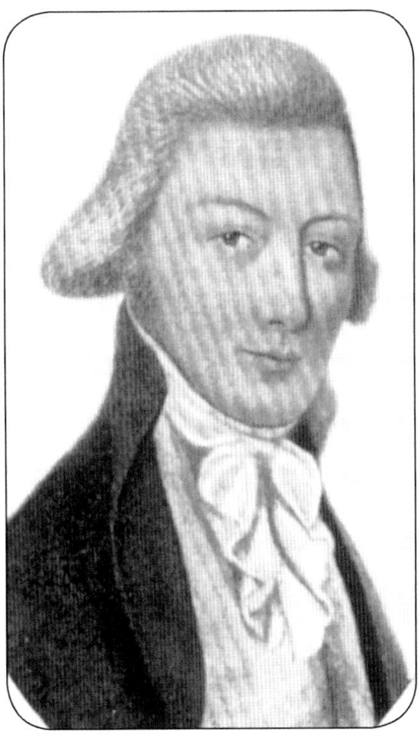

COLONEL JOSEPH HIGHT [*sic*] (*c.* 1780). Colonel Hight was born in 1739, the youngest son of John and Mary Hight, and died in 1795 after having served in the American army with General Daniel Morgan. John and Mary Hight reputedly founded Hightstown in 1721. They settled in this area, having purchased 3,000 acres of land from the British crown. On the north side of Rocky Brook, currently the site of the Hightstown firehouse, they erected a log cabin. Later they built a mill, blacksmith shop, and at least two other buildings nearby. (*Hightstown New Jersey Bicentennial 1721–1921*, Official Program)

Contents

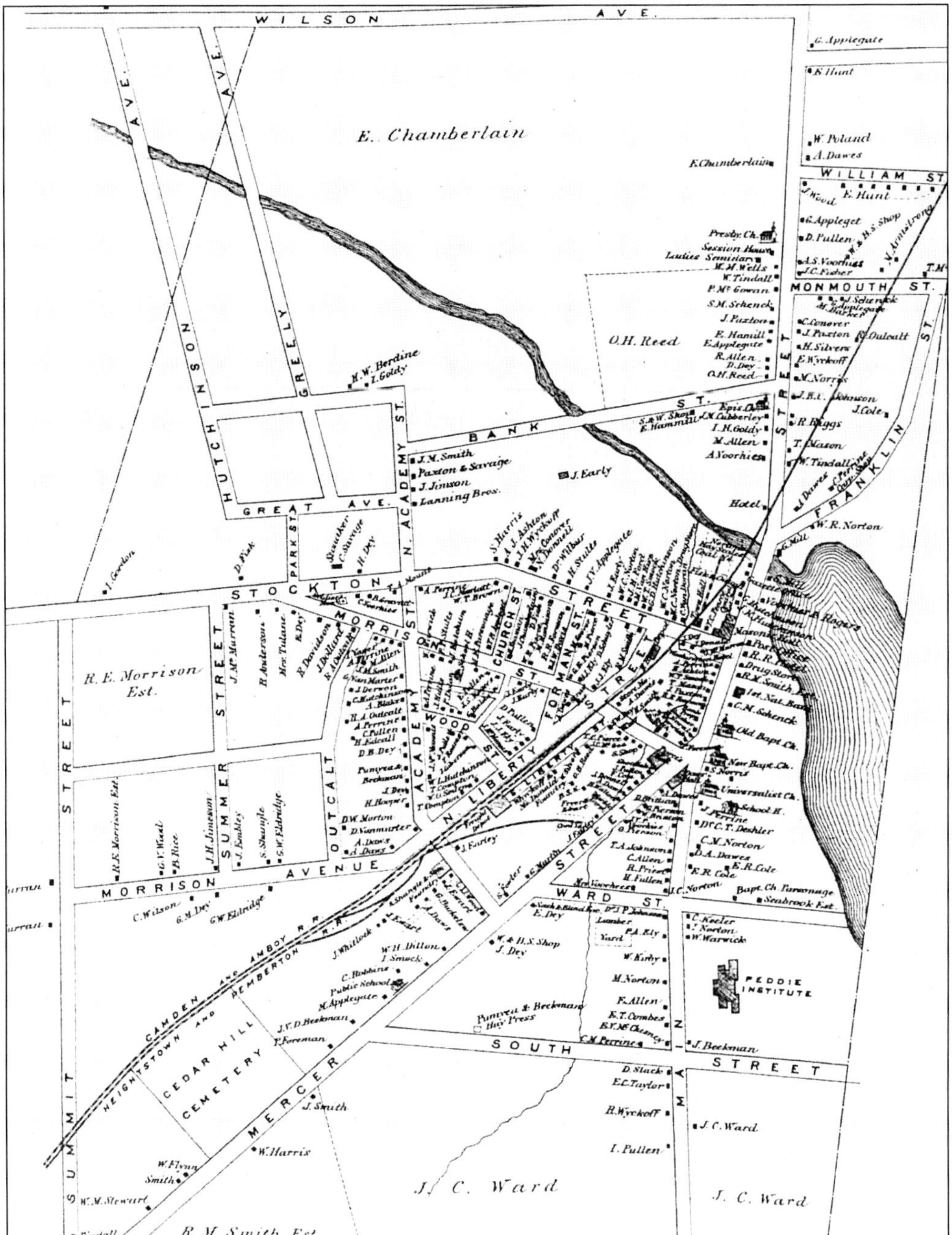
WILSON AVE.
E. Chamberlain
HUTCHINSON AVE.
GREELY AVE.
WILLIAM ST.
MONMOUTH ST.
O.H. Reed
BANK ST.
GREAT AVE.
N. ACADEMY ST.
STOCKTON STREET
MORRIS ST.
CHURCH ST.
FORMAN ST.
FRANKLIN ST.
R. E. Morrison Est.
SUMMER STREET
SUMMIT STREET
OUTCALT
ACADEMY
WOOD ST.
N. LIBERTY ST.
MORRISON AVENUE
CAMDEN AND AMBOY R.R.
HIGHTSTOWN AND PEMBERTON R.R.
CEDAR HILL CEMETERY
MERCER STREET
WARD ST.
MAIN ST.
SOUTH STREET
PEDDIE INSTITUTE
J. C. Ward
R. M. Smith Est.

Hightstown

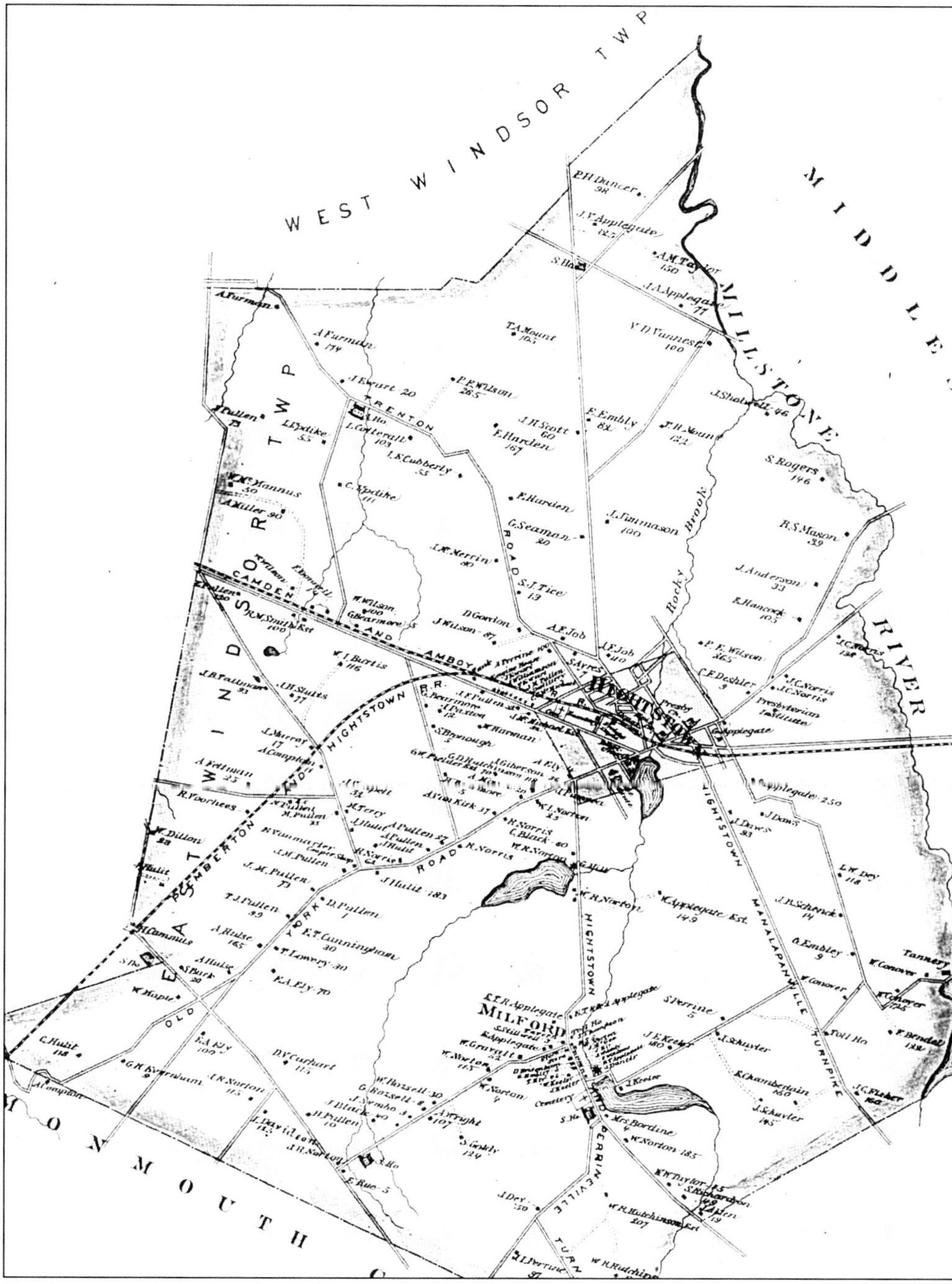

East Windsor

Introduction

This book provides a visual excursion into the history of two contiguous communities, the Borough of Hightstown and the Township of East Windsor. Celebrating its 275th anniversary in 1996, Hightstown is one of the oldest towns in New Jersey. East Windsor Township will commemorate its 200th anniversary in 1997.

At one time Hightstown and East Windsor were the hub of agricultural activity, the center of rural mercantile endeavors, and were famous for their stagecoach stops during early times. Later they would also become well known as a passenger and freight center on newly developed railroad lines. The John Bull, one of the first steam locomotives, saw service here beginning in 1833.

These communities welcomed well-known national figures: Clara Barton taught school here, the Marquis de Lafayette visited before the Battle of Monmouth, Horace Greeley and Phineas T. Barnum attended the Universalist church dedication, and former Vice President Thomas R. Marshall spoke during the celebration of Hightstown's 200th anniversary.

Today the dirt roads and the railroads have disappeared. Little remains of the deeply rooted agricultural heritage. Some of the charming residential buildings have been replaced by structures typical of the last decades of the twentieth century. However, the reader will notice that many well-known family names of bygone years are still familiar today. At present many descendants of these early residents are active in the social, governmental, religious, and educational life of these communities.

This book presents selected glimpses of Hightstown and East Windsor from 1834 to 1950; its sketches, snapshots, and captions attempt to provide the reader with some insights relative to life during these years. Unfortunately, the scope of a book such as this is limited to the period when photography was relatively popular, and essentially excludes the period from the towns' settlement to the middle of the nineteenth century. Also, the limitations of space required our chronological cut-off in 1950; perhaps a sequel could include the last half of the twentieth century.

As Hightstown celebrates its 275th birthday and East Windsor looks toward its 200th anniversary, we anticipate that the book will launch an imaginative trip into the past for those too young to recognize the subjects of these images. At the same time we hope that this collection will provide a nostalgic recall for those who lived in these communities during the period encompassed by the book.

Note: Unless otherwise stated, identifications of individuals in captions are in the usual order, from left to right.

One

1834 to 1879

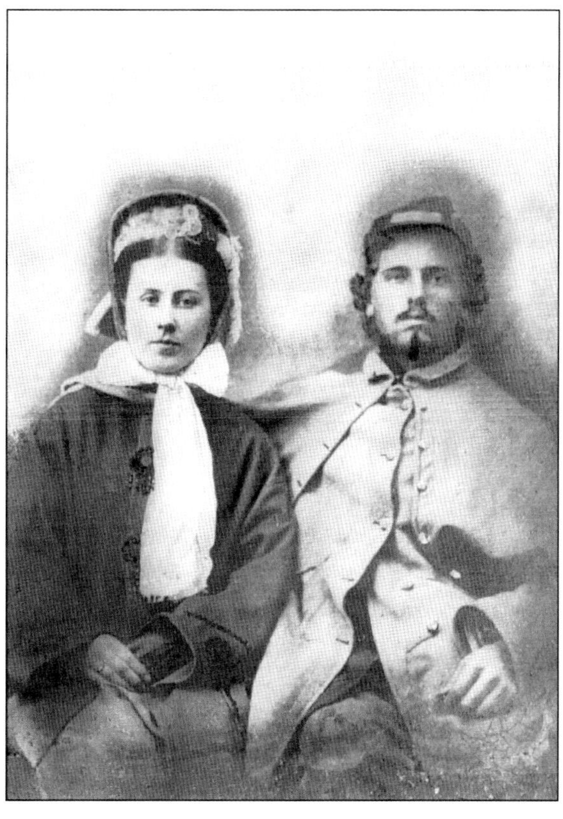

A WARM REUNION (1863). George Washington Conover (1843–1926) returned to Hightstown in January from duty in Washington, DC, and posed for this photograph with his future wife, Emeline Hutchinson Hudnek; they were married in 1865. George then returned to the front along the Potomac. He was a member of the Union forces that witnessed the surrender of General Lee to General Grant at the Appomattox Court House on April 9, 1865. (Brenda Dey MacMurray)

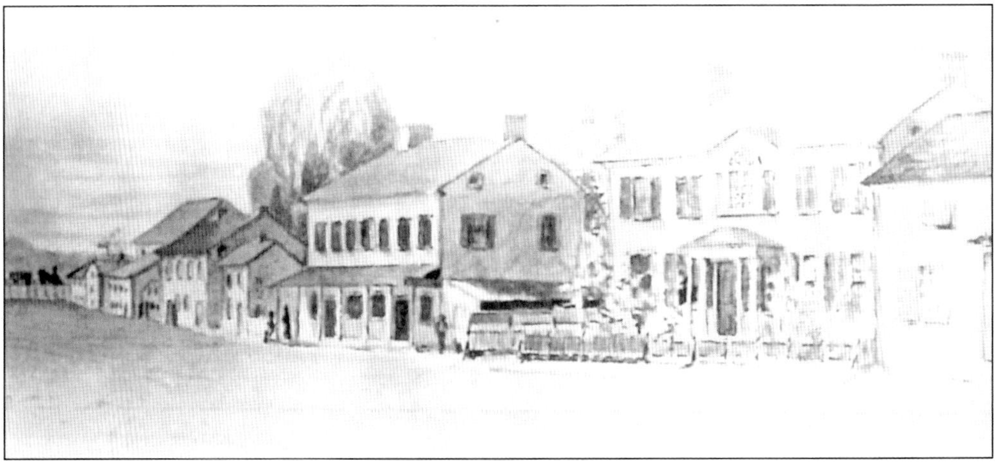

CENTER OF HIGHTSTOWN (1834). Mrs. Eliza P. McChesney, widow of Dr. Charles G. McChesney, the New Jersey secretary of state from 1840 to 1851, made this pencil sketch of the eastern side of Main Street. At that time Hightstown contained six stores, a grist and a sawmill, and five hundred inhabitants. Shown from the left are: the miller's house; a fulling mill, which adjoined the gristmill, the roof of which may be seen in the rear; Andrew Segar's tin shop, which later became a residence; Segar's house; "Aunty Purdy's" house where she sold homemade cakes, candies, and root beer; the hotel kept by David Perrine; the residence of Mrs. McChesney; and the store of R.M. Smith (the latter two buildings were destroyed by fire in 1838 in a blaze started by an explosion of gunpowder in the store's attic). (Hightstown-East Windsor Historical Society)

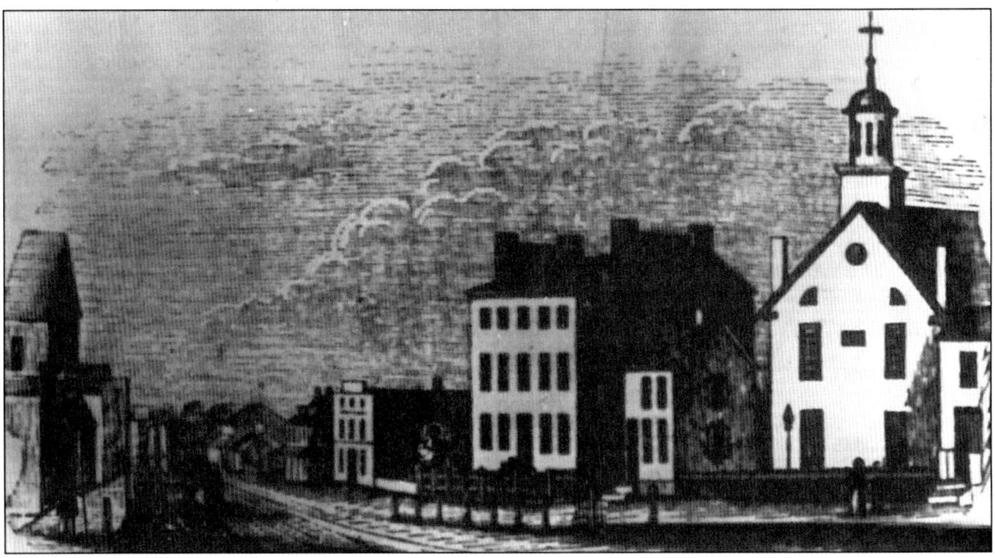

MAIN STREET (1840). The Baptist church, at right, was established in Cranbury in 1745—the seventh Baptist church to be established in New Jersey. In 1785 the congregation moved to Hightstown and built a meetinghouse where the Eaches Memorial Chapel stands today. In 1842 Hightstown had six stores, a grist and a sawmill, a variety of mechanics, Methodist, Baptist, and Universalist churches, an academy, from eighty to one hundred dwellings, and a population of approximately five hundred. In 1841 a local store sold: calicoes at 25¢ per yard; coffees at 13¢ a pound; teas at $1 per pound; butter at 34¢ a pound; eggs at 5¢ a dozen; palm hats for 25¢ each; and pairs of boots for $5. (Hightstown-East Windsor Historical Society)

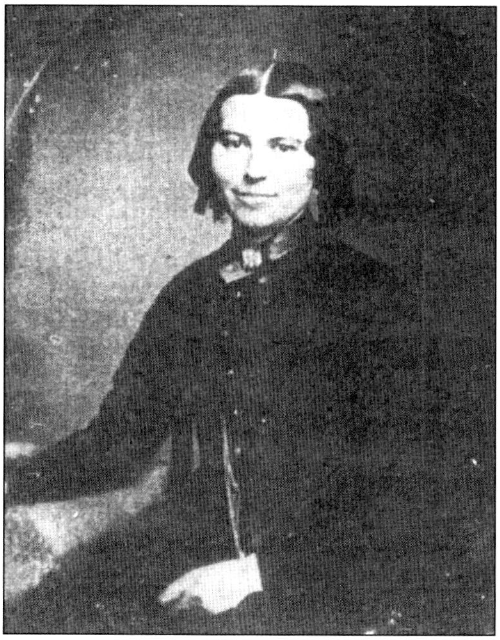

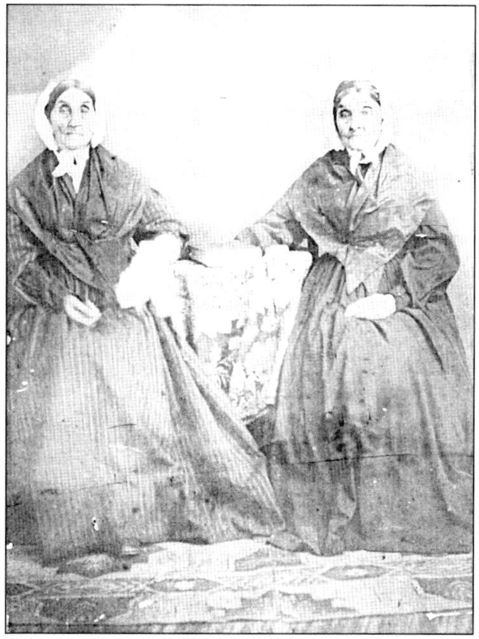

CLARA BARTON (c. 1851). Clarissa Harlowe Barton (1821–1912), founder and first president of the American Red Cross, taught at the Cedarville Road School in East Windsor Township from 1851 to 1852. During the Civil War she met one of her former students, Hart Bodine, on a Virginia battlefield. (Hightstown-East Windsor Historical Society)

SISTERS (1850s). Rebecca Holman Rue (1777–1871) and Ann Holman Perrine (1775–1870) were two of the nine daughters of Joseph and Nancy Holman. All of the girls married and raised large families: Rebecca married William Rue and Ann married Enoch Perrine. Family members traveled to Cranbury to attend the First Presbyterian Church. (Hightstown-East Windsor Historical Society)

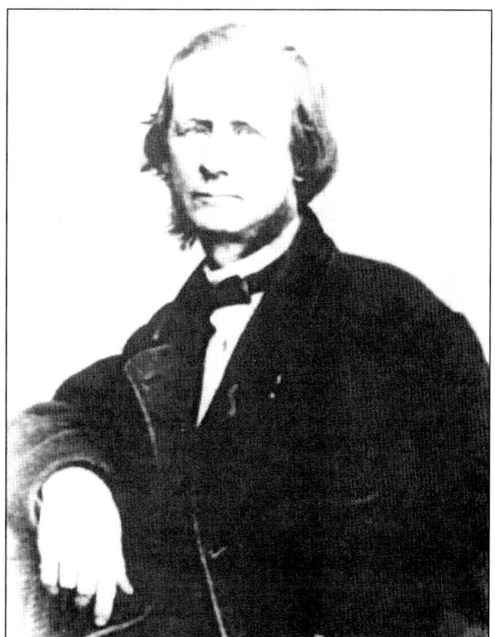

CLARK S. HUTCHINSON (c. 1858). Born in the spring of 1824, Clark was the son of John Tindall and Elizabeth D. (Ward) Hutchinson. After his marriage in the fall of 1848, Clark was listed in the 1850 census as a wheelwright, and in the 1860 census as a lawyer with offices in Hightstown and Burlington. From 1853 to 1855 he served as Hightstown's tax assessor. He held a U.S. patent for a machine that made tags. (Richard S. Hutchinson)

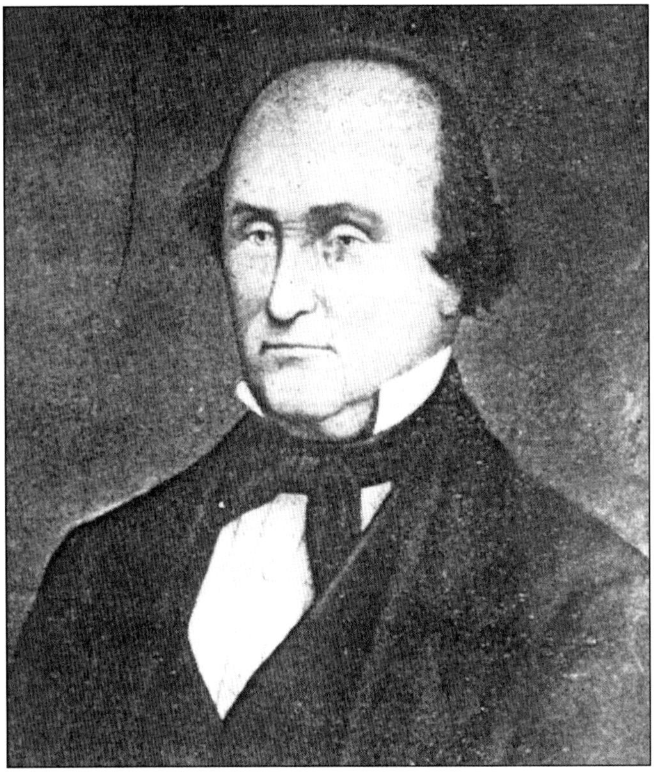

BENJAMIN REED (1850s). In 1834 thought was being given to fire protection in Hightstown, and one of the town's leading citizens, Benjamin Reed (1808-1864), negotiated in Princeton for an old hand-pumped fire engine, securing it in trade for a mule. It is recorded that the deal was not a great success for the "engine proved as balky as the mule." For Reed, an experienced dealer in horses and mules, the trade necessitated a 9-mile walk to Princeton. Sixteen years later, a fire company was organized in Hightstown. ("One Hundredth Anniversary Engine Company No. 1, Hightstown, N. J.," 1935)

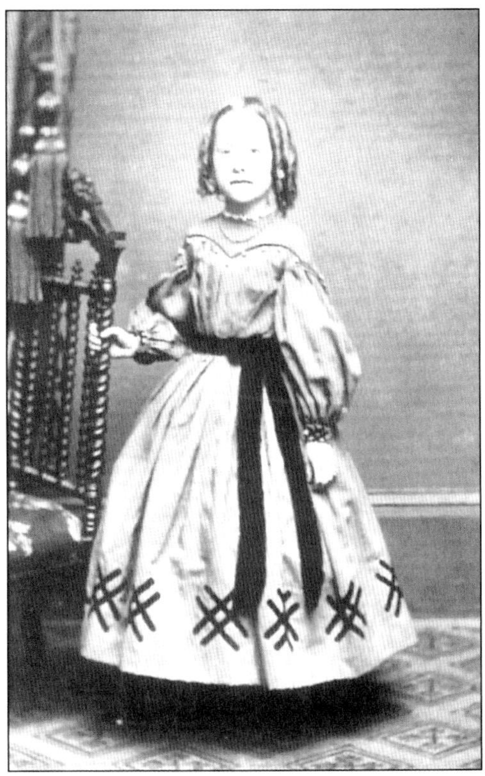

PORTRAIT OF A TEN YEAR OLD (1865). Addie A. Walling, born in 1855, was the daughter of Mr. and Mrs. Augustus Walling. Her curls and long dress are typical of the Civil War era. She married Runey R. Forman, Jr. in May of 1881 and remained in Hightstown until her death in 1937. An organist at the Methodist church for thirty years, Addie was the composer of more than three hundred hymns, children's songs, and musical pieces. It was under the name R.R. Forman that much of her work was written. Not even her publishers knew that she was a woman. (Hightstown-East Windsor Historical Society)

AUGUSTUS WALLING (*c*. 1866). A house-painter by trade and one of the best-known citizens of the community, Augustus (1818–1890) married Elizabeth Davison of Dutch Neck on February 24, 1842. His obituary stated that his advertisement as a painter appeared in the first issue of *The Village Record* and remained in the columns of local papers as long as he was in business. He was one of the founders of what is now known as the Cedar Hill Cemetery. (Hightstown-East Windsor Historical Society)

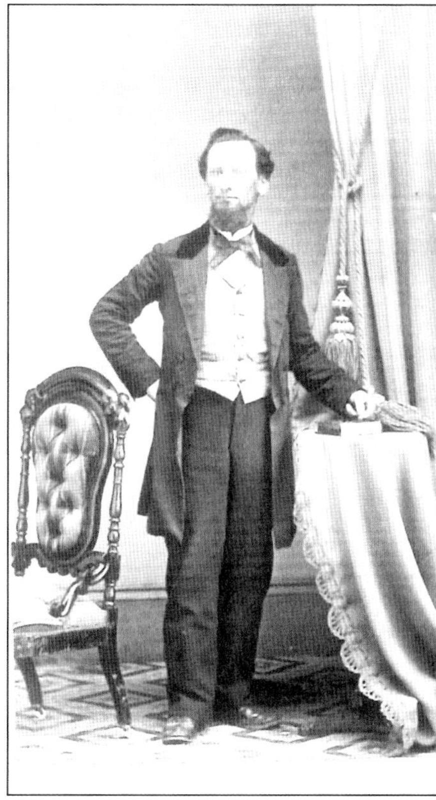

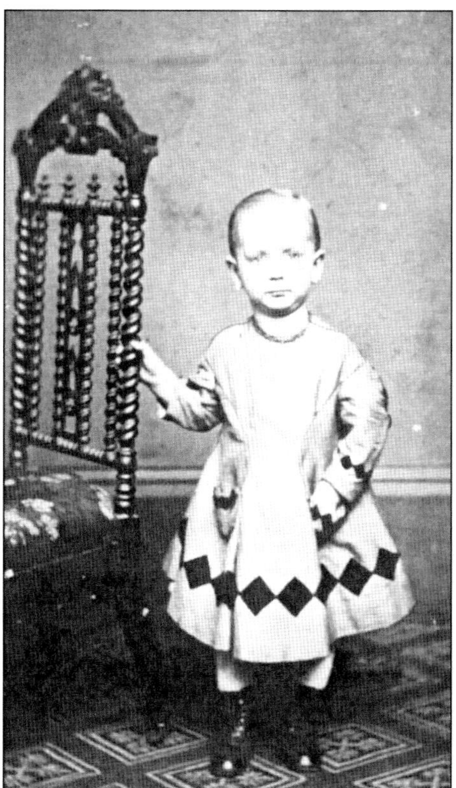

CHARLES E. STULTS (*c*. 1866). Charles E. was born in Prospect Plains in 1864, the only son of Cornelius Bodine Stults and Amanda Silvers Stults. After attending Cranbury's Brainerd Institute, he clerked at the general store of Mason & Allen in Hightstown before taking a position as salesman with J.S. Silvers & Brother in Cranbury (his mother's brother's business). He met Adelaide Bennett of Cranbury here, whom he later married. After moving to Hightstown, Charles began a partnership with John E. Allen, who was married to Laura Silvers (Mr. Stults' mother's sister). Allen and Stults—who began as undertakers—purchased the insurance business of Edward Cunningham in 1893 and became "Allen & Stults Co.-Insurance, Real Estate, Commissioners of Deeds, Settlers of Estates, Notary Public, Investors of Money" as well as undertakers. Charles E., who died in 1917, was the Hightstown borough collector, a board of education member, the custodian of school funds, postmaster, and an active Baptist, Mason, and Republican committeeman. (C. Stults Family-Allen & Stults Collection)

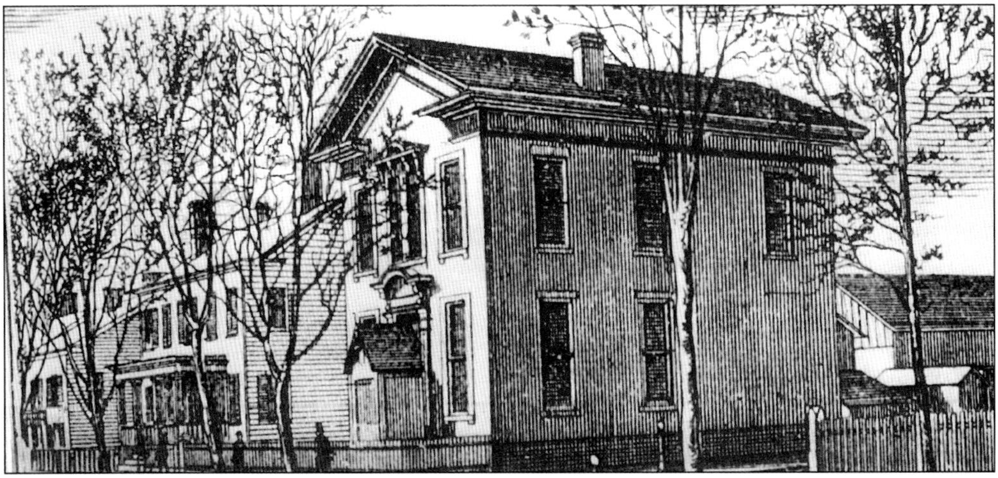

EARLY LOCATION OF CENTRAL BANK (1860s). The Central Bank of New Jersey in Hightstown was established as a state bank in 1852 in a building on the southwest corner of North Main and Bank Streets. The Reverend R.E. Morrison was elected president and T. Appleget, cashier. This pen-and-ink sketch was undoubtedly done before the bank moved and the building became the Episcopal church in 1869. The congregation diminished after World War II and the structure was torn down in 1950. In the photograph, the Ely House, currently the location of the Hightstown-East Windsor Historical Society, is adjacent to the bank. (Norris Robbins Collection)

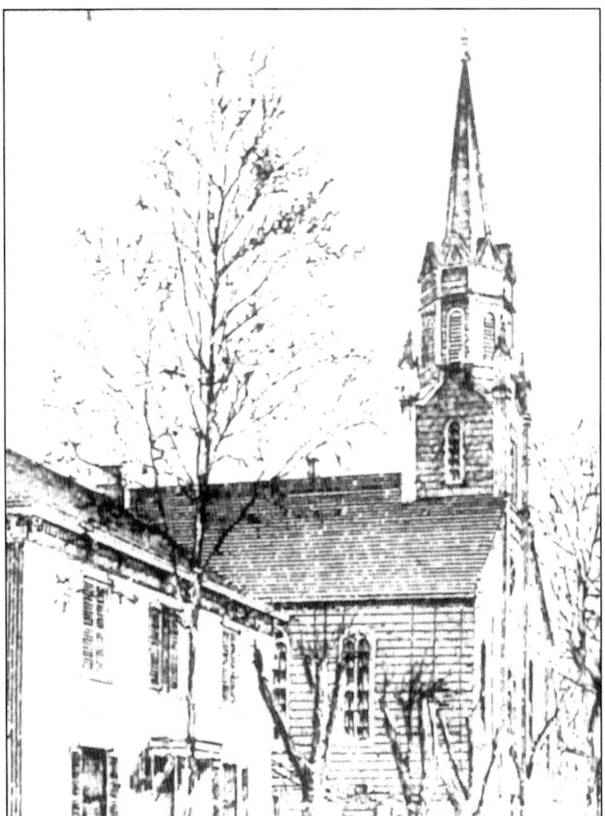

EARLY METHODIST CHURCH (1860s). This pen-and-ink rendering shows the first two buildings used by the Methodists. The building in the rear burned in 1929; the one in the foreground is currently 171–173 Stockton Street. In 1835 the congregation moved from Etra to a brick church they had built on the corner of Stockton and Church Streets. In 1857 they erected a church at the rear of the original brick building. This church was abandoned in 1899 in favor of the present stone church built the same year. After the 1857 church burned in 1929, some of the old-timers shook their heads and declared that it was a "judgment" because the Methodists had sold it to M.P. Chamberlain for use as an opera house (rather than a building dedicated to the service of God). (Hightstown-East Windsor Historical Society)

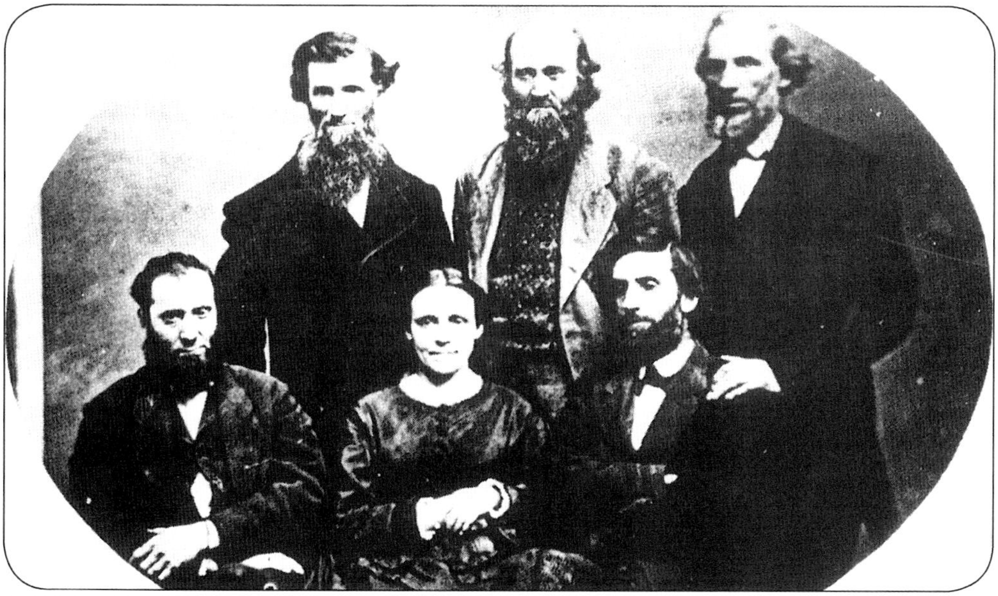

RICHARD NORTON FAMILY (1860s). During the 1851–52 school year, Clara Barton taught at the Cedarville Road School and lived with this family on Windsor-Perrineville Road. The Nortons had seven children, one of whom died in infancy. The six remaining children are: (front row) Charles (a student of Clara, later the editor of the Universalist publication, *The Hightstown Excelsior*), James (architect for the 1869 Universalist church), and Mary (the youngest child and only daughter, who was instrumental in having Clara Barton live with the family); (back row) Wyckoff (grandfather of Grace Norton Rogers), William R., and Joshua N. (builder of the remarkable Norton Tower in the Ely Cemetery). Charles' *Excelsior* battled the Baptist-inspired publication, *The Hightstown Gazette*, for many years. (*The Princeton Recollector*)

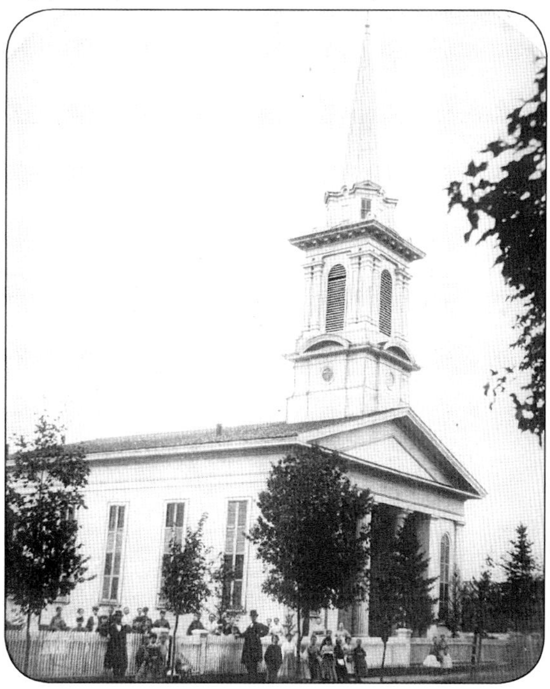

OLD FIRST CHURCH (1869). Gathered outside the First Presbyterian Church (1857–1930) are Dr. John McClusky and his students at the Hightstown Young Ladies Seminary, founded in 1864. The group used the Session House at left on weekdays. The gentleman at the right (also in a beaver top hat) is believed to be Dr. Jesse B. Davis, the church pastor from 1869 to 1887. The stables of the Hightstown station on one of the New York to Philadelphia stage lines were once located where the First Presbyterian Church stands today. (Hightstown-East Windsor Historical Society)

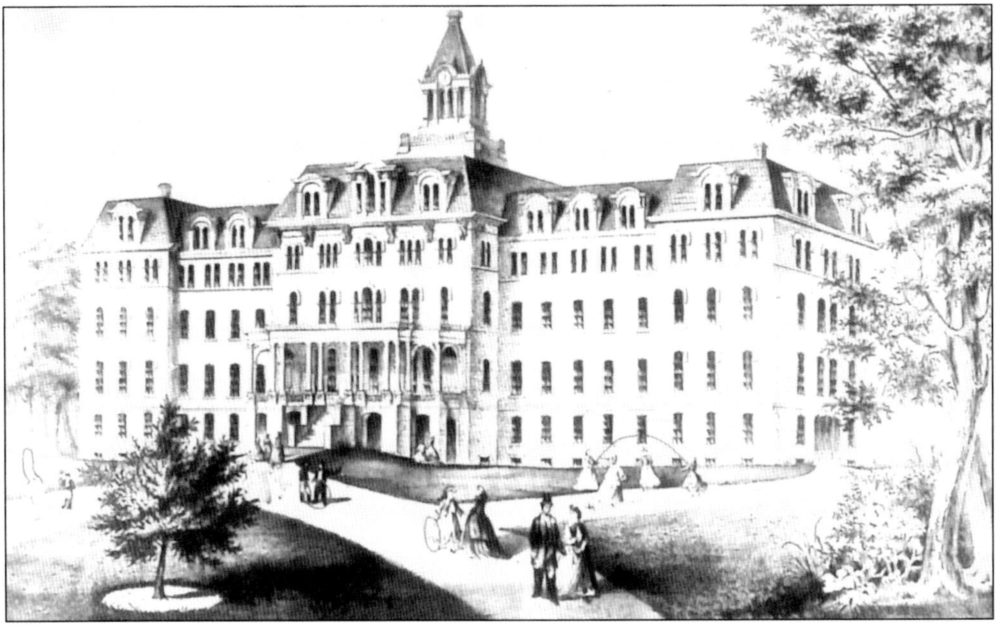

WILSON HALL (1869). Hoop-rolling and rope-skipping are enjoyed by students of The New Jersey Classical and Scientific Institute, which later became The Peddie School. The building had room for 150 students and 10 masters. It was constructed in 1866 and named for William B. Wilson, president of the board of corporators at that time. (Hightstown-East Windsor Historical Society)

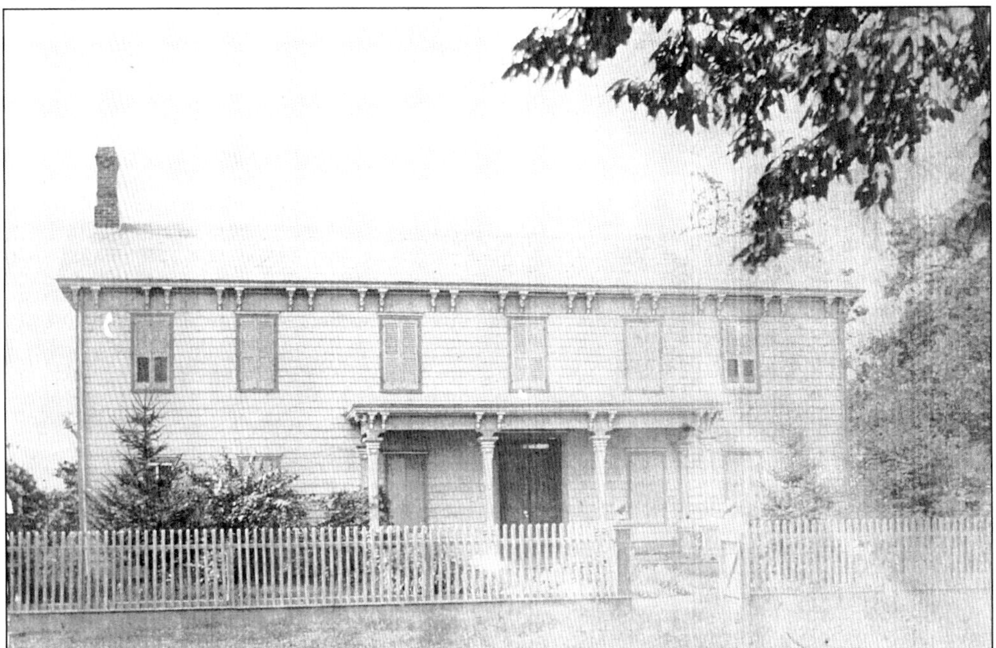

LEE FARMHOUSE (c. 1870). Bought by the Lee family in 1868, the house had been built in two sections—the left part about 1802 and the other side about 1830. It was one of the first farms to have running water (in 1908), electricity, and central heat. (The Lee Family)

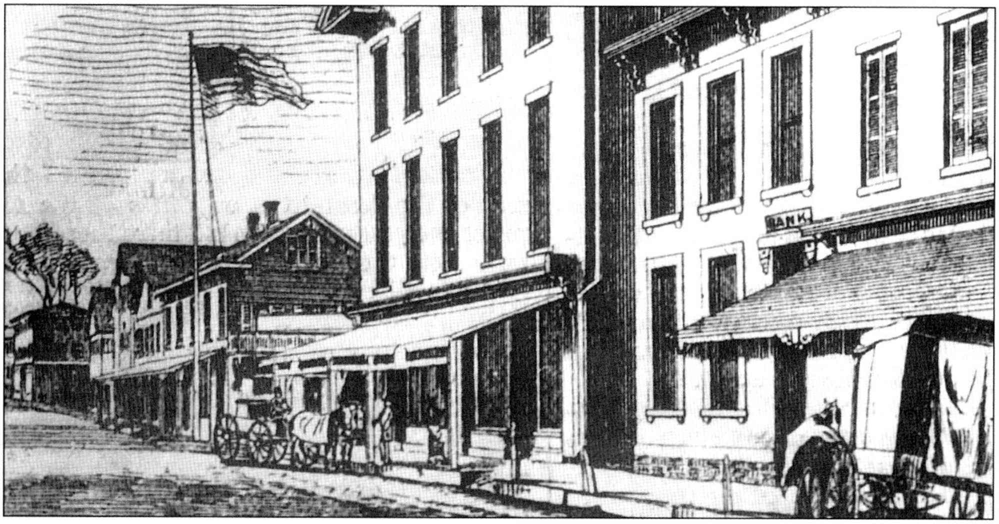

WEST SIDE OF MAIN STREET (early 1870s). The building to the rear of the flagpole was the Britton Tavern in the early 1800s and the Washington Hotel, owned and kept by Alfred Smith, during the mid-1800s (it is currently the site of Cunningham's). To reach the barroom on the second floor of the rickety Britton Tavern, patrons were obliged to ascend a broad flight of stairs. The bank on the right, established in 1852 at Bank and North Main Streets, moved to this location in 1869 when it was organized as a national bank. In 1879 its assets were liquidated and consolidated with those of The First National Bank. The three-story building in the center is currently the site of Allen & Stults Company. (Norris Robbins Collection)

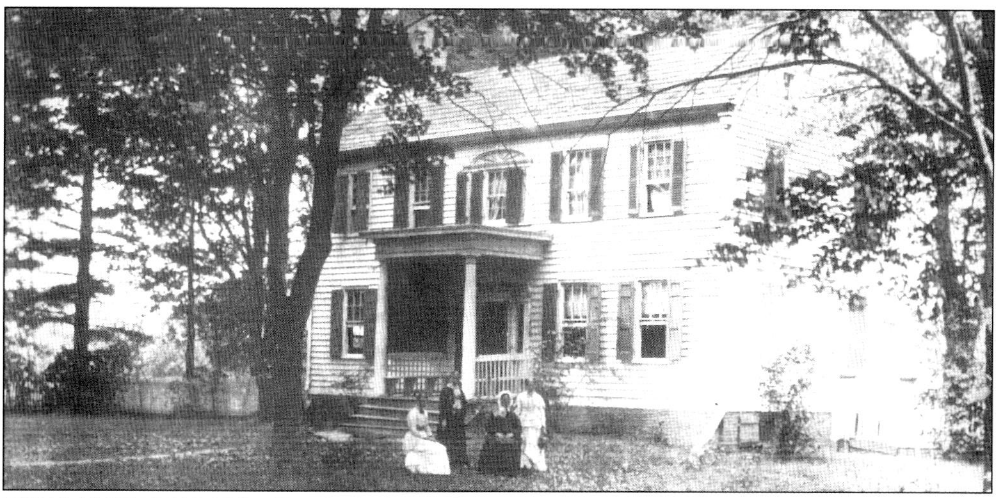

THE MORRISON HOMESTEAD (1870s). Mrs. Robert E. Morrison (Martha Swift) (1799–1896), with lace bonnet, poses with three of her daughters in front of the Morrison Homestead, currently 234 Morrison Avenue. Originally from Pennsylvania, Martha was born in the same house in which Robert Fulton was born in 1765. She and the Reverend Morrison (1800–1873) purchased the Hightstown homestead and many adjacent acres in the 1840s. A "retired" Methodist minister, Morrison was a financial and community leader. The couple had five daughters: Margaret Swift (1829–1897), Elizabeth E. (1830–1911), Hester Ann (1833–1890), Mary Swift (1835?–1854), and Martha Jane (1838–1923). Several of the Morrison daughters were gifted musicians and music teachers. The authors of this book currently reside in this home. (The Frank J. Brennan, Jr. Family)

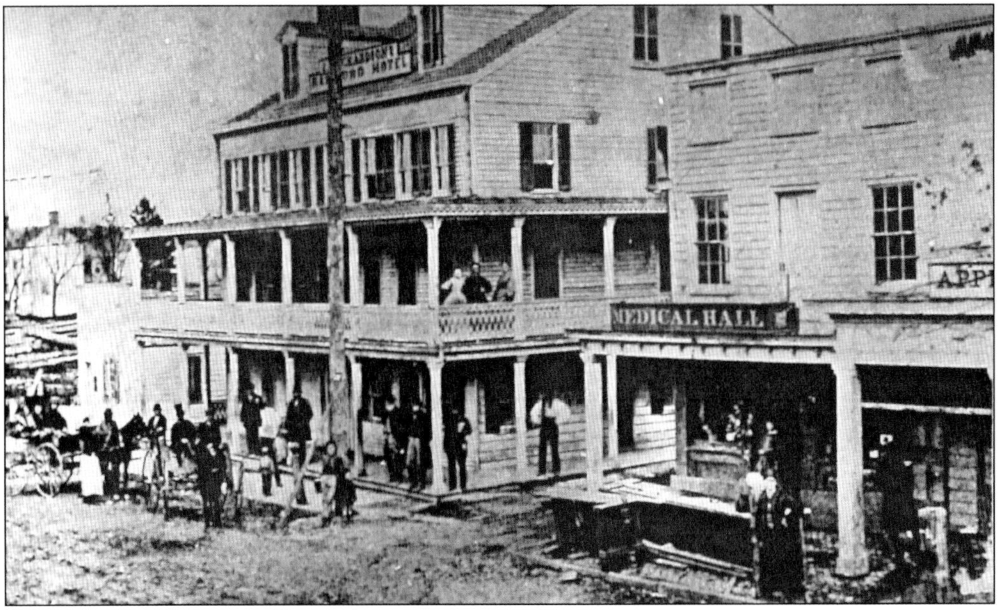

J. RICHARDSON'S RAILROAD HOTEL (*c*. 1876). Built in 1783, the hotel was known for much of the 1800s as the "Railroad Hotel." Visitors and locals are shown gathered around the "political pole." Richardson's was also a stop on the stage run between Princeton and Freehold. Logs for use at the adjacent sawmill may be seen on the left. In 1850, Rescarrick M. Smith (1804–1865), treasurer of the State of New Jersey for fifteen years, owned the hotel shown here. An Irish servant girl wrote to her mother, "I live in Hightstown with the R.M. Smith family. He keeps a large hotel. I like it here very much indeed. I get five dollars a month, which is two dollars more than I got at the other place." (Hightstown-East Windsor Historical Society)

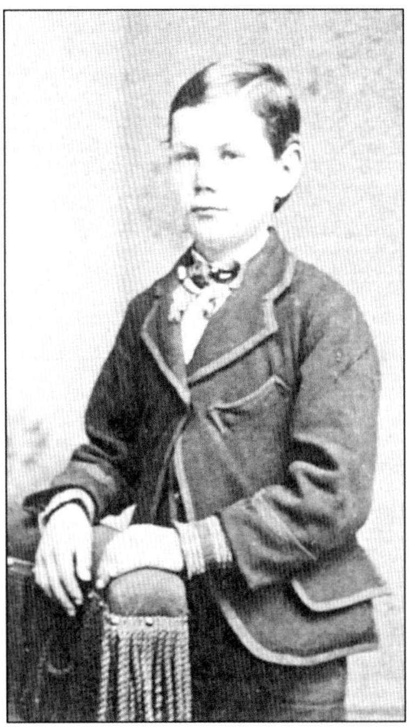

WALTER C. BLACK (*c*. 1877). Born on Valentine's Day in 1867 to Joseph H. and Sarah Shinn Black, Walter Black died in August 1962 at the age of ninety-five. It is anyone's guess as to what is contained in his left-hand jacket pocket! Village Nurseries, begun in 1853 by Walter's father, is operated today by family member Joseph Black Locke. Walter C. built his home on the current site of the Peddie Golf Course. William Thompson, C. Stanley Stults (Walter's son-in-law), Walter, and a few other local businessmen built the golf course and presented it to Peddie during the Depression of the 1930s. A Peddie graduate, Black later became a member of the school's board of trustees, served on the local board of education for fifty-six years (part of that time as board president), and was honored by having a local elementary school named after him. In 1961, at the age of ninety-four, Mr. Black resigned as the East Windsor tax collector, a position he had held for fifty-nine years. At that time, he was the oldest tax collector in the country and had a 100% collection rate, many times paying residents' taxes himself. (C. Stults Family-Allen & Stults Collection)

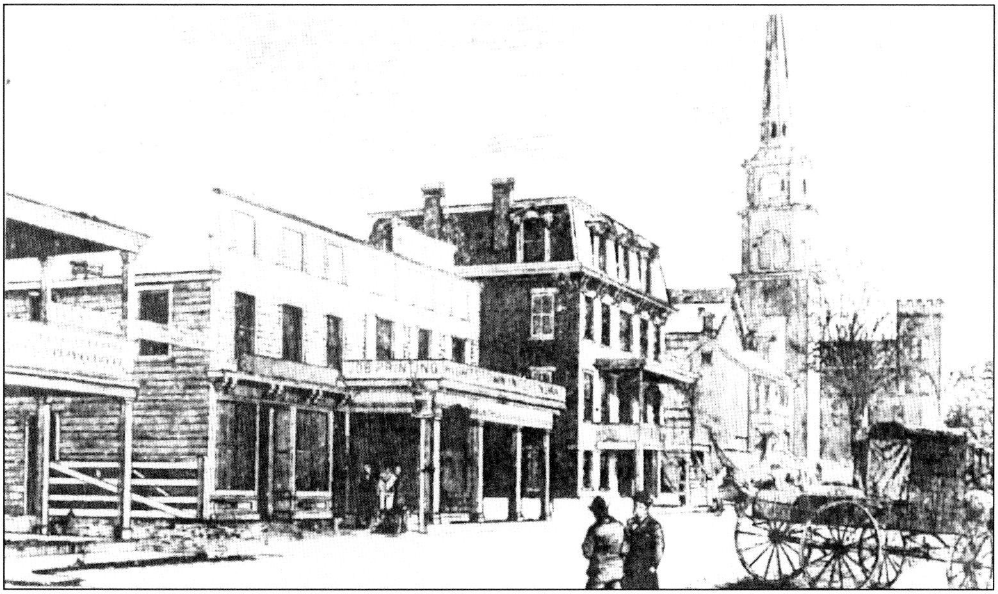

ARTIST'S SKETCH OF DOWNTOWN (1879). This artist's rendering of the east side of Main Street shows a portion of the Railroad Hotel at the left and next to it the entrance to the livery stables. At the right are two churches: the Baptist, built in 1859, and the Universalist, built in 1871. The First National Bank was located in the three-story Smith Building from 1870 to 1879. (C. Stults Family-Allen & Stults Collection)

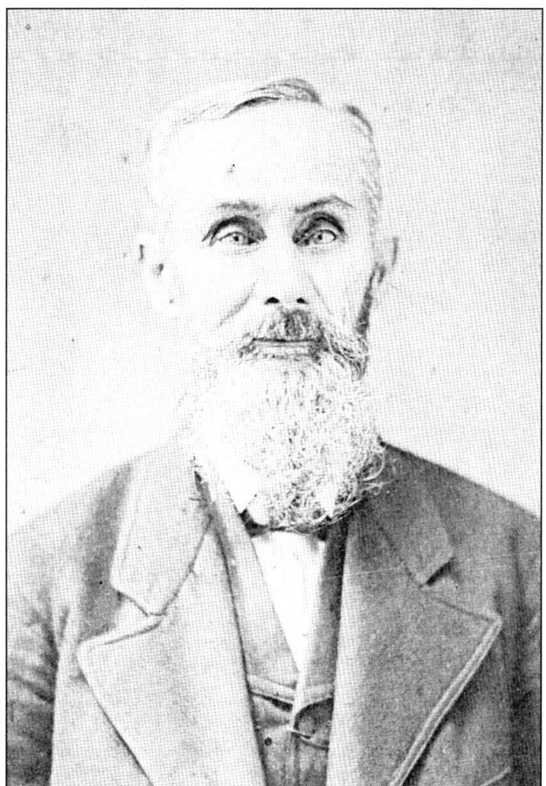

EZBON R. COLE (1870s). For many years the only undertaker in town, Ezbon (1810–1882) operated the Cole Funeral Home. Married in 1836, he was the father of four sons, one of whom, Charles E., joined him in his South Main Street business. At his father's death, Charles moved the business to a location between the Baptist and Universalist churches on Main Street. Ezbon, a forty-year member of the Baptist church and a Democrat "who voted for principle and not men," had years before his death prepared a plain but substantial metal casket for his remains. (Richard S. Hutchinson)

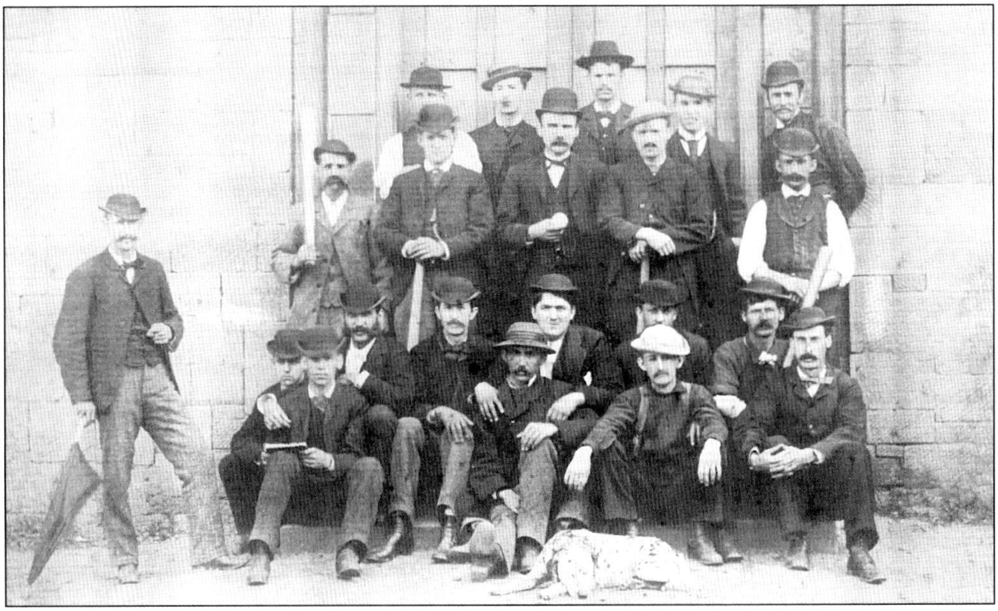

PEDDIE SCHOOL BASEBALL SQUAD (1879). It's not a hat show . . . just the Peddie baseball team with a pet Dalmatian in the foreground. Baseball was Peddie's earliest sport; the first game was played in the fall of 1870 against a Freehold team. It was not until 1885 that the Peddie baseball team engaged in interscholastic competition. This photograph was taken at the side entrance to Wilson Hall on May 21. (Hightstown-East Windsor Historical Society and The Peddie Archives)

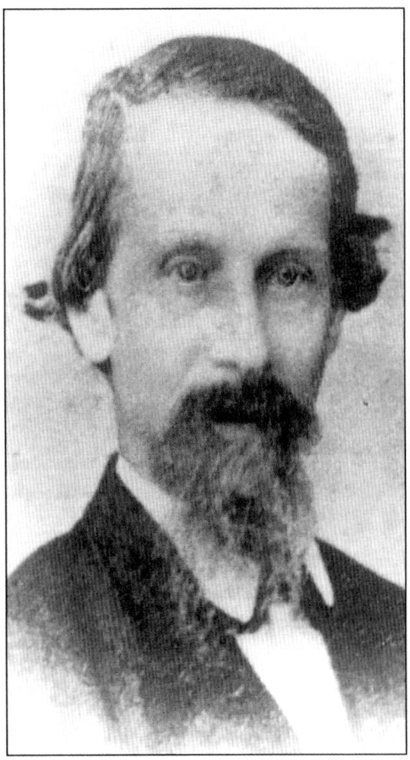

EDWARD CROWL TAYLOR (*c.* 1879). Born in New York in 1822, the son of Wilson and Susan Murray Cunningham Taylor, he was the first master of the Hightstown Masonic Lodge, #41, serving from its inception in 1856 to 1859. Other lodge charter members included James S. Yard, Jacob Stults, William D. Davis, Charles Bennett, Jehu Patterson, the Reverend F.S. Wolfe, Charles Keeler, Ira Smock, and Thomas Appleget. Married to Mary Elizabeth Stults, Taylor had been an editor and proprietor of *The Village Record*, and was at one time associated in its management with his brother-in-law, Jacob Stults. Taylor held principal positions in the Central Bank and at the time of his death was on the board of directors of the First National Bank. For many years, he was superintendent of the Universalist church Sunday school, and at his death was considered one of the town's wealthiest citizens. (Ernest Thompson and the Hightstown Masonic Lodge, #41)

Two

1880 to 1899

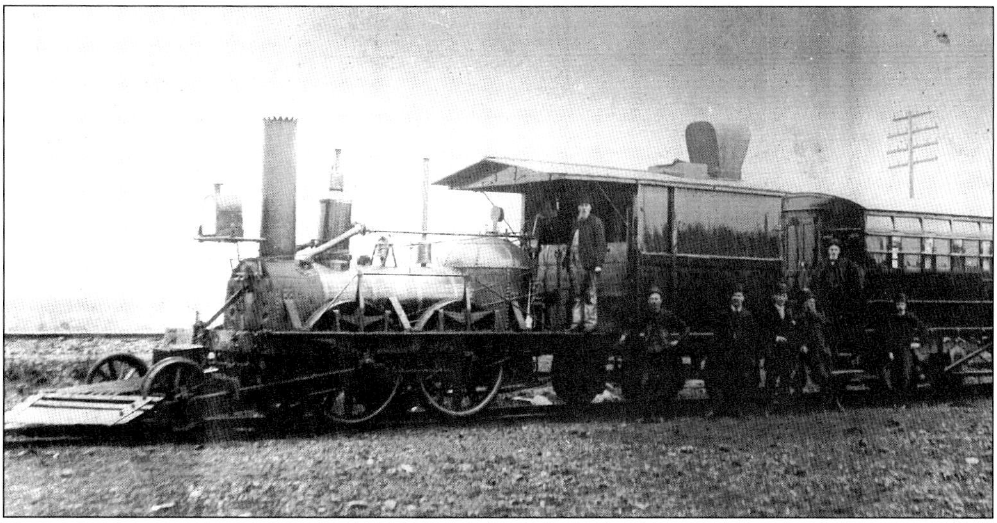

THE JOHN BULL (1880s). In September of 1833, what is probably the nation's most famous old steam engine, the John Bull, was placed in service. The railroad had come to Hightstown two years earlier (in 1831) using a horse-drawn conveyance. The John Bull, now recognized in the Smithsonian Institute as the oldest operative locomotive, chugged through Hightstown regularly on the Camden & Amboy Railroad, the first in New Jersey. It made a daily round trip from Bordentown to South Amboy as the first regularly scheduled passenger run from New York to Philadelphia. Connections from South Amboy to New York City and from Bordentown to Philadelphia were made by steamboat. The time for the 61-mile trip was seven hours, and the cost was $3. According to an account of the John Bull's first trip through Hightstown, "the town crowds sat on fences and stood in the fence corners. The carriages filled the roads. Hurrahs and hand clapping were deafening." Removed from service in 1866, the John Bull was later repaired, renovated, and restored. It made the trip to the Columbian Exposition (the Chicago World's Fair) in 1893, where it provided rides to visitors for 25¢. The photograph above shows the cow catcher, headlight, bell, covers for the wood box and passenger coaches, and a cabin for the engineer, John West, Sr., who is standing on the engine. A Hightstown resident, West was considered one of the nation's oldest train engineers in 1887. (Hightstown-East Windsor Historical Society)

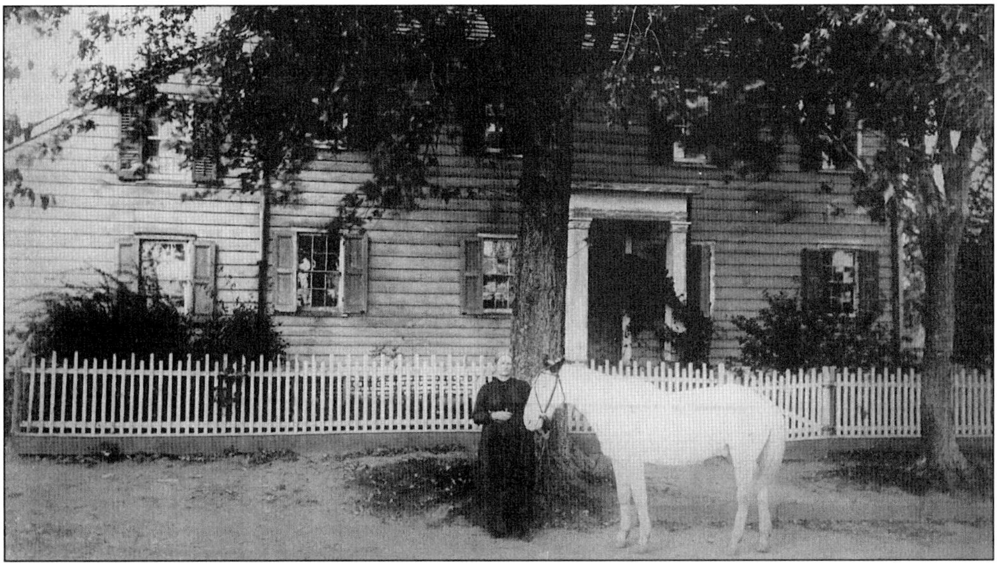

CEDARVILLE ROAD FARMHOUSE (*c.* 1880). Elizabeth Vancleaf Roszel (1840–1923) poses with a horse in front of her East Windsor farmhouse. Originally from Monmouth County, she had married William Roszel of Hightstown in November 1858 at the Baptist parsonage in Freehold. Her son Eugene, born here in 1860, was the grandfather of Lillian Roszel Black and Howard "Howie" Roszel. (Lillian R. Black)

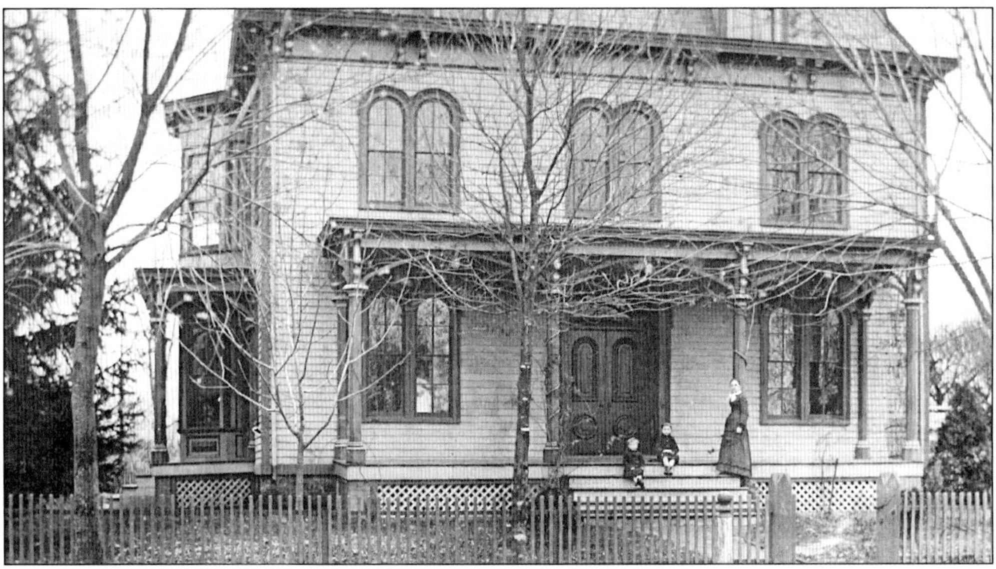

THE WYCKOFF HOMESTEAD (*c.* 1881). Mrs. Elston Hunt, the former Mary J. Runyon (1827–1894), is standing on the front porch of her North Main Street home with her grandchildren, Ernest (1878–1962) and Virginia (1874–1954) Wyckoff. Edna Wyckoff (1881–1968), in the window wearing a white dress, is being held by the children's mother, Mrs. Abraham Bergen Wyckoff. Edna and Virginia were never married and lived in this house until their deaths. The house, built by Mr. Elston Hunt (1825–1879) in the 1870s, has a mansard roof and Italianate arches. The windows on the first and second floors are paired with oval tops, and the windows in the dormers have oval tops and oval cornices. The front door has an arched transom and circles carved in the double doors. (Hightstown-East Windsor Historical Society)

SERING SHANGLE (*c*. 1884). In 1857 Sering established himself in Hightstown and was the proprietor of a foundry that produced castings for various agricultural machines. Born in 1827, he was a charter member of the Presbyterian church and served as its superintendent from its founding in 1857 until his death in 1899. He was the mayor of Hightstown for three terms in the 1860s, 1870s, and 1880s, and was also a justice of the peace and commissioner of deeds. (Bob Pierce)

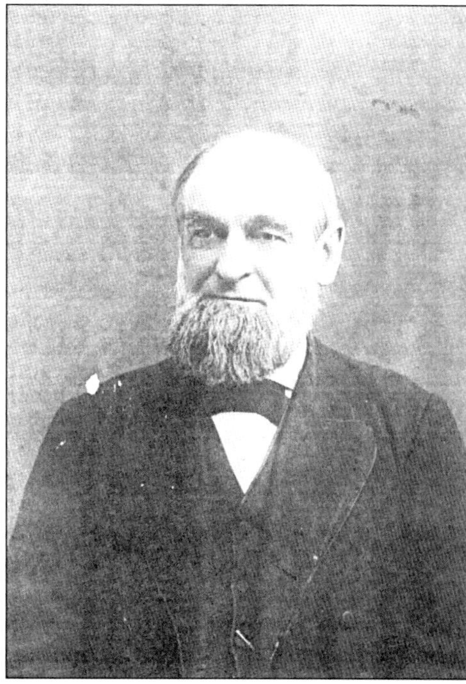

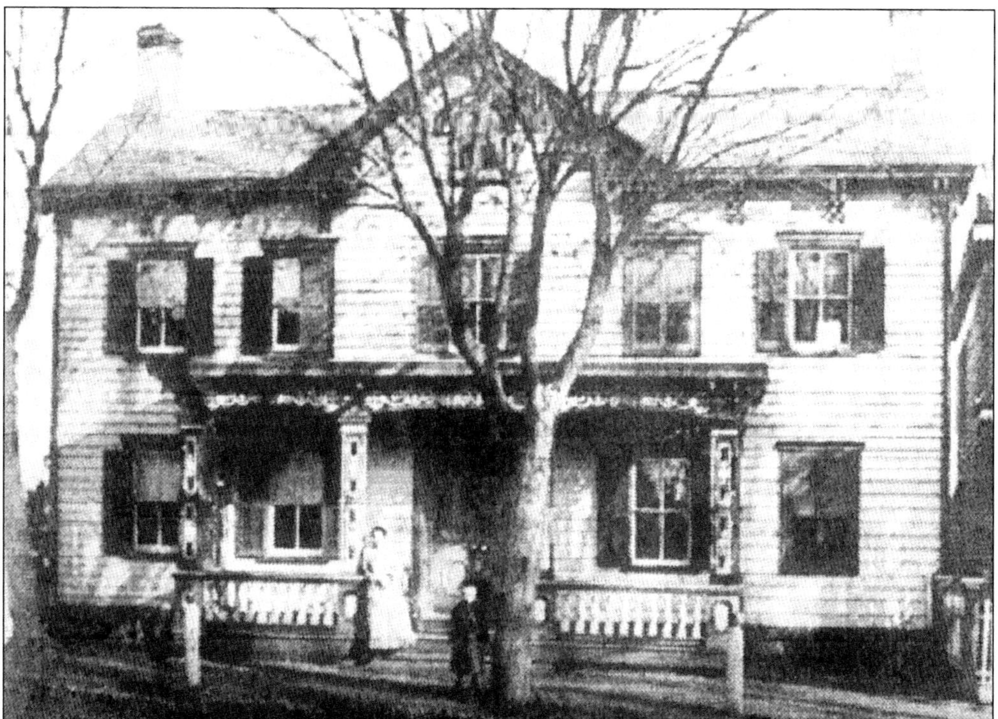

THE ASHTON HOUSE (*c*. 1884). The current owners of this house believe that the individuals standing on the porch are Melvin Ashton and his mother. The back kitchen portion of A.J. Ashton's Stockton Street home existed in the 1820s and was probably there much earlier, according to the recollections of Jacob Stults. (Jim and Barbara Walker)

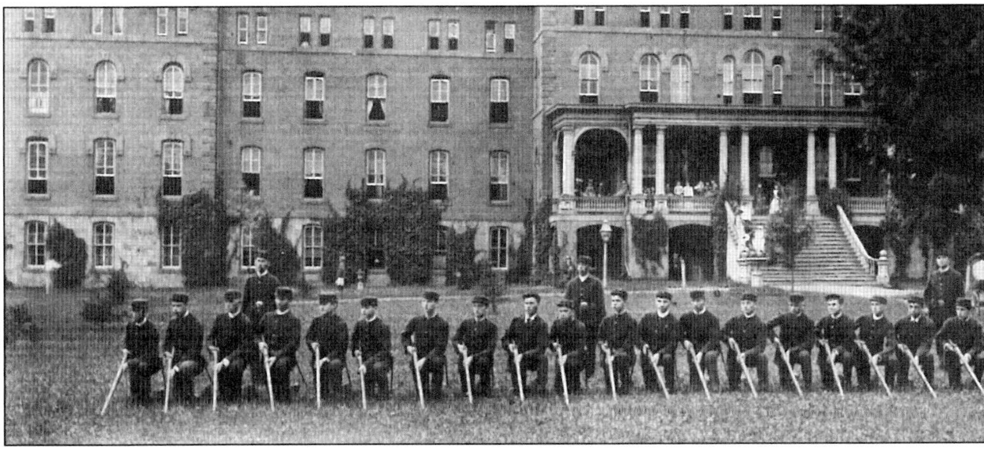

PEDDIE INSTITUTE GUARDS (1885). A voluntary cadet corps was organized at Peddie, and military drills were provided to all who enlisted. Note the female students observing the corps from the porch of Wilson Hall. During the principalship of the Reverend Dr. John Greene (1882–1889), the following notable events occurred: the school acquired its first endowment fund, the standards of scholarship were raised, one of the students ate twenty cream puffs in eleven minutes on a wager, and in the north boys' wing, foul-smelling lanterns were hung 3 or 4 feet from the ceiling in order to be out of reach of mischievous students. (Hightstown-East Windsor Historical Society)

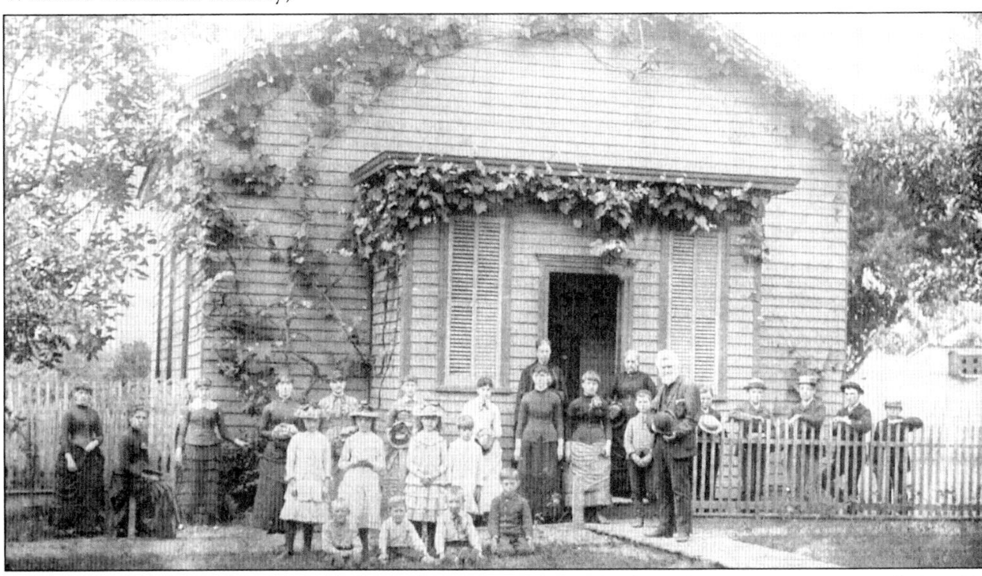

WELLS SCHOOL (1884). The Hightstown Young Ladies Seminary, organized by Dr. McClusky as a day school in 1864, was taken over by the Reverend William M. Wells in 1870. Among those near the door are teachers, Miss Baldwin, and the Reverend and Mrs. Wells. The students are: (seated) Willie Brown, Melville Ashton, and Archie and Charlie Everett; (middle row) Emilie Deshler, Virginia Wyckoff, Laura Davison, and Evie Townsand; (back row) Maude Everett, Eva Davis, Irene Everett, Helen Schenck, Lizzie Ketchem, Annie E. Applegat, Hattie Magaum, Annie Perrine, Celia Ivans, Luke Voorhees, Lemuel Black, Joe Morgan, Bobie Woodward, Grandan Sharich, and Charlie Black. The Presbyterian school was continued in the home of Reverend Wells at 302 North Main Street; later it was sold to Frank D. Budlong, who continued it for a number of years. (Hightstown-East Windsor Historical Society)

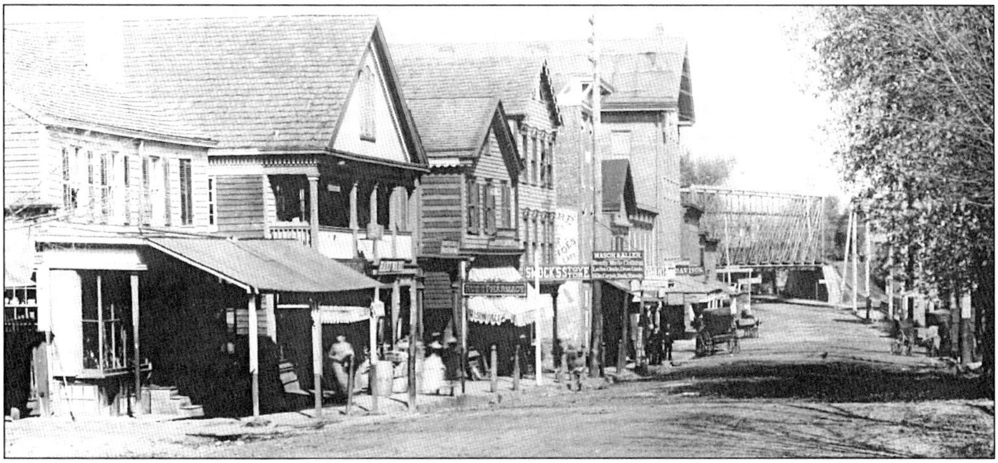

RAILROAD AND CARRIAGE ERA (1886). On a fall day, patrons are shopping at the stores on the west side of Main Street. Pictured are a hardware store, (Harvey) Rue's Pharmacy, Smock's Stove Store, the Mason & Allen general store, and Davison's dry goods store. In 1893, the year he turned eighty, Joseph J. Dey wrote in his diary that Mason's and Smock's were destroyed by fire in September. (C. Stults Family-Allen & Stults Collection)

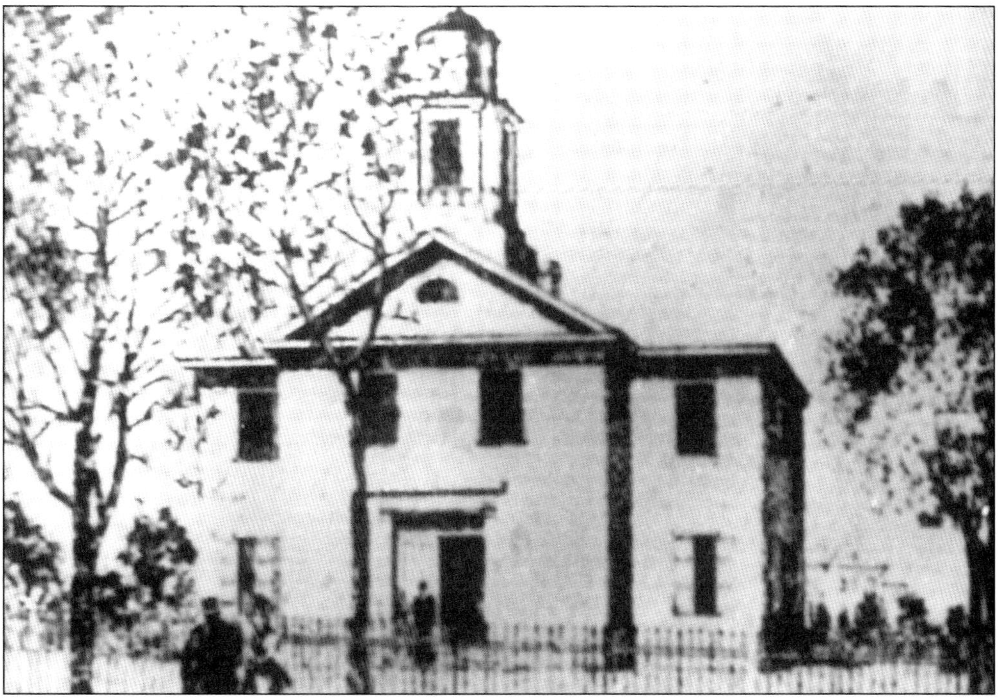

HIGHTSTOWN ACADEMY (1880s). Known as the Academy, the first public school was a two-story, two-room structure built in 1841 on Mercer Street. By 1859, 250 pupils crowded into the school and two additional rooms were added. This was a "part pay" school originally, but in 1871, a free school system as started. In 1880, there were 417 school-age students in the district: 235 were enrolled in the Academy, 50 attended private school, and 132 did not attend school. The one male teacher received $62.50 per month; the three female teachers each received $28.33 per month. In 1894, the Academy was torn down and the Mercer Street School was built on the site. (Hightstown-East Windsor Historical Society)

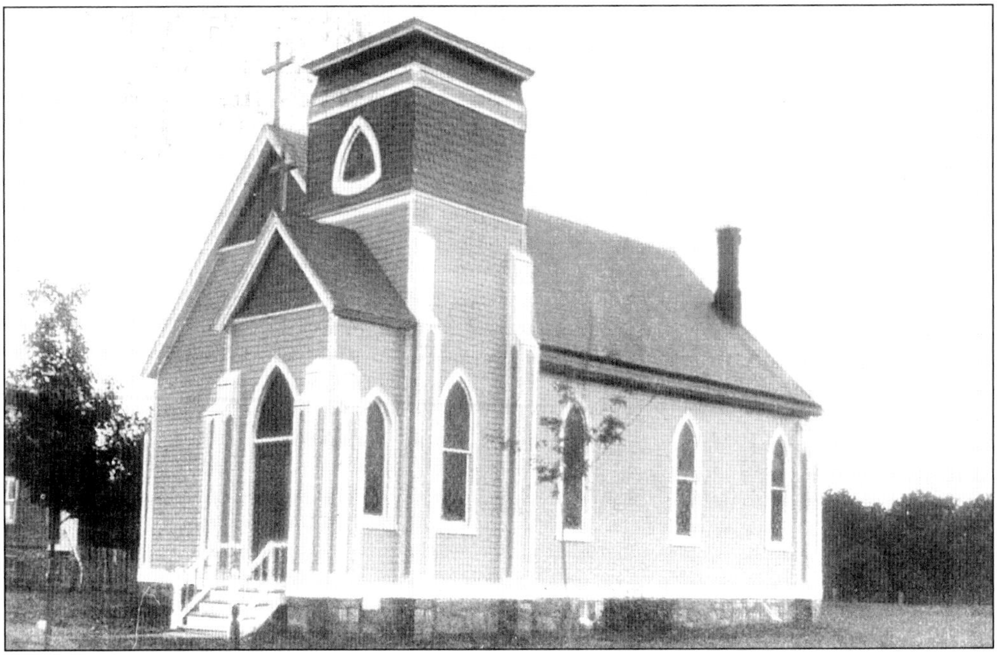

ST. ANTHONY'S R.C. CHURCH (1886). In the mid-1800s Thomas Collins, Stephen Courtney, and Thomas Conway carted lumber from the Roebling Lumber Yard to build the first Catholic church in Hightstown. This parish, organized in 1874 with a congregation of twenty-five, held services at the Stockton Street home of James Dullard. In the early 1880s, after attending mass in Allentown for a few years, the Catholics held services in a little building on South Main Street near the corner of Mercer Street. (Norris Robbins Collection)

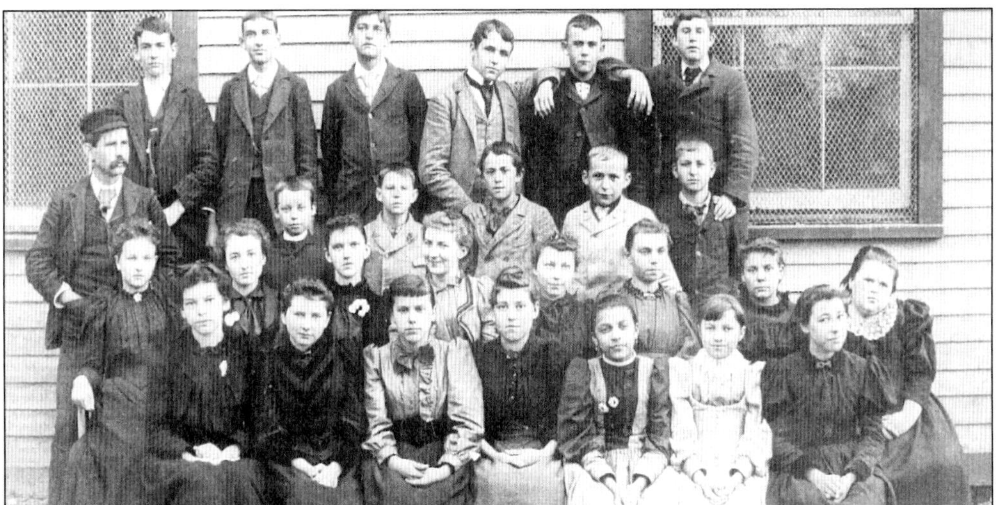

ACADEMY STUDENTS (*c.* 1889). Professor Theodore Green—in hat and mustache—poses with his students: (front row) Jessie Tracy, Amanda Donnell, Amanda Carr, Edna Conover, Mattie Wilson, and Iva Doyle; (second row) Minnie Hoagland, Sadie Taylor, Etta Lott, Sadie Farr, Emma Dennis, Luella Lewis, Sadie Cole, and Gertie Smith; (third row) Joe Shinn, Fred Voorhees, Eddie Blackell, Harry Weller, and Horace Ayers; (back row) James Taylor, Herbert Lewis, Frank Pullen, Elmer Chamberlin, Harry Messler, and George Craig. (Dorothy Petty Dey)

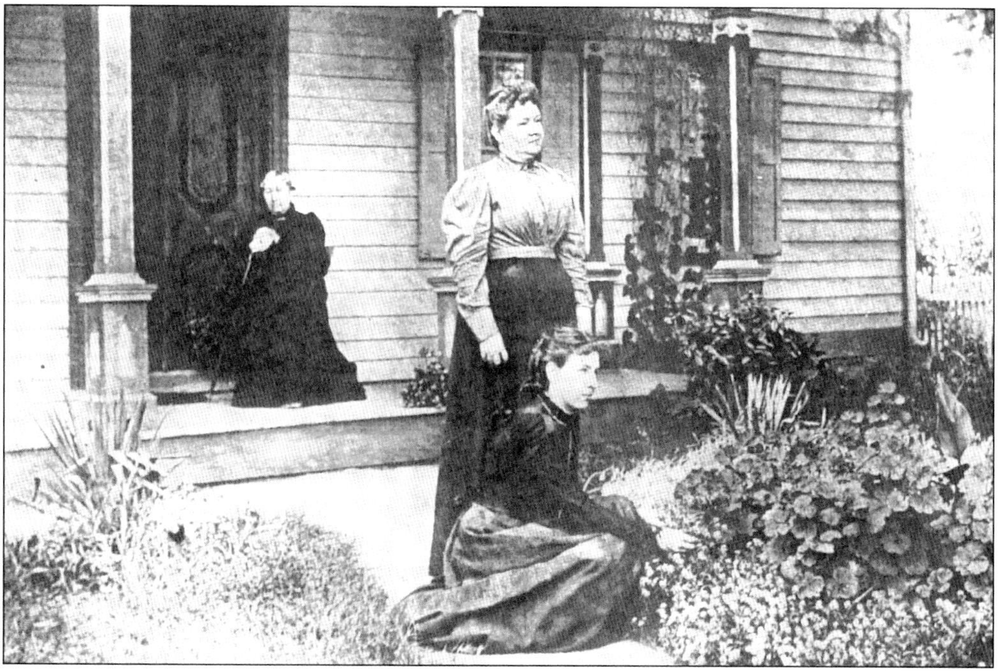

THREE GENERATIONS (*c.* 1890). Kneeling in front of the Lee home is Lamattie Updike Lee, the first of her family to be born in this farmhouse. Standing behind her is her mother, Abbie Updike, and seated on the porch is Abbie's mother, Edna Appelget. The spiked plants on either side of the walkway, known as century plants, are still there today. (The Lee Family)

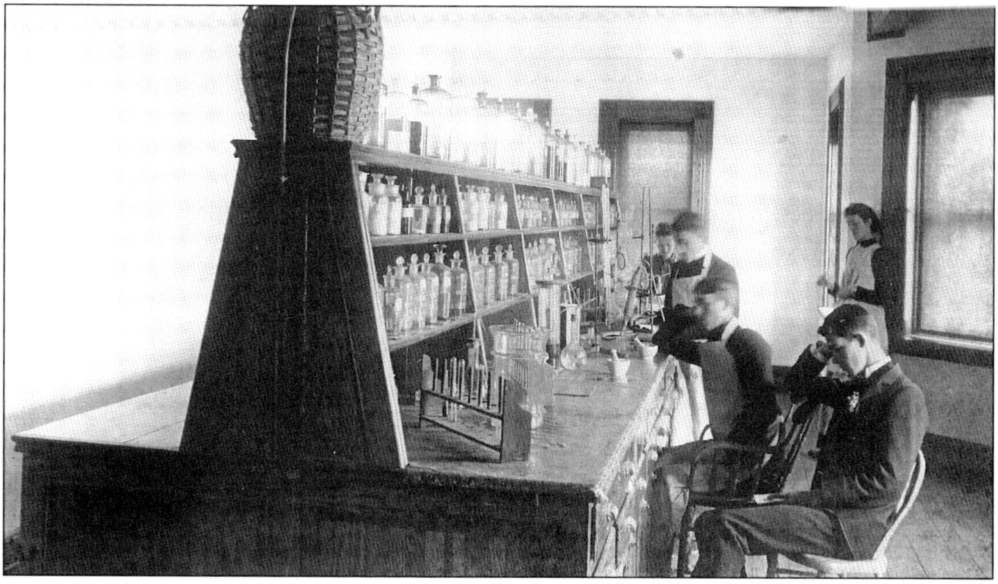

SERIOUS LAB STUDY (1890). Peddie students are absorbed in their science laboratory studies in Longstreet Hall, which opened in 1889. Herbert E. Slaught had come to Peddie as a mathematics teacher upon graduation from Colgate University in 1883. After Dr. John Greene's departure as principal in 1889, Slaught became the youngest man to head the school. During his administration, the Longstreet library and science building was erected. Currently, the building is being used for instructional purposes. (Peddie Archives)

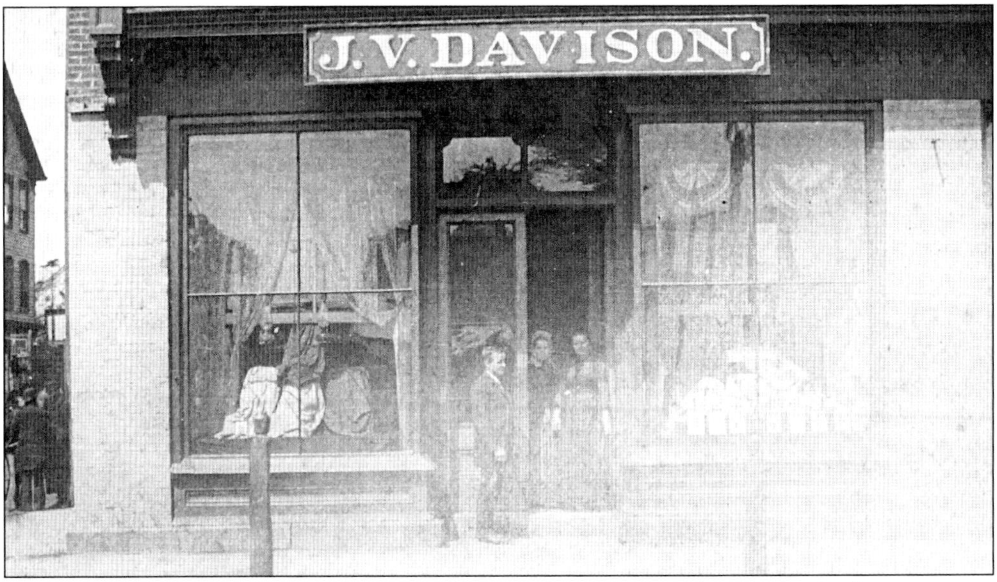

WAITING FOR CUSTOMERS (c. 1893). In early 1885, Joseph Van Doren Davison, one of ten children in the Davison family, purchased the general store of C.W. McMurran at the corner of Main and Stockton Streets. It opened on May 2, with the first day's receipts totaling $20. When Davison, who had previously been in business in New York City, purchased the store, its stock was limited to dry goods. Soon it was expanded to include grocery and clothing departments. Davison sold to his sons in 1906, and the store became known as J.V. Davison's Sons. In 1907, Joseph V. Davison purchased a controlling interest in the Hightstown Smyrna Rug Company. (C. Stults Family-Allen & Stults Collection)

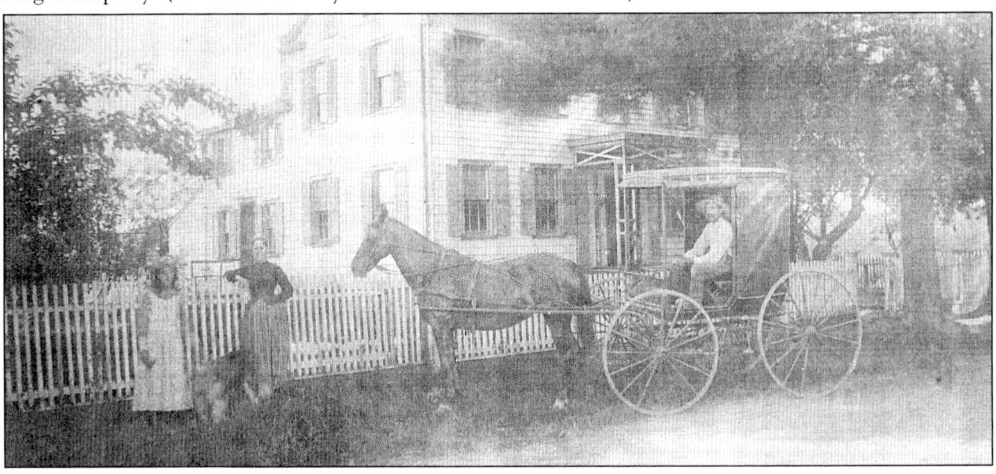

COX-TAYLOR FARMHOUSE (early 1890s). Fran Cox (Early) (1881–1958) and her mother Annie E. Cox (b. 1852) watch Samuel J. Cox (1851–1919) as he arrives at his Mercer Street farmhouse in East Windsor Township. Built in the late 1850s, the house was acquired by Samuel in 1889. His daughter, Bertha Cox Taylor, bought the property in 1916. The property was subdivided during relatively recent years to include the following municipal and commercial concerns: the Hightstown Swimming Pool (1934), the FCA (1937), the Jersey Central Power and Light Company (1959), and the East Windsor Regional Board of Education (1967). The house was purchased by the Harold C. Cox family in 1969 and moved to South Main Street. (Vinton and Maribelle Taylor)

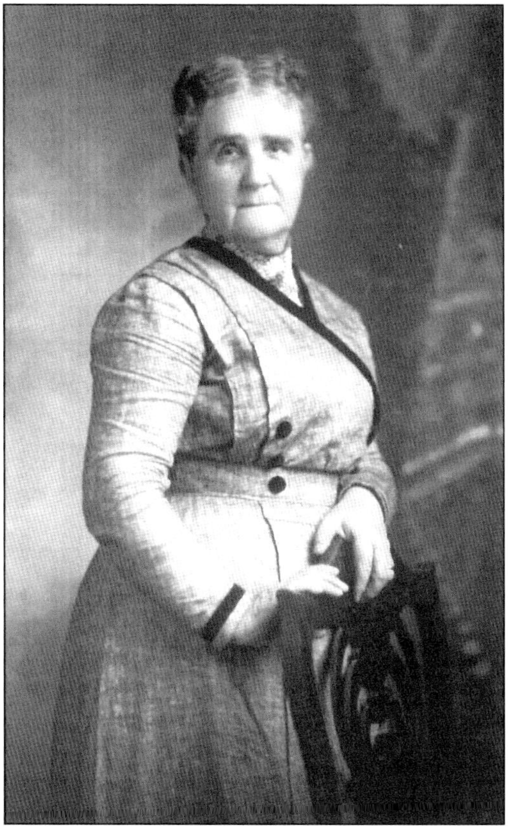 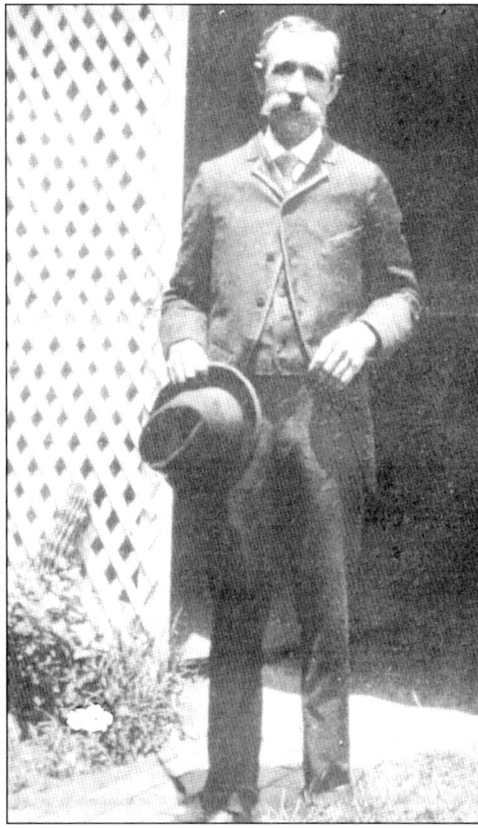

A FARM COUPLE (*c.* 1895). Annie E. and Samuel J. Cox, the parents of Fran Cox (Early) and Bertha Cox (Taylor), were married on December 15, 1875, and in 1889 bought what would later become known as the Cox-Taylor farm on Mercer Street. (Vinton and Maribelle Taylor)

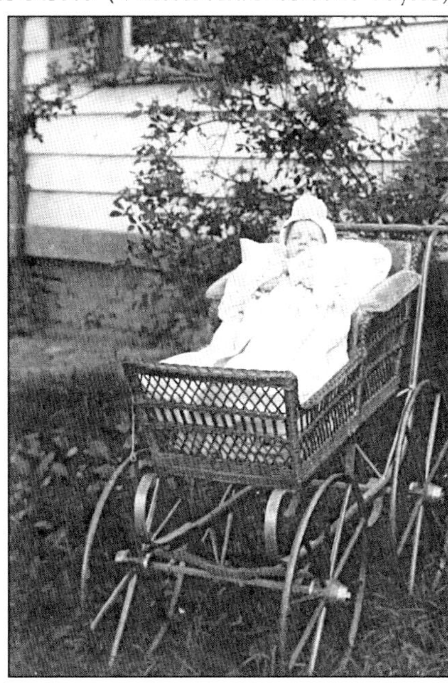

NAP TIME IN A WICKER BUGGY (1895). C. Stanley Stults (1894–1982) relaxes in his carriage outside the home of his parents, Charles E. and Adelaide Bennett Stults, at 201 Stockton Street. As a youngster, he traveled by train from Hightstown through Bordentown to Trenton daily to attend Trenton High School, from which he graduated in 1912. Some of his early jobs were as a postal service mail sorter on the Washington, DC, to Boston run and as assistant postmaster in Hightstown. Following the death of his father in 1917, he became president of Allen & Stults Company. (C. Stults Family-Allen & Stults Collection)

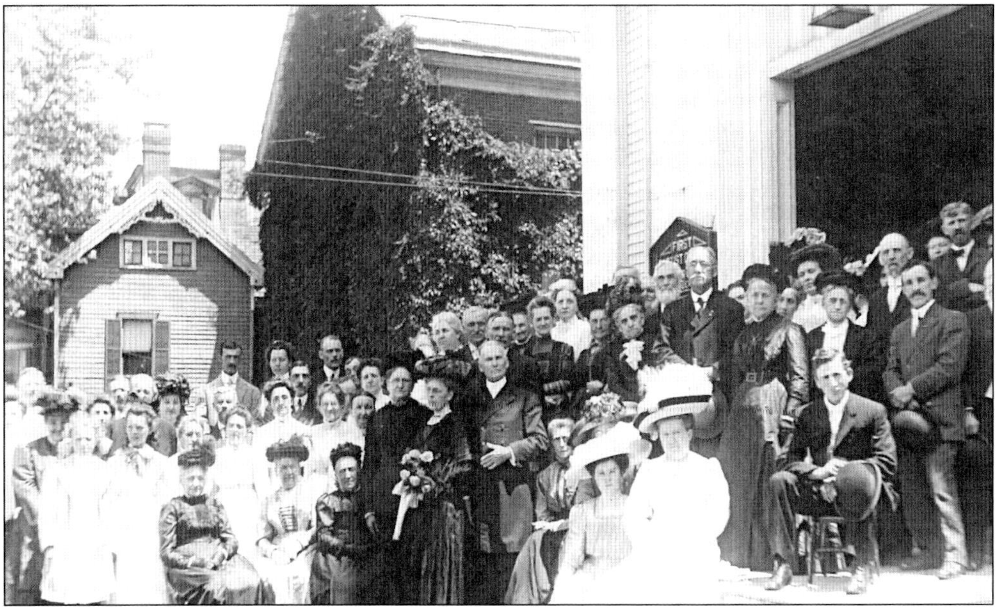

TWENTY-FIFTH ANNIVERSARY CELEBRATION (1895). Dr. and Mrs. O.P. Eaches are surrounded by well-wishers at a May celebration of the doctor's 25th anniversary as pastor of the First Baptist Church. The women's upswept hairdos were considered stylish at this time. (C. Stults Family-Allen & Stults Collection)

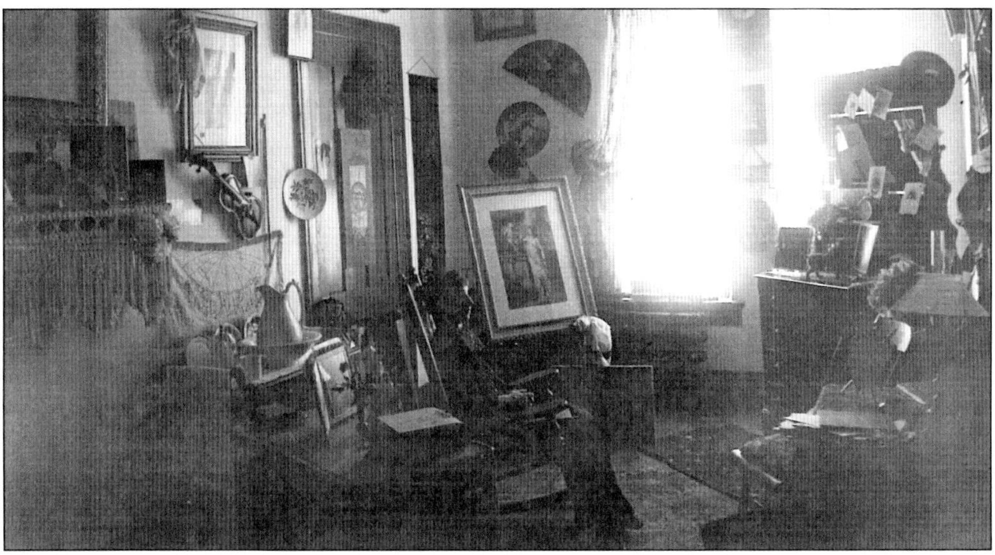

DORM ROOM AT PEDDIE (c. 1893). Resting in a rocker, a female student is shown surveying her rather cluttered room in Wilson Hall. Of interest are the wash pitcher and basin on the stand at left. Peddie's principal at this time was the Reverend Dr. Joseph E. Perry, and it was during his administration (1892–98) that a "dining room building" was constructed (at a cost of $30,000), the Octagon House was acquired, and 8 acres to the south of the campus and the Peddie Woods were purchased. In 1897 the school was recognized as "one of the eleven schools having the largest endowments and the finest facilities for education in the entire country." School rates at this time ranged from $200 to $250 per year for boarding students. (Hightstown-East Windsor Historical Society)

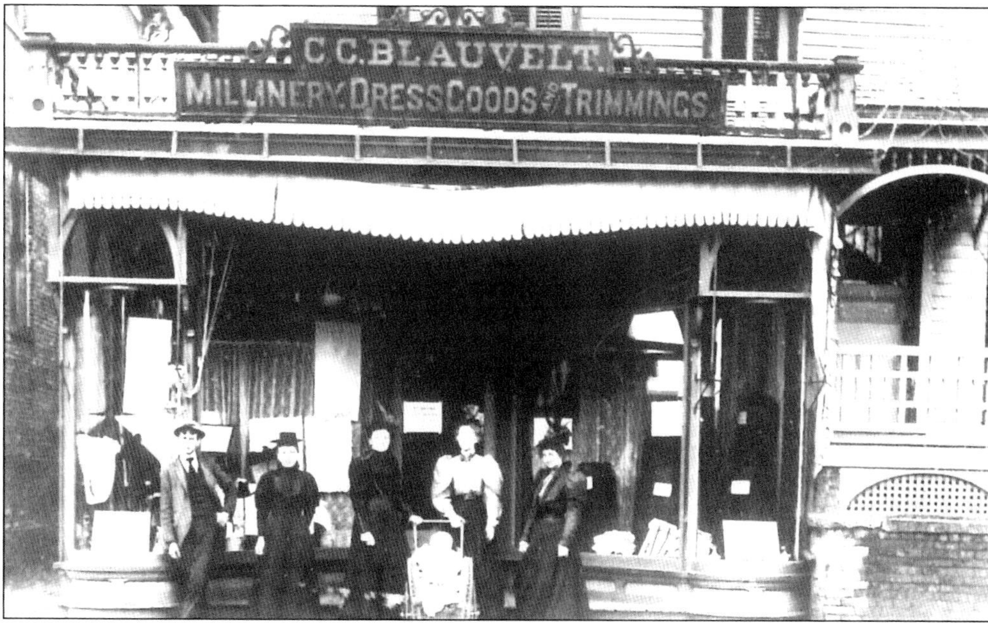

FASHIONS OF THE TIMES (1890s). In April of 1883, Blauvelt's, which was first located on Stockton Street, moved to this location next to Eaches Memorial Chapel. Bargain prices on silks, velvets, buttons, gimps, and fringes were advertised in the *Hightstown Gazette*. Mrs. Nellie Blauvelt operated a millinery department on the second floor. (Hightstown-East Windsor Historical Society)

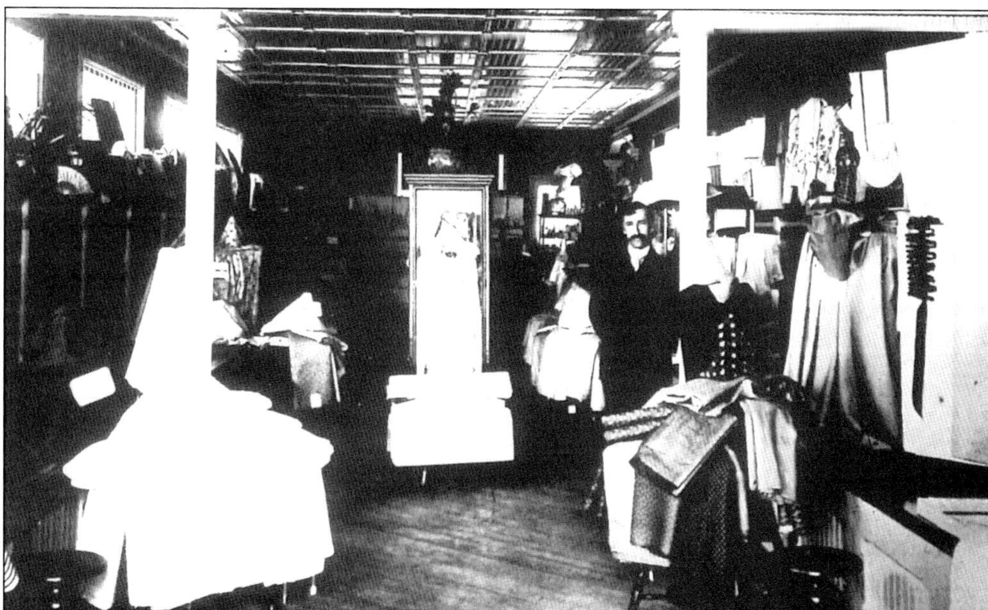

INSIDE BLAUVELT'S (1890s). The latest in silks, trimmings, and fashionable millinery are displayed in this well-known Hightstown shop. Proprietor Charles Coatsworth Blauvelt (shown here) served as mayor from 1911 to 1914. His father, Joseph S. Blauvelt, was mayor from 1859 to 1861, and his grandfather, Dr. Charles G. Blauvelt, was the town's first mayor, having served from 1853 to 1855. (Hightstown-East Windsor Historical Society)

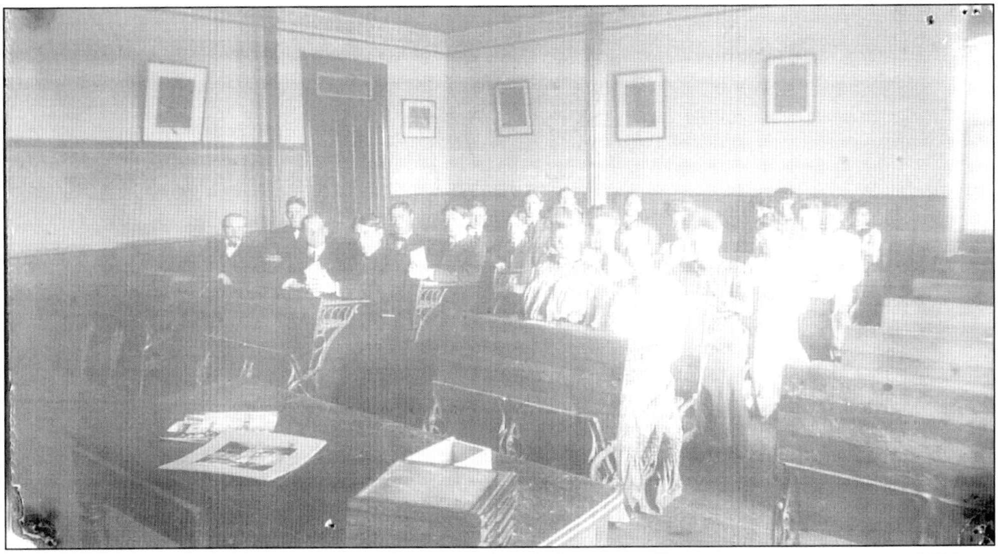

COED DAYS AT PEDDIE (1890s). Boys and girls (separated) await instruction in a Wilson Hall classroom. By 1898 the school rates were $250 a year. This included room, board, oil for light, heat, tuition, and laundry (twelve pieces a week). There were six men and six women teachers, and their salaries ranged from $400 to $650 per year, in addition to free lodging and food. (Hightstown-East Windsor Historical Society and Peddie Archives)

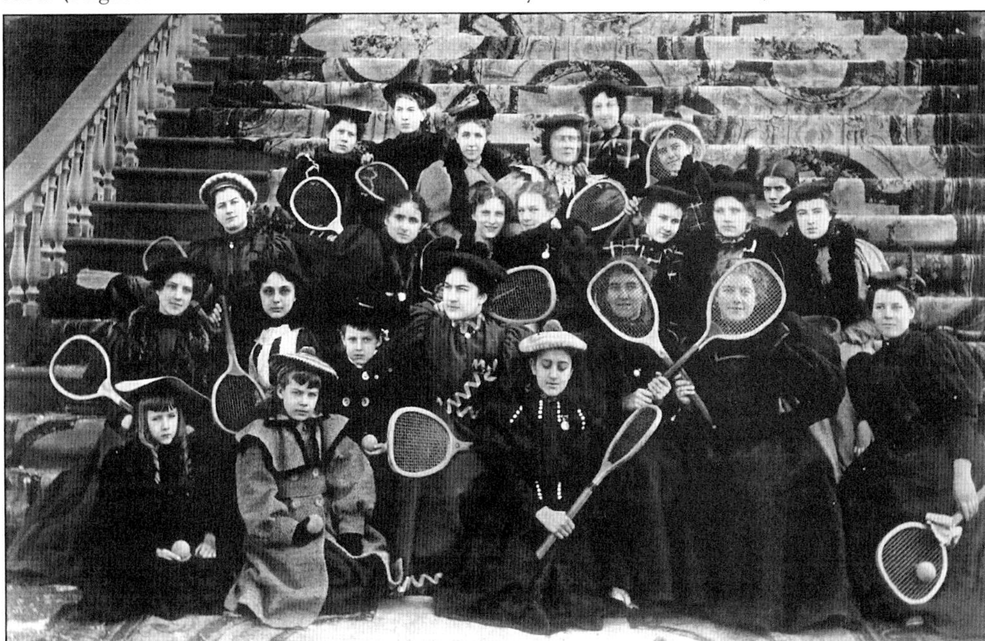

"ALERT TENNIS CLUB" (1896). Tam-o'-shanters were part of a woman's tennis costume in the mid-1890s. These Peddie club members posing during the spring season on a carpet covering the steps of Wilson Hall are: Estelle Cramer, Evelyn LeMay, Marianne Reed, Edythe Black, Maude Reed, Grace Harding, Helen Baker, Louise Chamberlain, Georgia Harding, Lizzie Perrine, Emily Swain, Matilda Craig, Helen Cook, Pauline Jennings, Gertrude Russ, Ethel Story, and Edna Williams. (Peddie Archives)

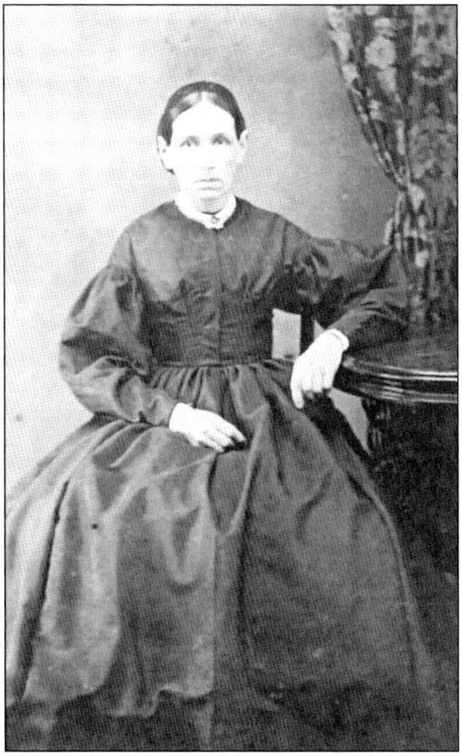

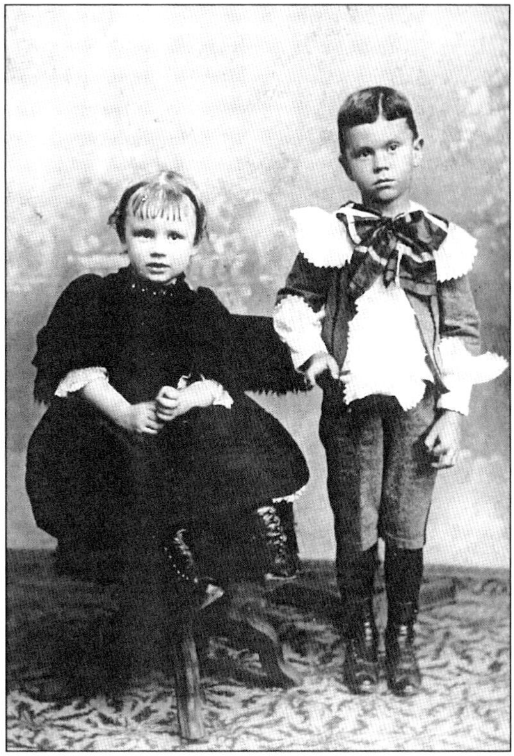

"AUNT MARY" CROSHAW (1890s). Mary Croshaw (1853–1921) was the wife of H.P. Croshaw and a relative of Nettie Black Stults. The puffed sleeves on her dress came into fashion in the late 1880s and continued to be popular during the early 1900s. (C. Stults Family-Allen & Stults Collection)

GROENDYKE CHILDREN (*c.* 1897). Wearing their Victorian finery, including high-button shoes, Edgar, age seven, and Ethel, age three, pose on a rug and chair typical of the period. (Lois Groendyke)

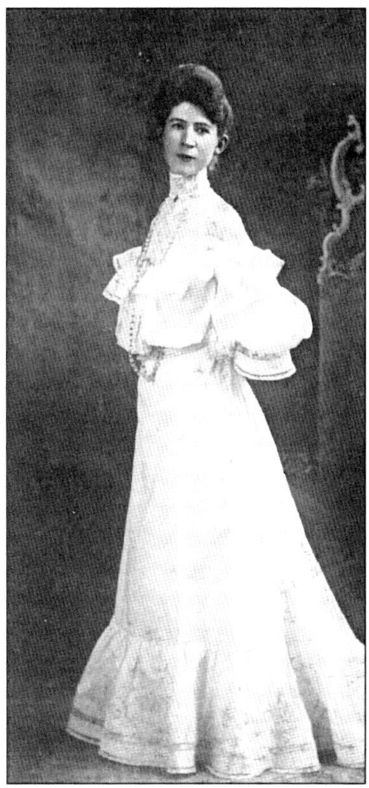

GRADUATION (1899). In a charming white dress with a high collar and gathered sleeves, Grace Ely is the image of girlhood at the turn of the century. The daughters of Joseph Addison Ely and Sara Fisher Segoine Ely, Grace and her sister Margaret graduated from Peddie in 1899. (Hightstown-East Windsor Historical Society)

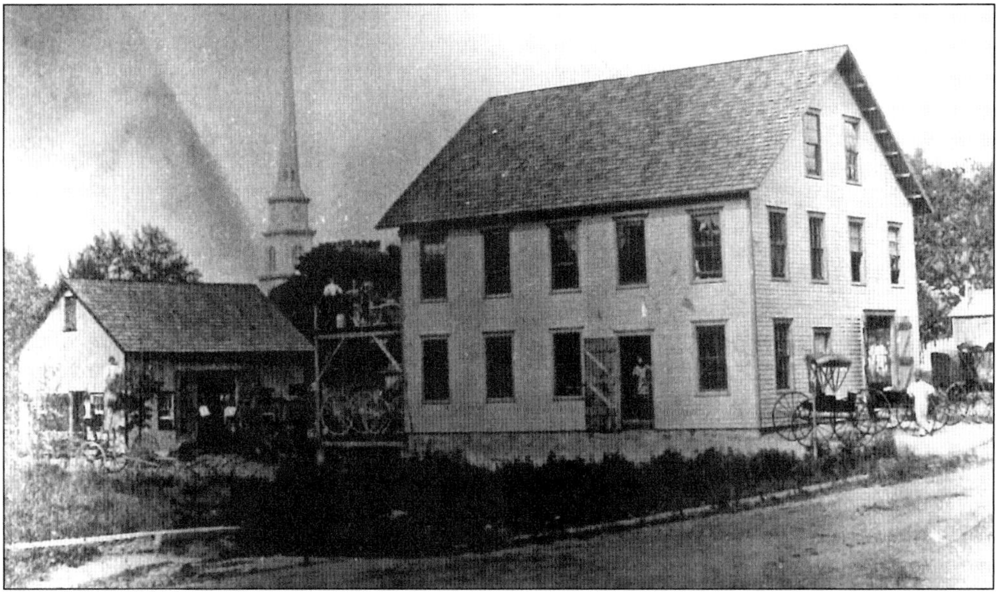

CARRIAGE SHOP (c. 1897). The Embley Carriage Works on the north side of Ward Street was in full operation when this picture was taken. Later the structure was converted to an apartment house and was recently razed to make way for a parking lot for the Hightstown Diner. The First Baptist Church steeple can be seen in the background. (Hightstown-East Windsor Historical Society)

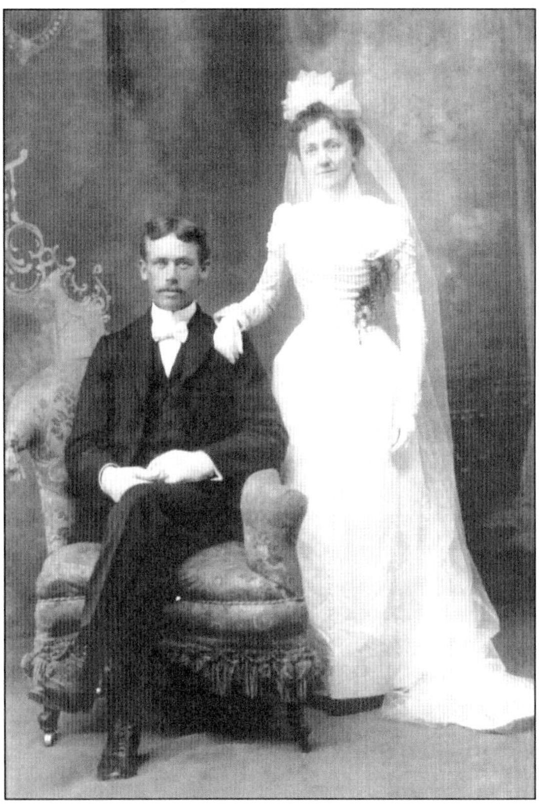

GROVER WEDDING (1899). Frank Grover and his twenty-six-year-old bride, Ella Rogers, pose on their wedding day, November 8, for the traditional photograph. Ella lived to be eighty-five. (Elizabeth Silvers)

Three

1900 to 1909

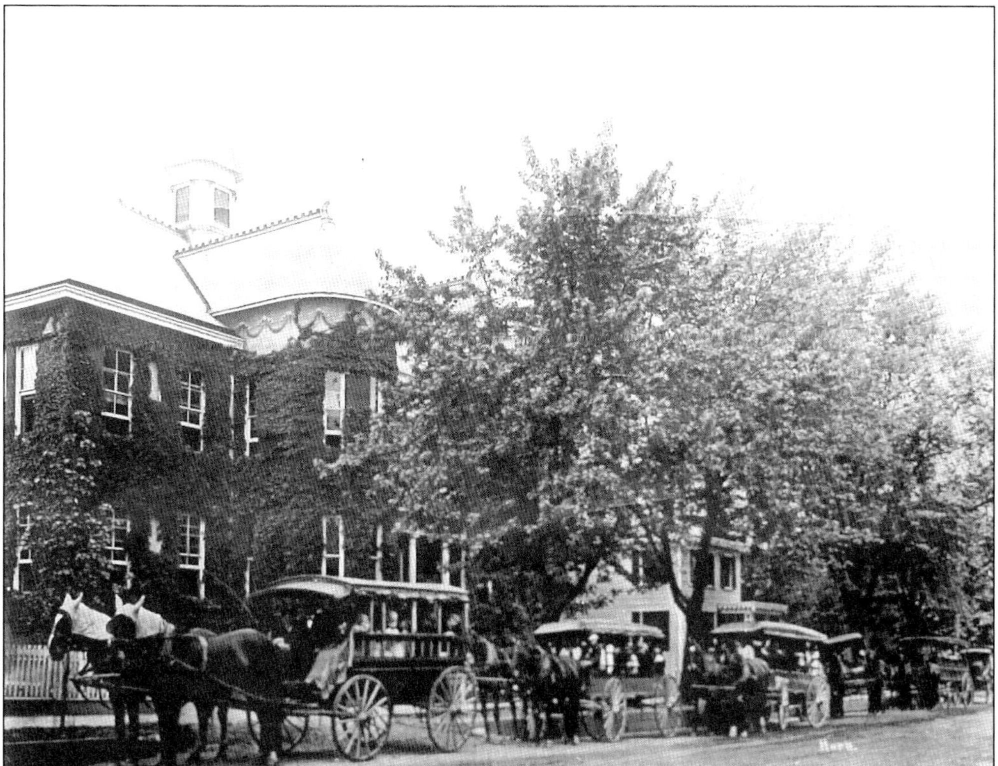

STUDENT TRANSPORTATION (early 1900s). Children were transported to and from the ivy-covered Mercer Street School in the early days of this century by horse-drawn wagons called carry-alls. Each vehicle held about fifteen to twenty students. The brick building shown here, built in 1894 at a cost of approximately $12,000, was Hightstown's only public school until 1913, when another school was built on Stockton Street. Along Mercer Street was a boardwalk, and one teacher recalled that the boys pushed each other off and often entered the school with wet and muddy feet. Teacher Edna Conover, who attended the Academy and whose father, George Washington Conover, was a local Civil War veteran, remembered children who lost many of their precious cooper pennies through the big cracks in the walk into the brook flowing underneath. (Hightstown-East Windsor Historical Society)

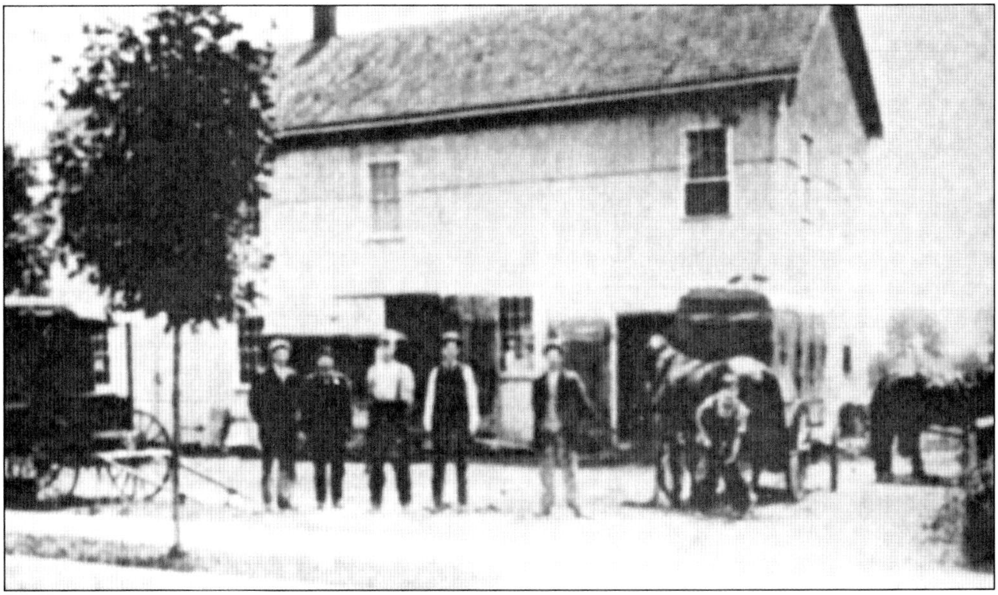

VILLAGE BLACKSMITH (1890s). Taylor's Blacksmith Shop on the corner of Broad and Monmouth Streets was a popular gathering spot for the local men. (Hightstown-East Windsor Historical Society)

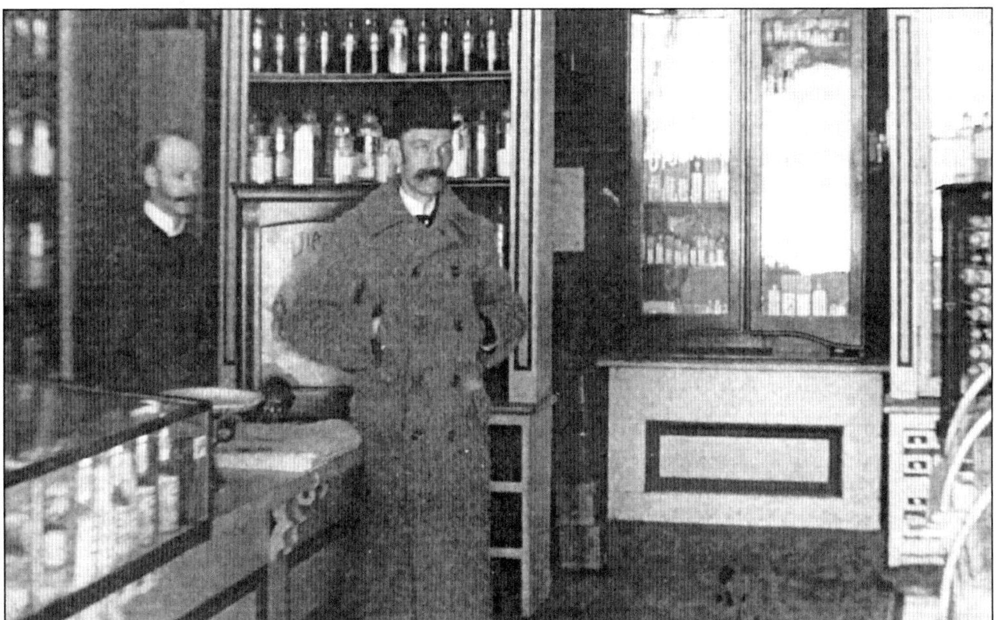

RUE'S PHARMACY (c. 1900). The hatless man is probably Harvey G. Rue, who ran this pharmacy for at least twenty years before this photograph was taken. The Harvey Rues were married on December 18, 1878, and The Friday Club Chorus sang at their 50th wedding anniversary celebration at their 326 South Main Street home. Rue, who graduated from Peddie in 1872 and then attended Yale, died in 1935 at the age of eighty-three. The pharmacy was later acquired by Ernest Thompson and then by George Burch. (Hightstown-East Windsor Historical Society)

WILLIAM ELY HUTCHINSON (c. 1900). A mail carrier for RD 1 in East Windsor Township, William Hutchinson (1877–1940) was probably the last carrier in New Jersey to make his rounds with a horse and buggy. In his last year of service he had an accident and his horse ran off without him. He spent his early days in the family home at 248 Mercer Street. Adelaide, one of his nine children, remembers spending many hours as a young girl shelling the lima beans her father grew and then selling them from house to house for 25¢ a quart. (Bob Hutchinson)

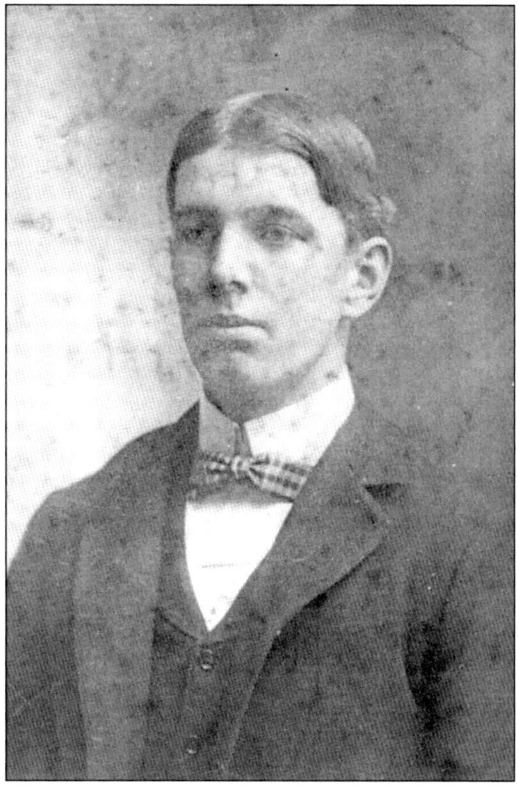

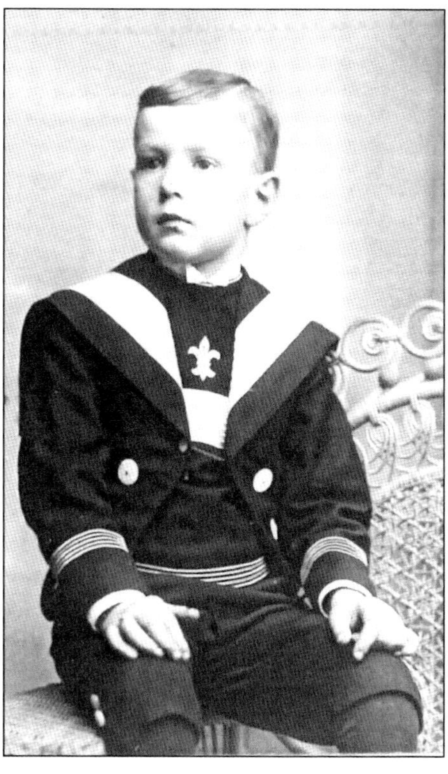

A YOUNG SAILOR (c. 1900). C. Stanley Stults appears somewhat stoic in this photograph. In later years, he was chief executive officer of the Hightstown Savings and Loan Association, founding director of the Hightstown Trust Company (currently CoreStates Bank), and treasurer and trustee of the First Baptist Church, the YMCA, and the local Masonic Lodge. He served as president of New Jersey and Mercer County Independent Insurance Agents as well as of the county real estate board. Elected to the New Jersey Assembly, he served from 1946 to 1948. C. Stanley, who died in 1982 at age eighty-seven, was a towering man, over 6 feet 3 inches tall, and is remembered by many for his Stetson, long cigars, and friendly smile. (C. Stults Family-Allen & Stults Collection)

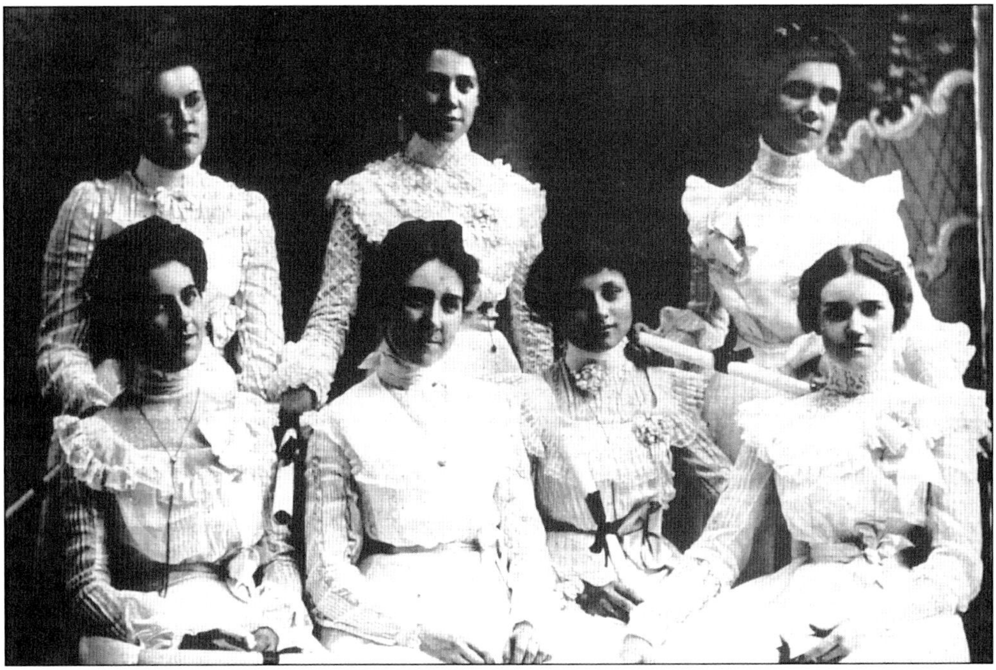

MERCER STREET SCHOOL GRADUATION (1901). On Friday, June 21, at 10 am, these girls graduated from the Mercer Street School, which at that time included a two-year high school: (front row) Nina Black, Miss H.D. Grover (teacher), Nola Swinger, and Sadie Van Dorm; (back row) Blanche Sutphin, Lettie Lee, and Bertha Cox. (Vinton and Maribelle Taylor)

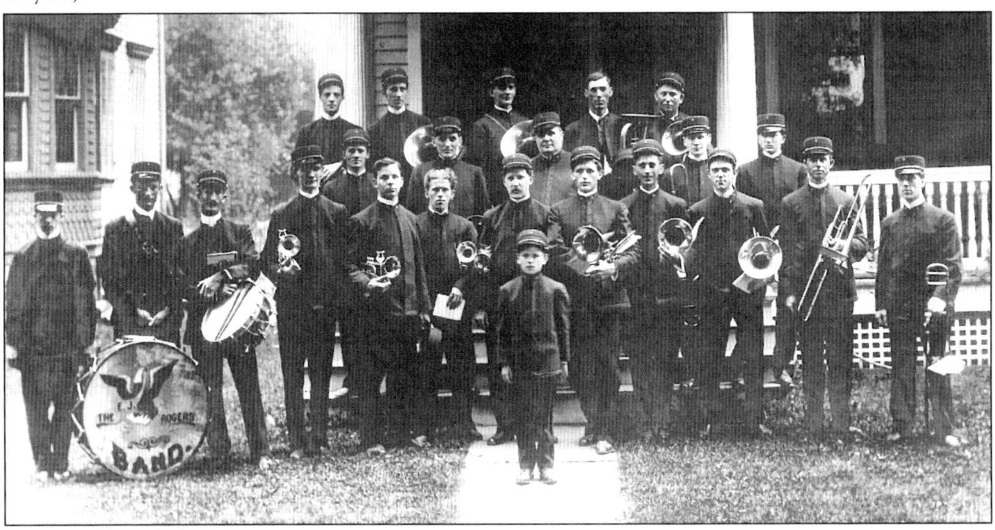

THE ROGERS BAND (1901). Bands were very popular in small towns around the turn of the century for both holiday parades and concerts. These band members, shown in front of the Rogers' 194 Stockton Street home, are: (standing) Davie Ray; (front row) Olie Masterson, N. Durphy, Charles Roszel, Fred Maple, Herb Davison, Art Dennis, John W. West, Elmer Rogers, James Johnson, Harry Morris, Walter Sutphin, and unknown; (middle row) Dave Ray, Morris Jessen, Pete Jessen, Norman Keeler, and Charles Gray; (back row) George Harron, ? Sickles, James Taylor, Tracey Norton, and Fred Pullen. (Beth Wham)

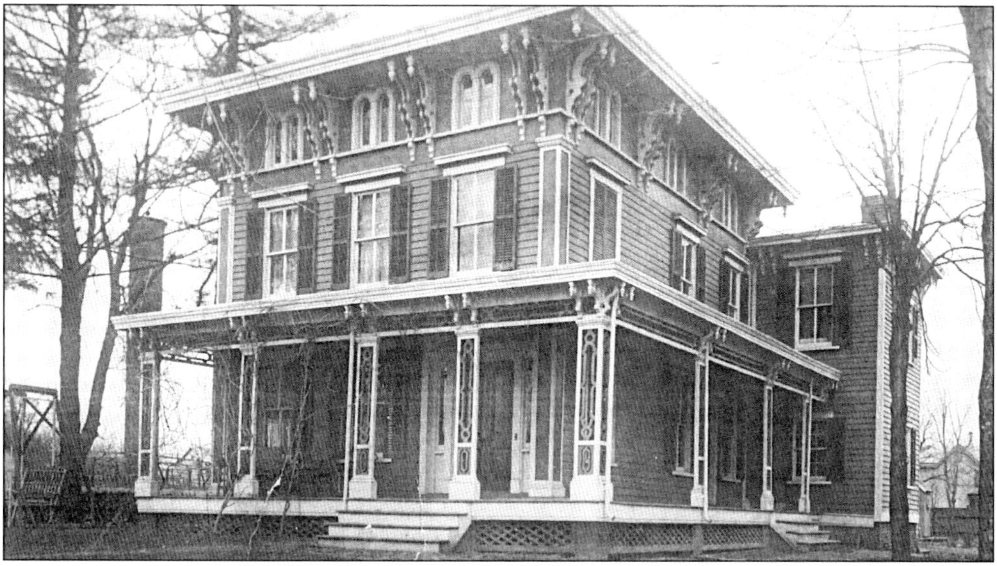

SHANGLE HOMESTEAD (c. 1902). Sering Shangle built this house in 1856. One of his sons, John R., served as Hightstown's mayor from 1907 to 1910 and was a numerator in the 1920 census. Mr. and Mrs. John R. Shangle's son Clifford was born there in 1882. Hightstown's water stand pipe (at left) was installed in 1893 and water from artesian wells was drawn into it. From the mid-1920s to the early 1930s, the structure was a NJ State Troopers barracks. The original hitching posts for the police horses are still in front of the home. A large garage at the rear of the building housed, at various times, the troopers' horses, their Harley-Davidson motorcycles, and the Buick Touring Cars used in police work. Currently this house with double windows and oval tops under the cornices is the Glackin-Saul Funeral Home, located on the corner of Morrison Avenue and Center Street. (Bob Pierce)

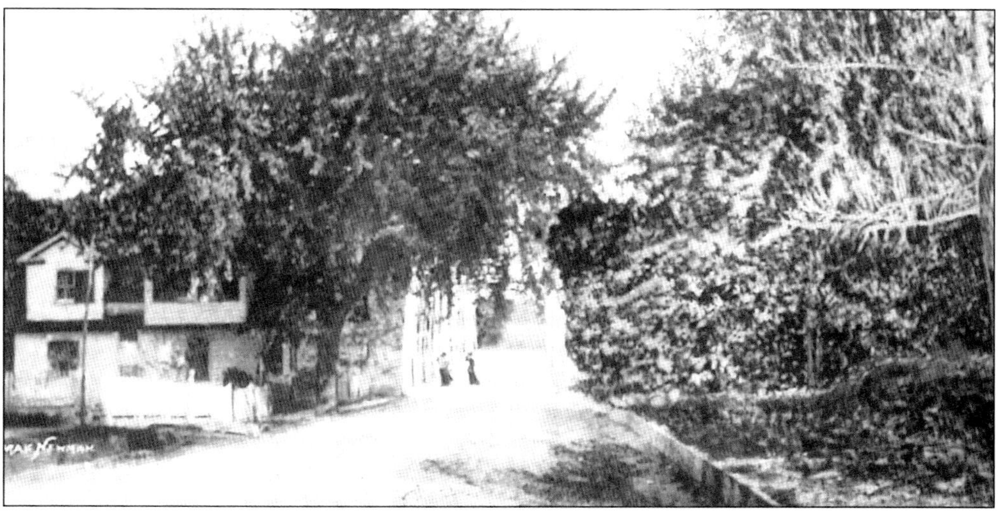

OUT FOR A STROLL (c. 1902). Two young ladies have just crossed the bridge on Lover's Lane that was built in 1896 across Hightstown Pond. The house at the foot of the bridge, built in 1900 by Albert M. Norton, has many balconies, gables, and dormer windows. With its hand-carved wood panels and clever use of space, it exemplified the emerging "Arts and Crafts" movement in house design. For many years, Norton operated a boathouse with boat rentals available at this location. (Brenda Dey Mac Murray)

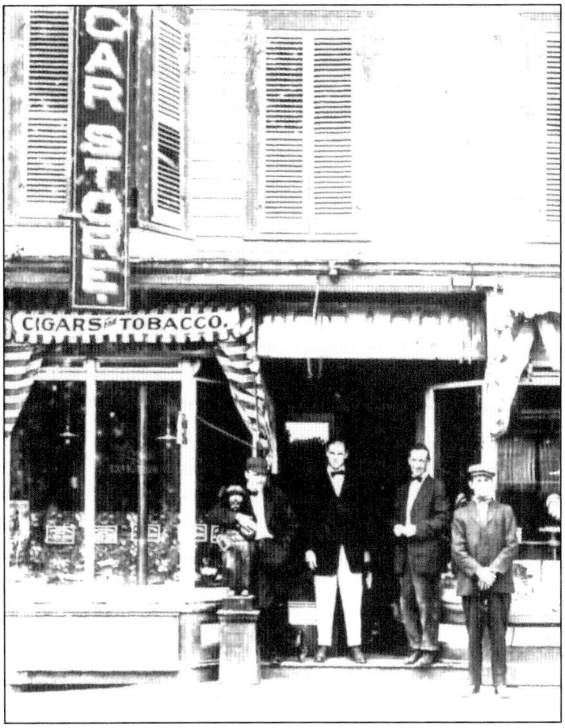

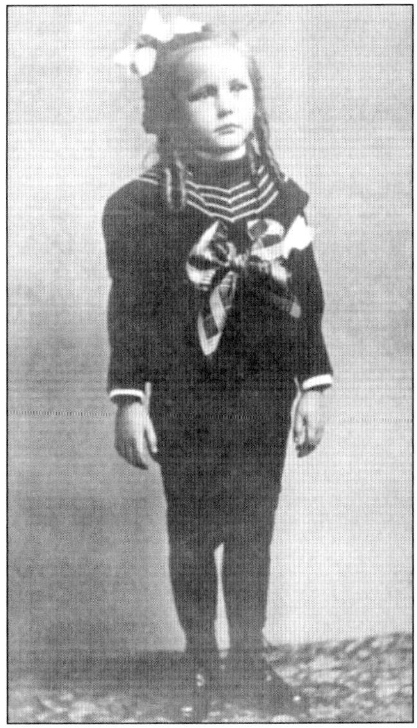

TURN OF THE CENTURY STORES (*c.* 1903). Not all cigar stores had wooden Indians in front of them—Weller's store sported a wooden "Turk," which a patron is embracing, near the door. Owner Henry Weller is third from the left in his doorway. (Hightstown-East Windsor Historical Society)

CURLS (*c.* 1903). Robert B. Roszel, while walking to Walter C. Black's home on the Old York Road, was often chased by gypsies calling, "ain't she got pretty curls." (Lillian Roszel Black)

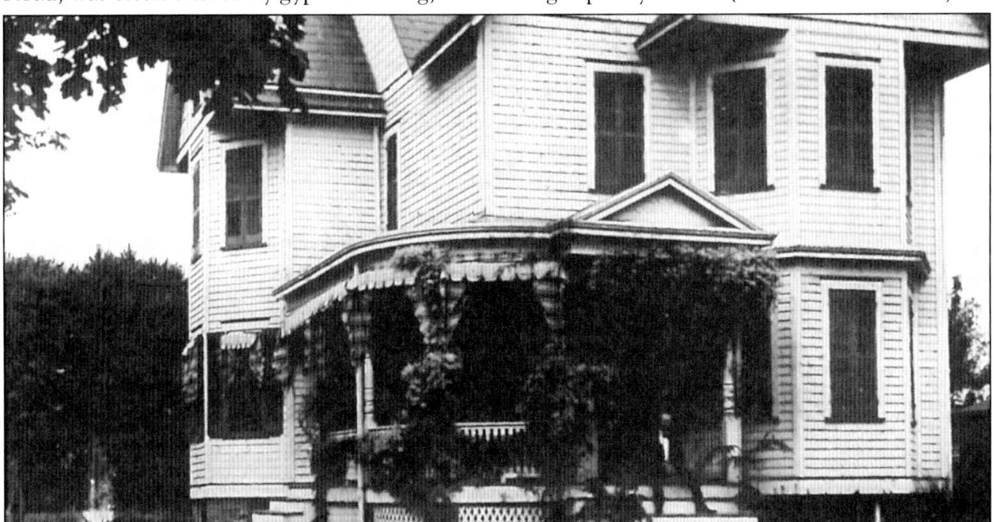

AWAITING FRIENDS (*c.* 1904). In the early part of the twentieth century, families spent much of their time conversing and socializing from the vantage point of front porches such as this one at the corner of Academy and Stockton Streets. (Beth Wham)

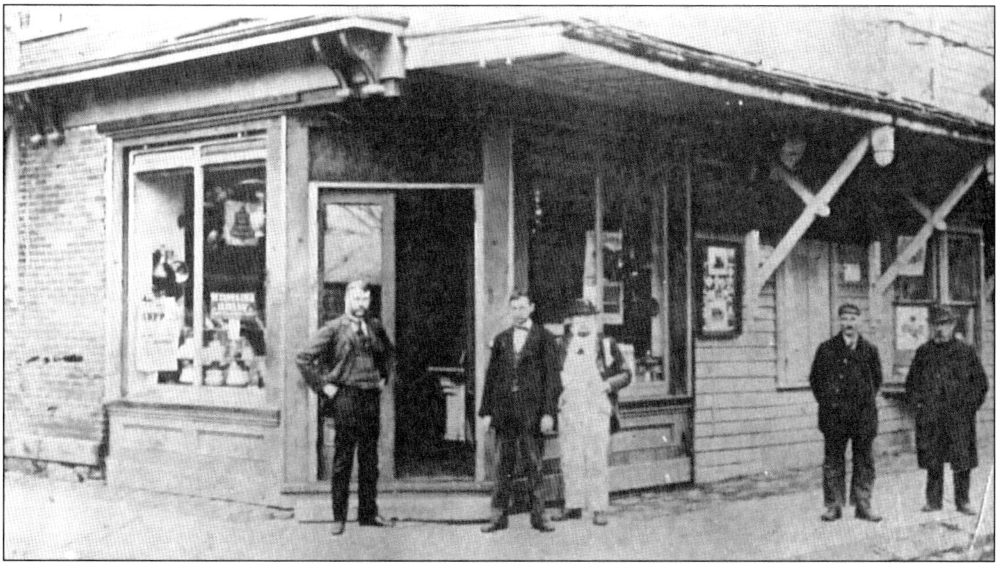

FIRST TELEPHONE (*c.* 1904). Will and D. Hart Cunningham stand on either side of the entrance to their pharmacy. In 1907 the building was changed into a three-story structure. The bell symbol in the left window indicated the location of a public telephone. In 1895, the first phone in town was installed here and the first long-distance call was made by Mayor W. Irving Norton to his brother, Dr. H.G. Norton, in Trenton, at a cost of 15¢ for five minutes. (Hightstown-East Windsor Historical Society)

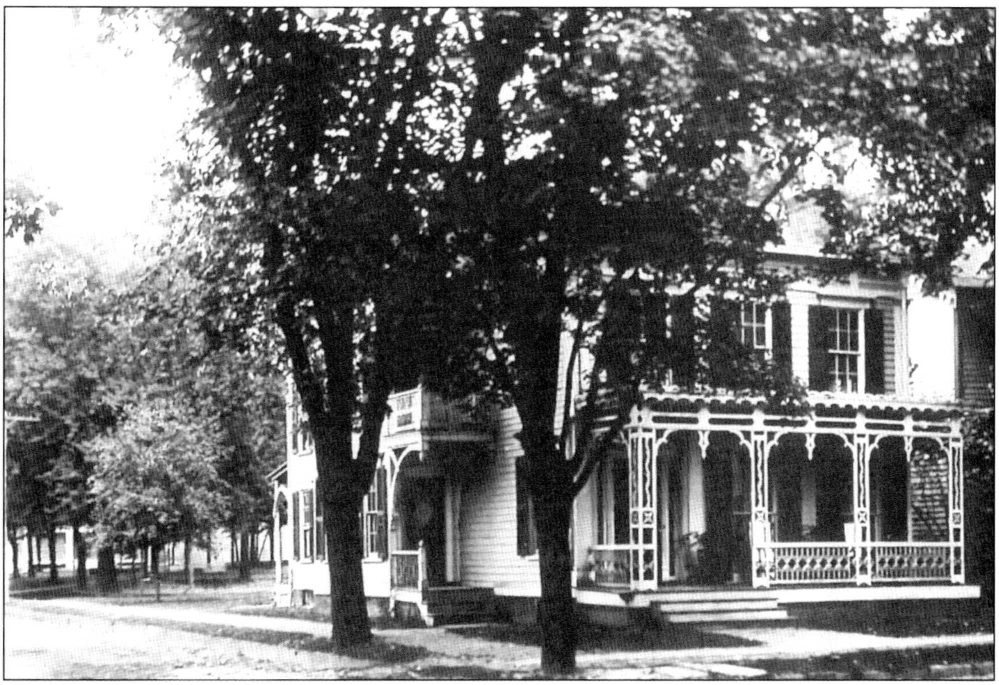

KEELER HOUSE (*c.* 1905). The home of Captain Charles Keeler on the corner of Ward and South Main Streets was purchased by Peddie in 1906, used as a dorm until 1913, and later torn down. Keeler served as Hightstown's postmaster for many years, being appointed in 1861 by Abraham Lincoln, in 1868 by Andrew Johnson, and in 1882 by Chester Arthur. (Beth Wham)

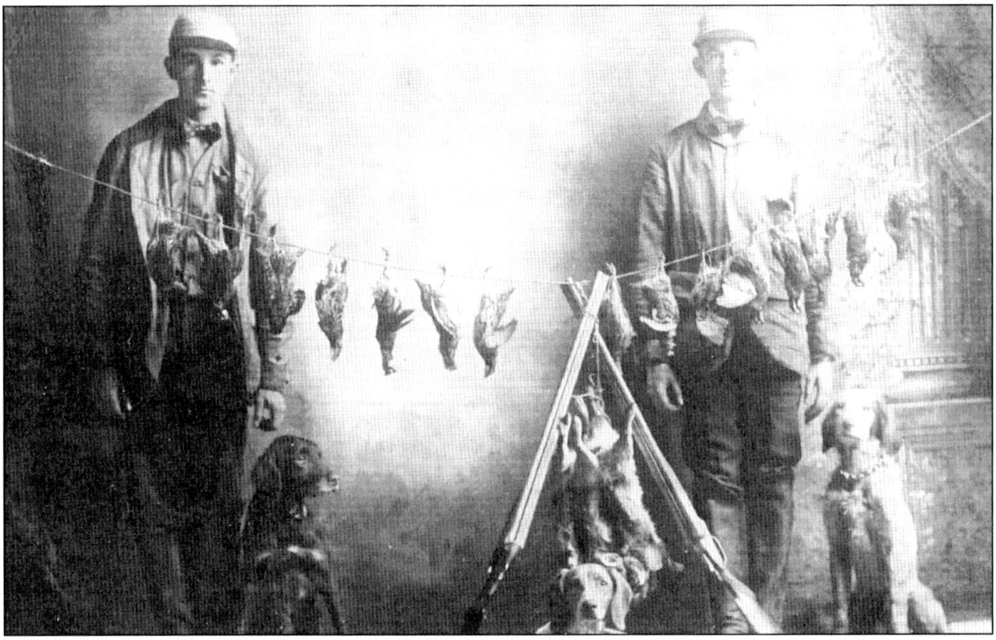

SUCCESSFUL HUNTING (early 1900s). If the number of rabbits and quail displayed are any indication, brothers David and Walter Cole and their bird dogs must have had a good day in the fields. David (1884–1939) ran Cole's Ice House, which was established by his father, David Sr. It was located off Cole Avenue adjacent to the lake. Walter, who died in 1945, served as secretary to the Masons in Trenton. (Hightstown-East Windsor Historical Society)

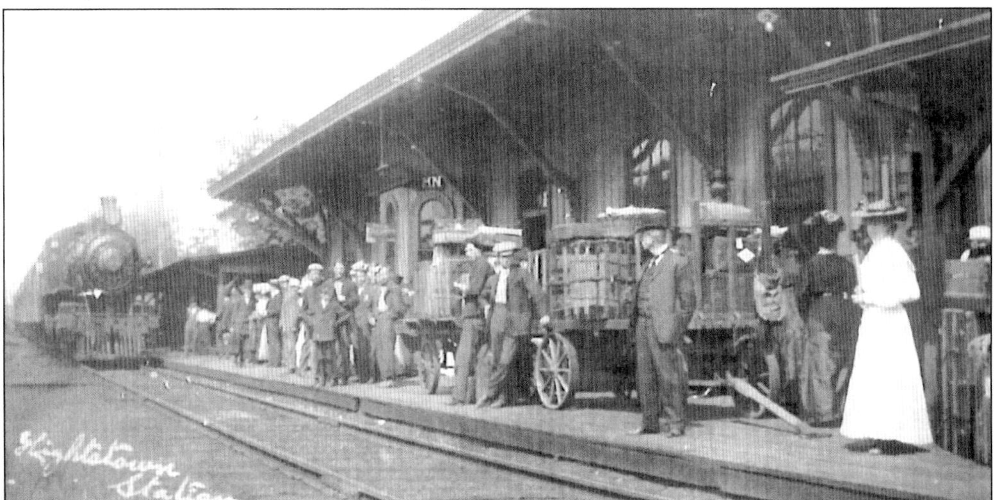

LADY IN WHITE (1906). Ethel Davison (Hutchinson)—in white—had just graduated and was awaiting the train to Newark or New York. Mr. Perrine, father of Isabelle Perrine Eldridge, is the man wearing a derby. Hightstown was a busy agricultural community and the railroad station was a bustling center of activity. In 1915 sixteen trains per day stopped in Hightstown. While on a tour of the country in 1860, the Prince of Wales appeared on the railroad platform in Hightstown. Townspeople noticed that he was wearing a "different kind of boot." Soon the local shoemakers were making ones just like it. It wasn't long before most of the local men had a pair of their own. (C. Stults Family-Allen & Stults Collection)

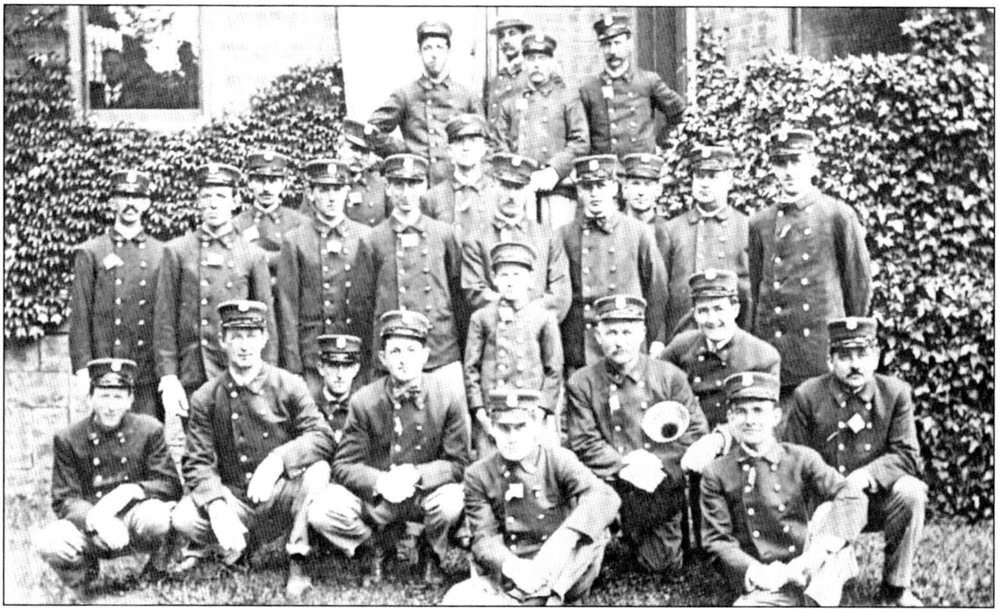

HIGHTSTOWN'S FIREFIGHTERS (1906). Ready for Decoration Day ceremonies are: (seated) Marsena Van Doren and James Taylor; (kneeling) Jack Mulvan, James Field, Walter McCue, David Cole, John H. Brandt (mascot), Chief Jeremiah Brandt, Charles Welsh, and Frank Weller; (standing in front) Elsworth Whitlock, Charles O'Hara, Forman Wright, Samuel McCue, Patty Ryan, Alonzo Pierson, William Hartman, George Norris, Fred Doyle, Harry Taylor, Charles Chamberlin, and William Taylor; (standing in back) Albert Hollenback, Albert Early, Robert Lanning, and William Scott. The photograph was taken by Peddie's Longstreet Library. Eight-year-old John Brandt became the company's mascot in 1905. He was born in a four-story building across from the old firehouse on Stockton Street that his father, Jeremiah Brandt, had purchased from John W. Dey in 1901. It had a restaurant and grocery store on the first floor where Brandt sold sea food, vegetables, and ice cream. (Cathy Simmons)

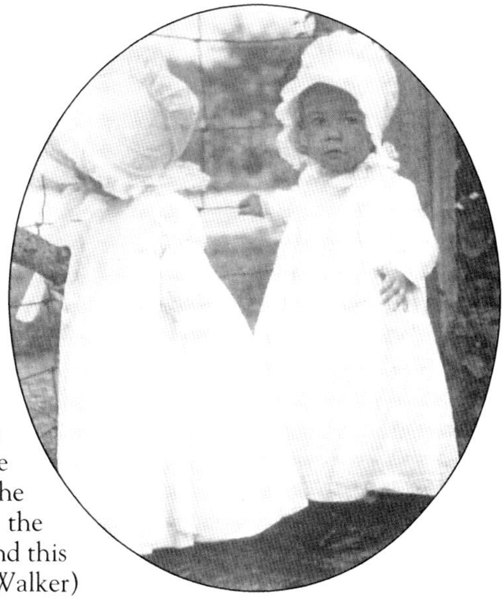

THE ASHTON TWINS (1907). On the occasion of their birth, March 10, 1906, Grace and Dorothy received silver spoons from The Friday Club. Their mother Grace had joined the group in 1898, the year the club was founded, and this gift began a club tradition. (James and Barbara Walker)

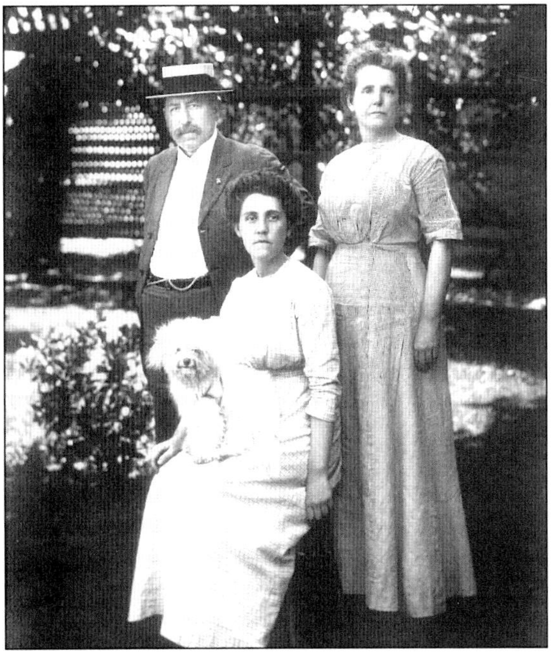

DR. TITUS' FAMILY (c. 1907). Dr. and Mrs. George E. Titus pose with their only child Katherine and their dog. In 1900, Dr. Titus persuaded the town to install a filter system for its water supply, and in 1913 to set up a sewer system. On November 2, 1912, Governor Woodrow Wilson, returning from a political rally in Red Bank, was involved in an accident when the car in which he was riding struck a mound of earth at the corner of Main and Monmouth Streets. Mr. Wilson was thrown against the top of the car and suffered a 4-inch long gash near his forehead. Local Doctors Titus and Franklin tended to him. Three days later Wilson was elected president. (Jeff Bond)

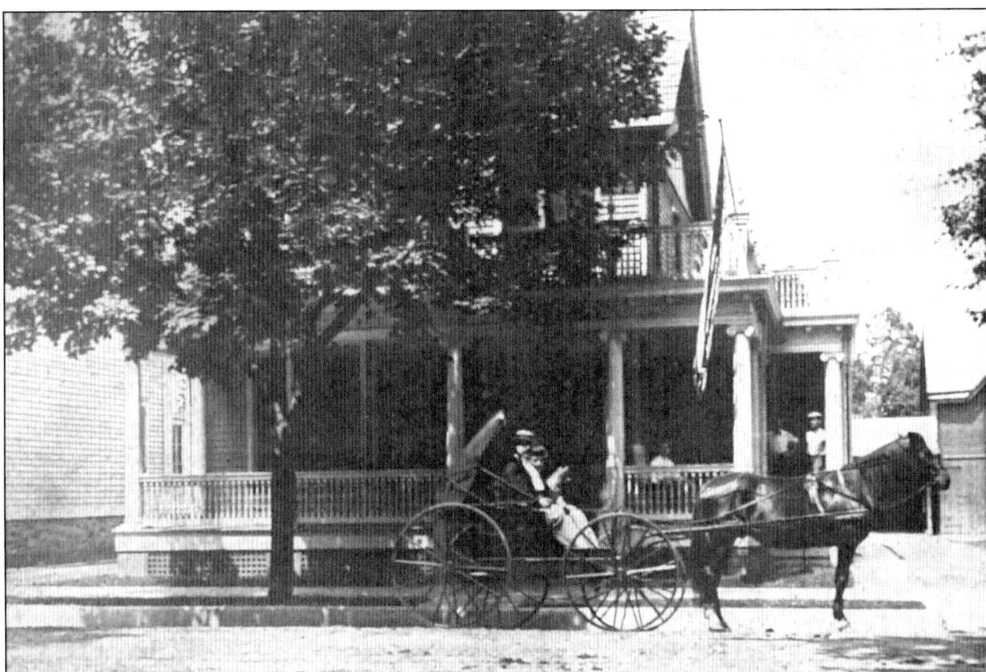

BUGGY RIDE (c. 1907). Dr. Titus (1855–1916) and his wife prepare to leave their home at 210 South Main Street. Dr. Titus graduated from Bellevue Hospital Medical School in New York City in 1877 and began practicing in Hightstown in the early 1880s. Dr. Titus served the town as a member of the borough council, president of the building and loan association, and master of the local Masonic Lodge. The Titus home was built in 1884 by George E. Pierson. The porch and side addition were built c. 1906. Titus' daughter Katherine, who married Lloyd Hulick in 1953, lived in the home until her death in 1980. (Jeff Bond)

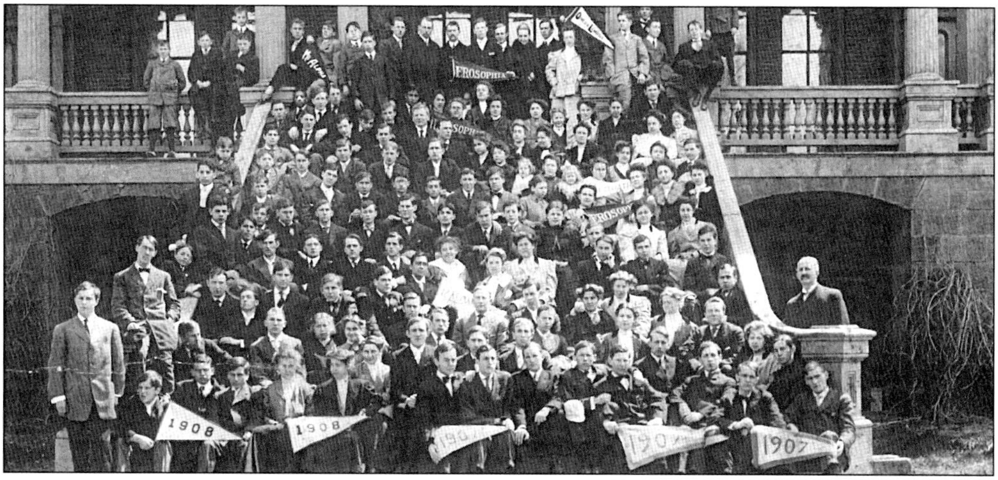

LAST DAYS (1908). Coeducation was ended at Peddie in 1908 by Dr. Roger W. Swetland, principal from 1898 to 1934 (shown standing on the right in this photograph). During the early coed era, girls were permitted to meet boys only in the classroom, chapel, and dining hall. All other contacts had to be approved by the principal. Harvey G. Rue wrote in his recollections of Hightstown, "In 1908 an adverse influence entered this Garden of Eden (Peddie) and the girls were banished from their little Paradise." Dr. Swetland's contributions to Peddie included enlarging the campus to 240 acres, increasing the faculty and enrollment, hiring a school physician, raising the endowment, and adding seventeen buildings to the campus. (Hightstown-East Windsor Historical Society and Peddie Archives)

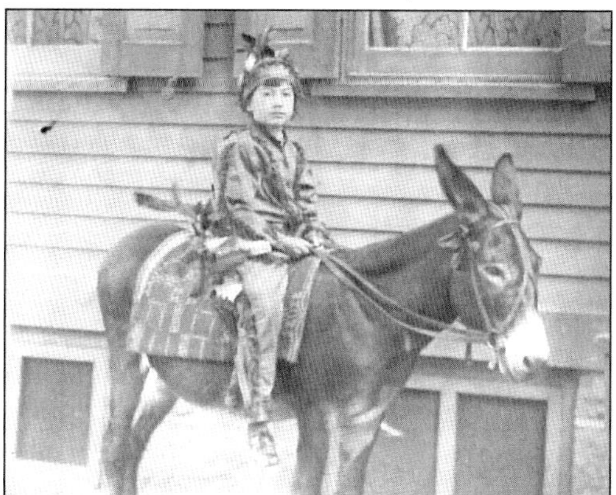

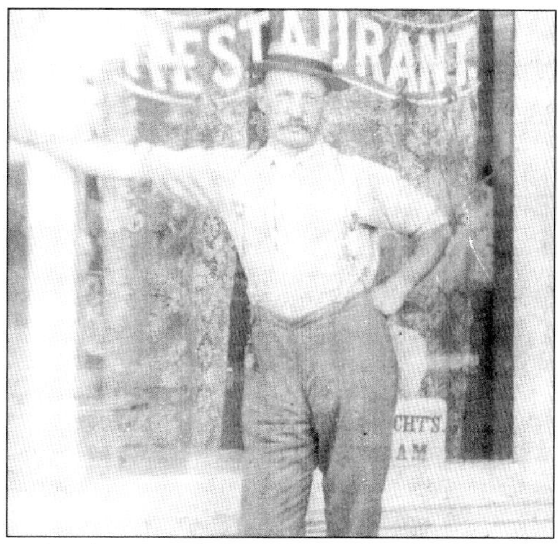

DOCTOR . . . INDIAN CHIEF (1908). Moving to Hightstown from Trenton in 1903 when he was three years old, Harold C. Cox, Sr. later became the town's favorite physician. He practiced from 1926 until his death in 1952. A graduate of the University of Pennsylvania Medical School, Dr. Cox, a true country doctor, served the borough and its surrounding area. Active in local affairs, he served as president of the Lions club, was a Mason, a member of Coterie, and president of the Mercer County Medical Society. (Harold "Skip" Cox)

GEORGE C. NORRIS (*c.* 1908). Norris (1866–1920) was born in Hightstown and for many years served as constable and police officer before becoming chief of police in 1919. Son of Mayor James Norris (1861–62 and 1871–72), George was a popular and efficient officer, known and highly esteemed by every person in town. At his death, he was the last surviving charter member of Engine Company No. 1, Hightstown Fire Department. (Evelyn Reynolds)

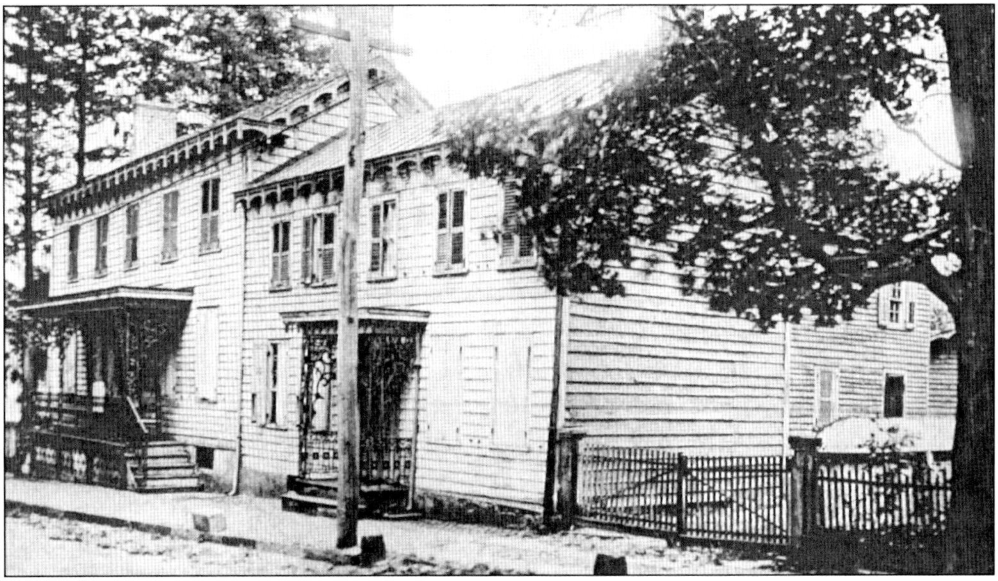

THE SMITH HOUSE (c. 1908). Probably the oldest house in town, the rear portion was built in the early 1770s by Israel Baldwin. Captain William Smith established a store in this building in 1783. In 1819 when Hightstown was large enough to have a post office, one was opened in part of this house with Robert Purdy as postmaster. Many went to the post office each day that the stagecoach arrived with mail, even though there was not the slightest chance of receiving a letter. This custom was never quite abandoned until the establishment of house deliveries in 1915. (Hightstown-East Windsor Historical Society)

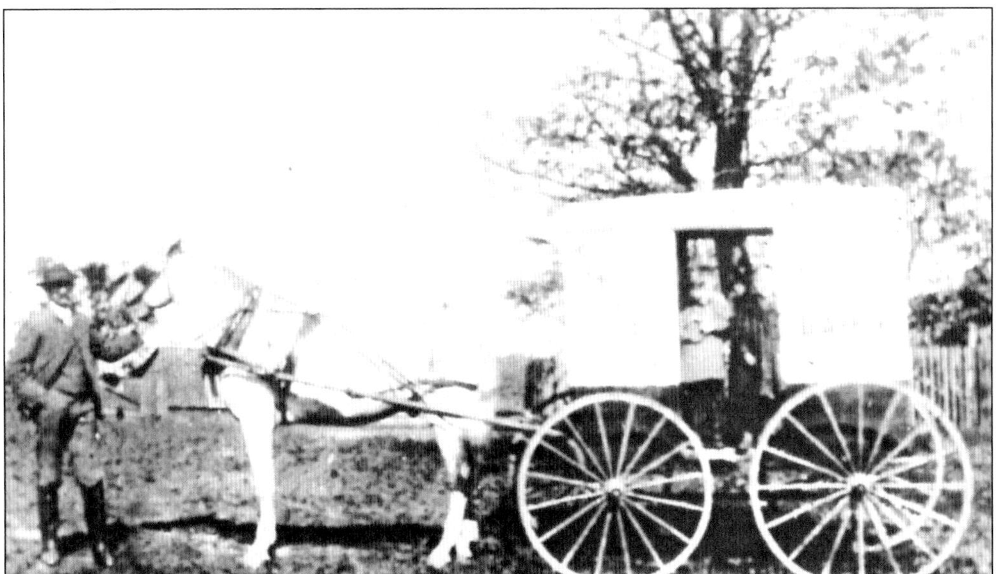

PICKERINGS DAIRY WAGON (c. 1909). Milk from Pickerings was only one of three daily food deliveries in the early 1900s. If it wasn't the milkman's bell, it was the butcher's horn or the baker's gong that brought residents rushing from their homes to make their purchases. There were no milk bottles; people had to supply their own pitchers. The price was 6¢ a quart. (Hightstown-East Windsor Historical Society)

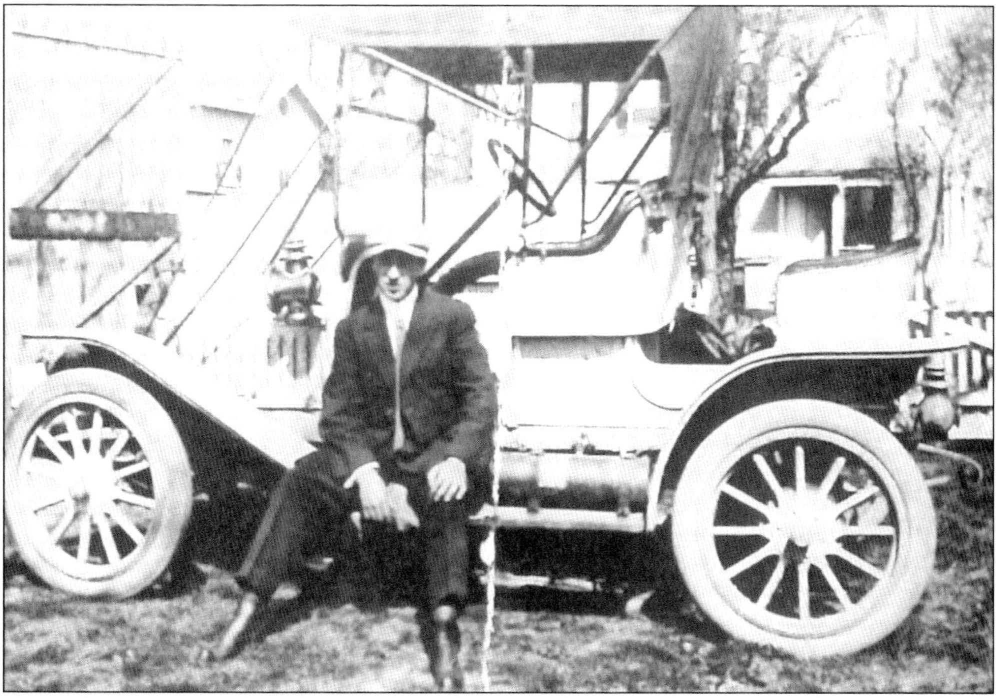

A NEW CAR (1909). Harry R. Field is relaxing on the running board of his father's first automobile—a 1909 Ford Roadster, which sold for $2,000 including extras and a special back. (Janet Field)

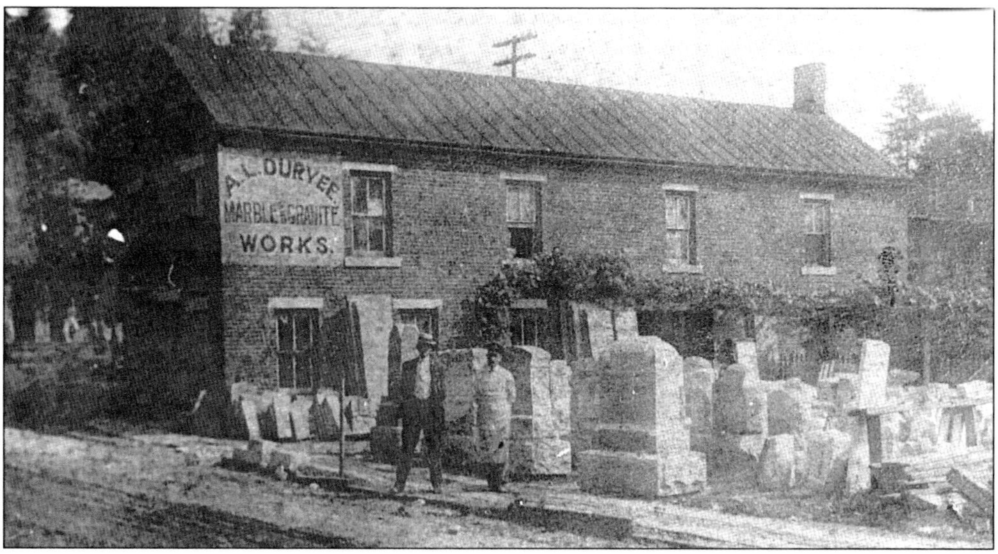

GRAVESTONES (c. 1909). About the time of this photograph, Arthur L. Duryee (left) had bought the marble and granite works that Samuel Fryer had started about 1884. It was located at the northeast corner of Rogers and Railroad Avenues. George Rue is standing next to his boss. Earlier, the brick building in this photograph had been used as a freight station—perhaps the first. The 1909 railroad station is at the extreme right. In the front of Duryee's building was an office, in the middle was a large room where monuments were lettered, and in the back was an apartment rented by John and Phoebe Dey. (Ken Duryee)

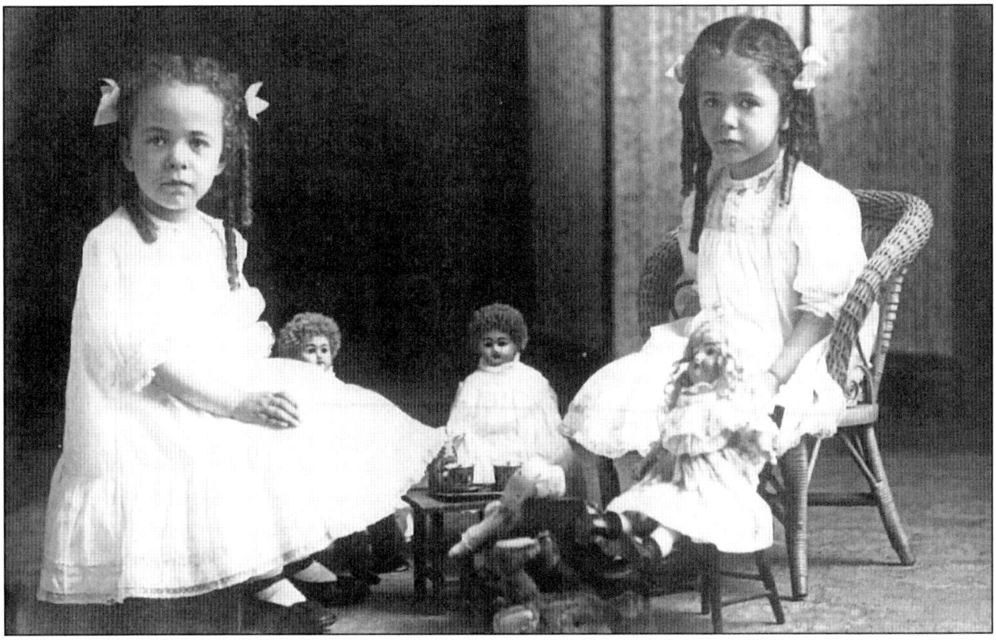

TEA PARTY (*c.* 1909). Twins Dorothy and Grace Ashton are ready for tea in their Stockton Street home with their dolls and teddy bear. (James and Barbara Walker)

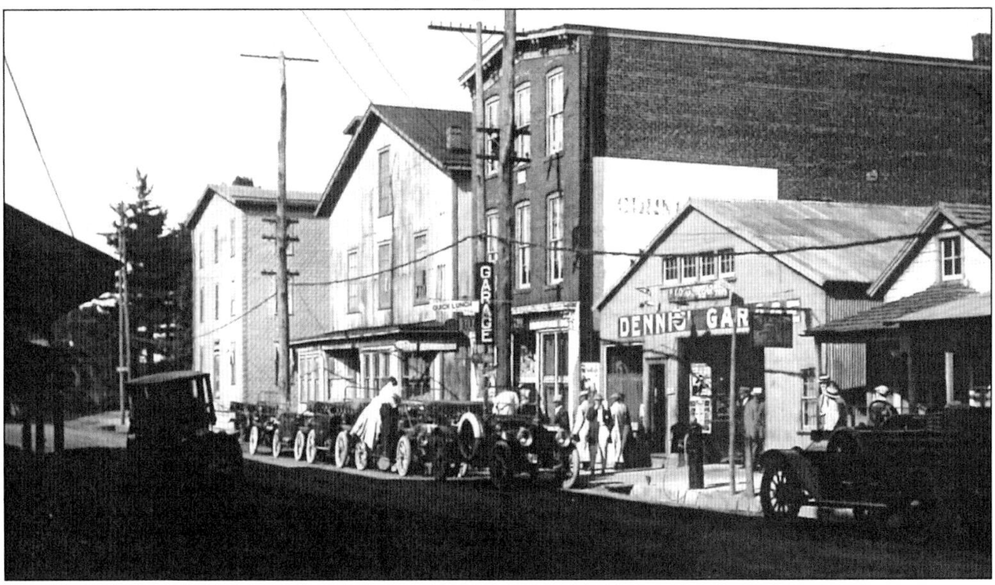

AUTO TOUR (*c.* 1909). These autos are part of a tour group—one has an Indiana license plate. The men and women are wearing long dusters in order to keep off as much road dust as possible. The buildings, from the left, are: the cereal mill, the mill's office, and a three-story building that housed the Electric Movie Theater on the first floor. The next building is Dennis' Garage. The first motion pictures in Hightstown were shown in the brick building. In his 1979 recollections, Calvin H. Perrine wrote: "One occasionally saw (or heard) a rat scurrying across the floor entirely unconcerned with the miracle of the 'flickers.' The price of admission was five cents for a twenty minute show which was quite in keeping with the quality of the movies." (Hightstown-East Windsor Historical Society)

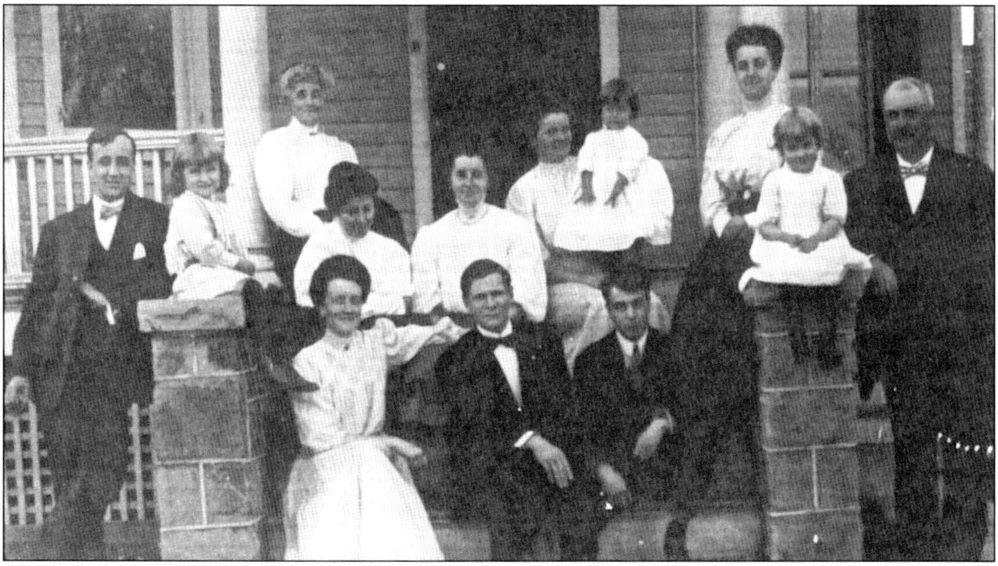

FRONT PORCH PORTRAIT (*c.* 1909). Members of the Thompson family on the front porch of their 352 South Main Street home are: (standing) William Homer Thompson, Sr. and Joseph Cook; (on bottom steps) Bessie and Norman Keeler and Ernest Thompson, Sr.; (at rear) Sarah Thompson, unknown, unknown, Ada Keeler Thompson, and Edith Thompson Cook. The children are: Homer, Katherine, and Blanche Thompson. Ladies of this era generally wore soft, white cotton blouses and long skirts. The coiffure of the period was the pompadour, drawn up high over a pad or roll of false hair. (Beth Wham)

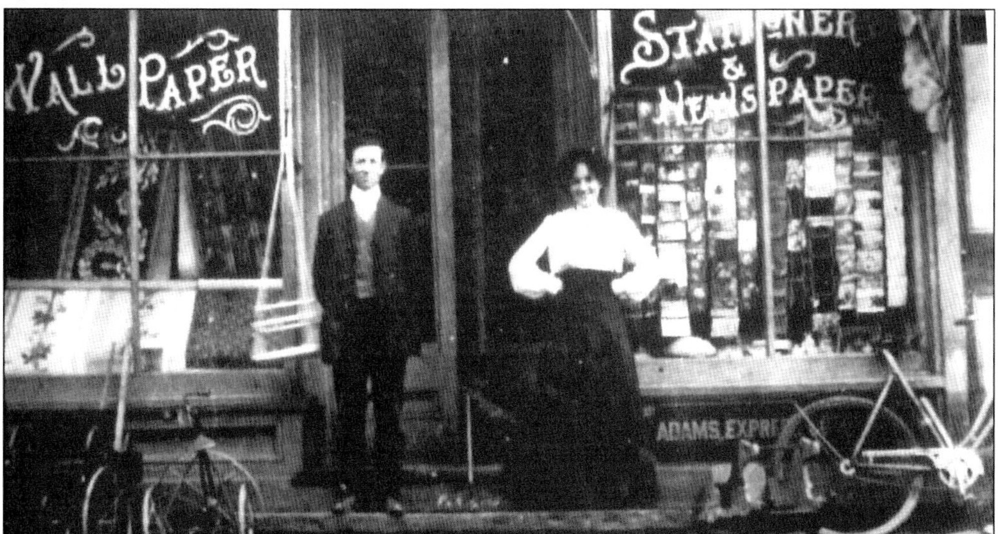

PERKY SHOPKEEPER (*c.* 1909). The lady in her fashionable blouse and skirt and the rather staid gentleman await customers at J.D. Mount's store on the eastern side of Main Street between today's dam and the Court Jester. Wallpaper is displayed in the left window and greeting cards in the right window. A tricycle, bicycle, and a rocking horse are in front of the store. Adams Express—below the right window—was the company the store used to mail packages. The store had been run by Frank Grover before the Mounts took over. (Hightstown-East Windsor Historical Society)

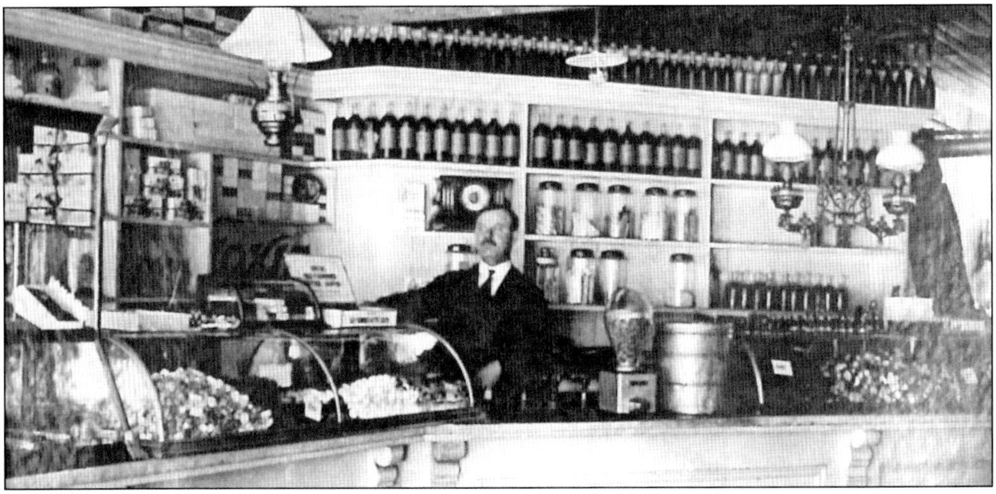

INSIDE PERDONI'S (*c.* 1909). Do you want a bottle of Moxie from the shelf or penny candy from the glass case? John Perdoni would be willing to sell you either. He is behind the counter of his well-known fruit and candy store on the western side of Main Street near Cunningham's. Notice the bare electric bulb on one of the light fixtures. Electricity had come to Hightstown in 1898 and was originally available only for a few hours at night. In 1901 it was provided for a few hours in the morning for early risers. By May of 1914, it was supplied on a twenty-four-hour basis. (Catherine P. Copleston and Phyllis Perdoni)

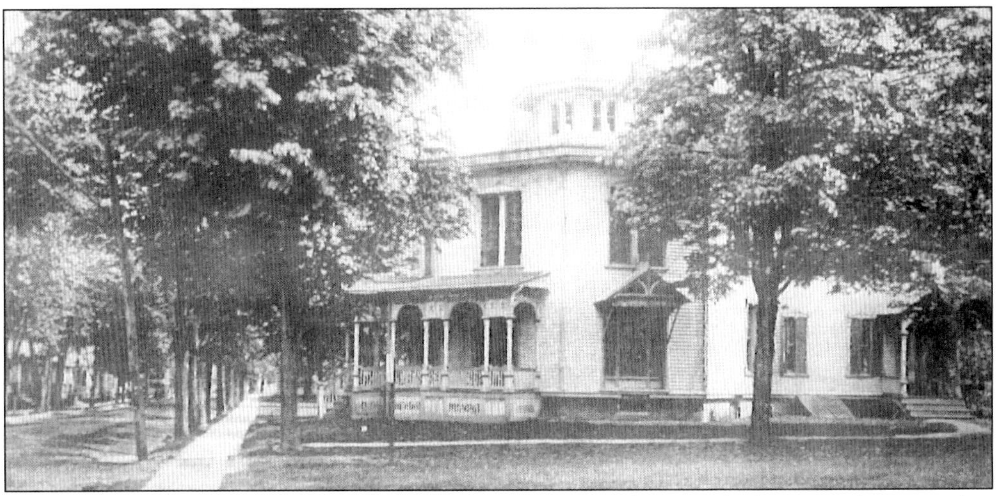

"OCTAGON HOUSE" (*c.* 1909). Built in 1857 by Dr. Calvin Bartholomew, a homeopathic physician who practiced in town for a short time, this house was presented to the Peddie School in 1896 by Hiram Deats of Flemington. Originally it had a stucco exterior, but when Carrie Hutchinson bought it she enclosed it with weather boards and built an addition in the rear. It was used by Peddie as the headmaster's house from 1900 to 1942. "Octagon House," architecturally one of the last of its kind remaining in New Jersey, was known as a "wedding cake" house because of its construction in tiers. Orson Fowler, who originated the design, claimed that the "wedding cake" was easy to keep clean because it lacked square corners. He also hailed it as a truly American design since it did not imitate European architecture. The style's advantages, according to architectural historian Robert Craig, are that it invites the sunlight in at every hour of the day and creates a large amount of living space with a small amount of building material. (Hightstown-East Windsor Historical Society)

Four

1910 to 1919

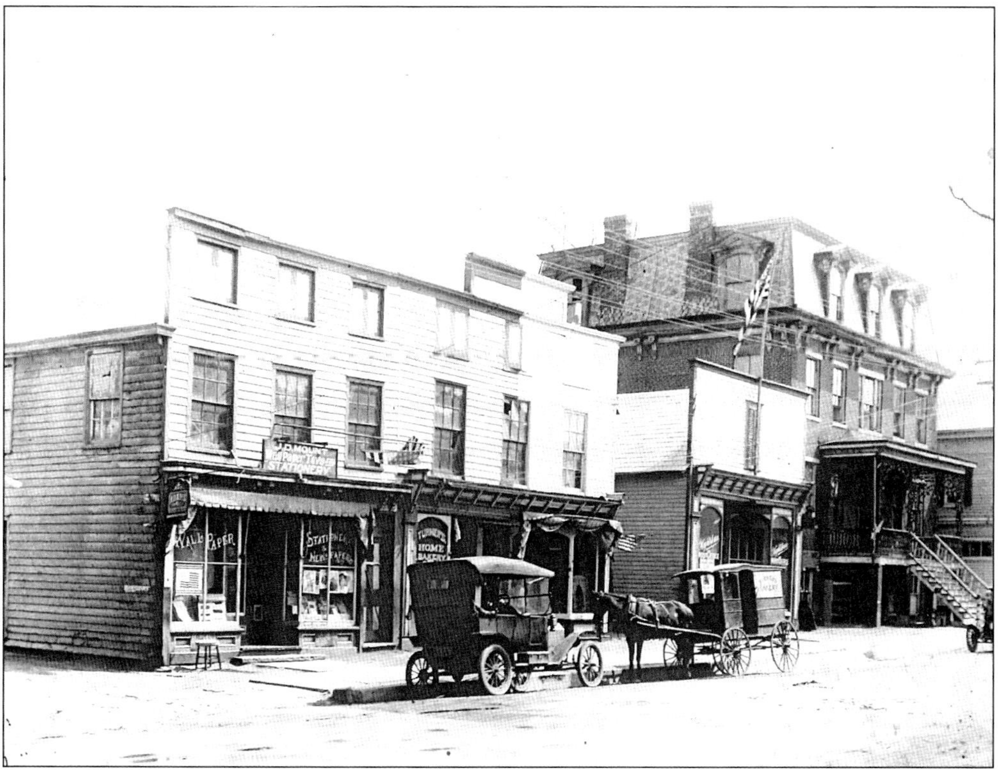

HORSELESS AND HORSE-DRAWN (*c*. 1915). The first auto was seen in Hightstown on June 7, 1900. This strange vehicle was an Orient Quadricycle; it resembled a carriage with bicycle-like wheels but lacked a horse. By September of that year, Ernest McIlevaine of Stockton Street had ordered and received the very first car owned by a resident of Hightstown—a Locomotive Steamer capable of burning up the road at 20 miles per hour. On a Sunday in July of 1903, a Mercer Street resident was able to see through the clouds of dust and count thirty-four cars passing by in one hour. The post office shown in the background with the flag above it was on Main Street facing Stockton Street. It contained four hundred boxes and its dimensions were 25-by-40 feet. To the left of the post office are Mount's Stationery Store and Turner's Bakery. To the right is the three-story Smith Building, which once housed the First National Bank. (Hightstown-East Windsor Historical Society)

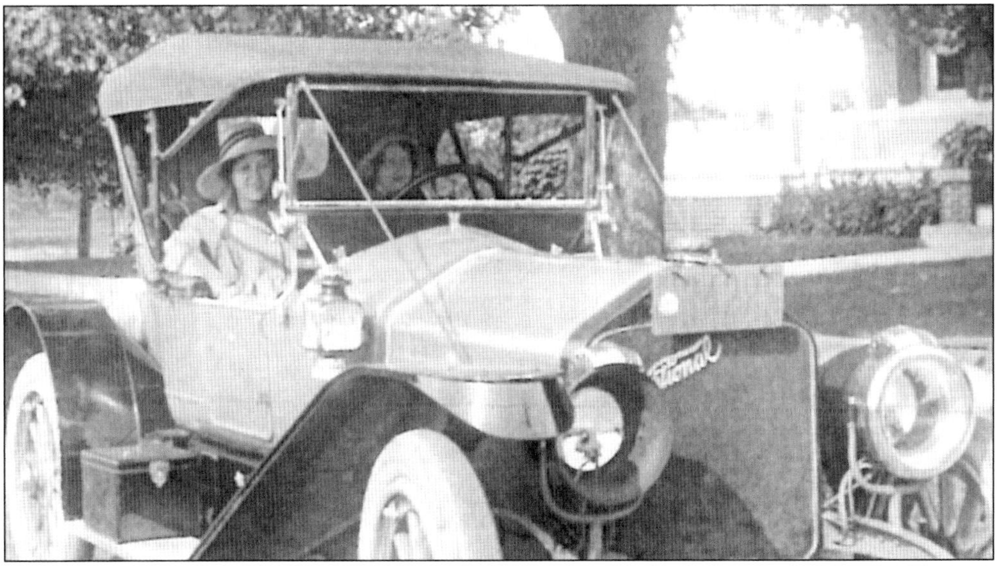

NETTIE AND ESTELLE BLACK (*c.* 1910). Nettie M. Black (Stults) and Estelle R. Black (Waite) are ready for a ride in their father's (Walter C. Black's) 1909 National. Reportedly, Nettie was the first female in Mercer County to receive a driver's license, about 1912. Both young ladies graduated from Wells College, Estelle being the first Hightstown woman to graduate from a four-year college. The sisters are in front of their home on the Borough-Township line where the Peddie Golf Course is located today. The house was razed in the 1970s. (C. Stults Family-Allen & Stults Collection)

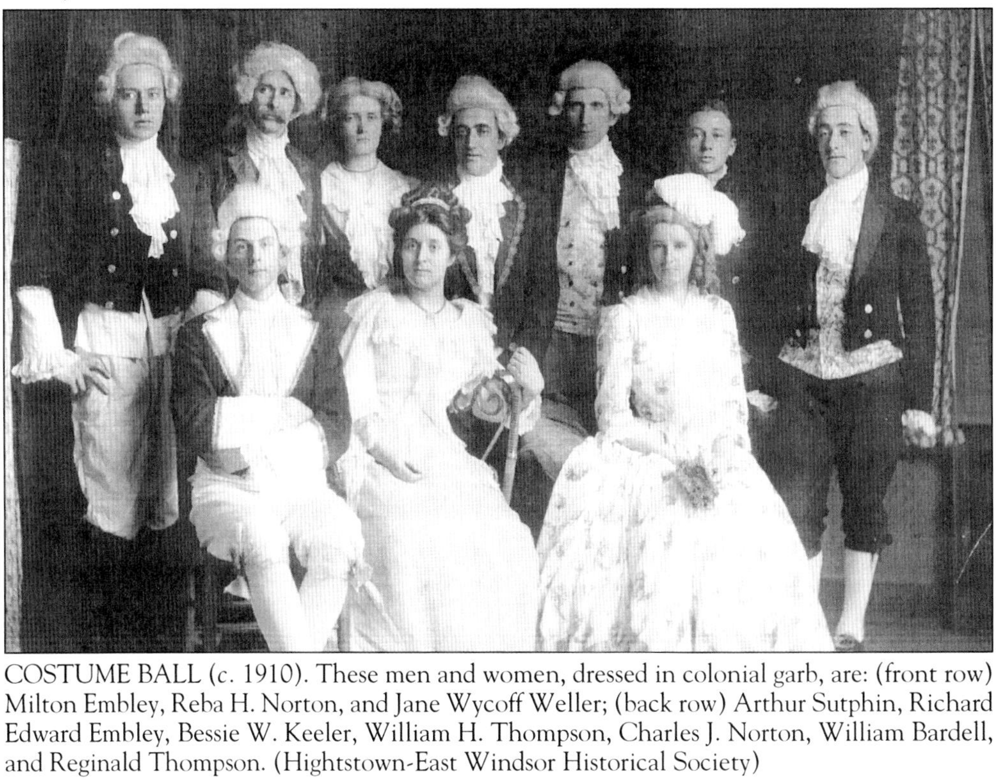

COSTUME BALL (*c.* 1910). These men and women, dressed in colonial garb, are: (front row) Milton Embley, Reba H. Norton, and Jane Wycoff Weller; (back row) Arthur Sutphin, Richard Edward Embley, Bessie W. Keeler, William H. Thompson, Charles J. Norton, William Bardell, and Reginald Thompson. (Hightstown-East Windsor Historical Society)

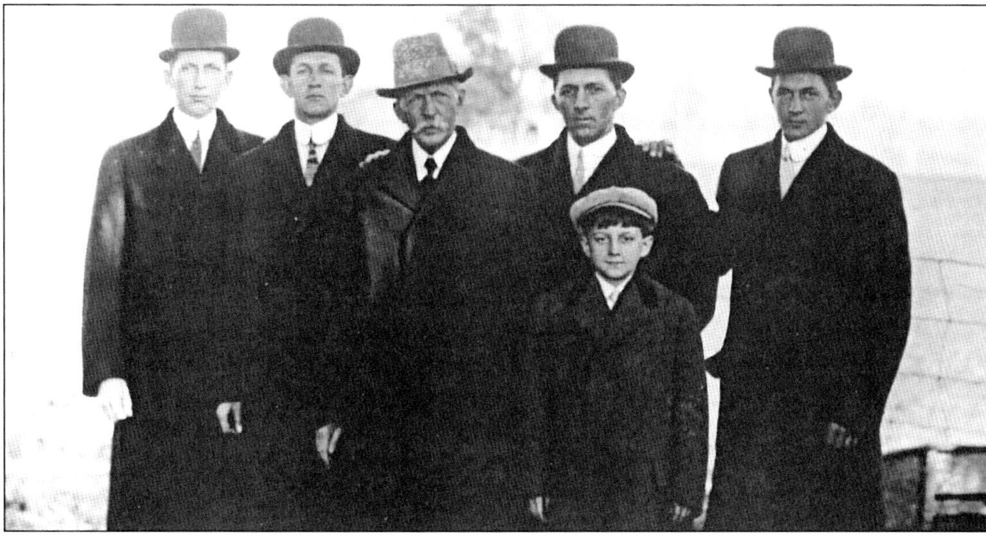

FATHER AND SONS (*c.* 1910). Watson Hancock (1851–1930) is surrounded by his five sons: Ernest (1886–1981), Elmer (1885–1947), Willis (1883–1959), Harry (1890–?), and (in front) John (1900–1947). Watson and his wife also had three daughters and lived on a farm on York Road near the East Windsor-Washington Township line. (Lois Groendyke)

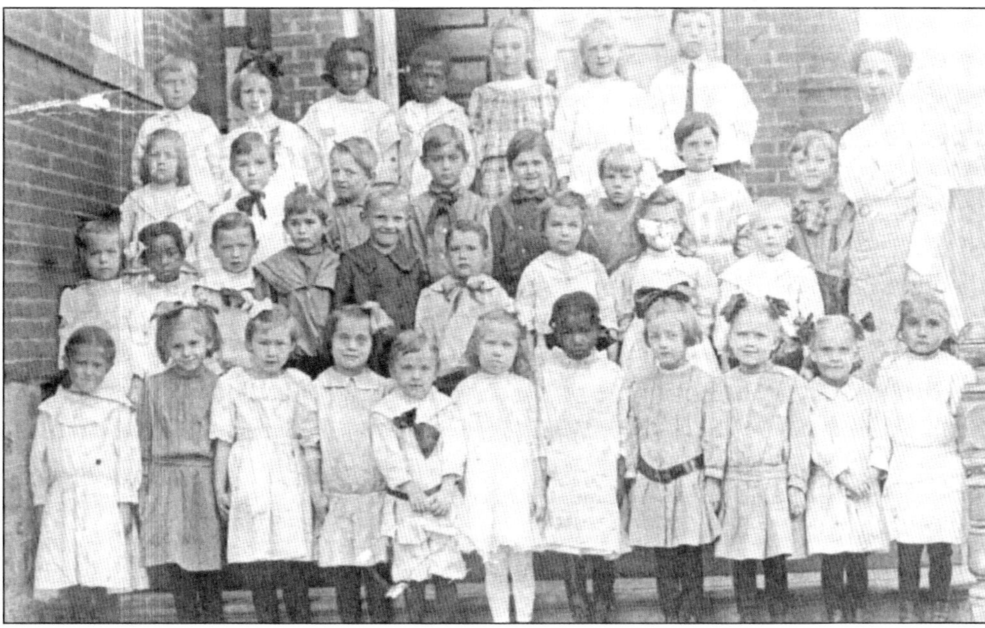

MERCER STREET SCHOOL KINDERGARTEN (1910). Elizabeth Grover Silvers, a youngster in this class, well remembers the outdoor toilets at the rear of the building. Those pictured are: (front row) unknown, ? Messler, ? Reil, unknown, unknown, Elizabeth Grover (Silvers), Viola Wormley, Isabella Lusby, Della Brown (Wiley), Edna Brown (Blake), and Mary Saltzer; (second row) unknown, unknown, Clarence Strang, ? Messler, unknown, Ted Hopkins, Jeanette Peterson, unknown, Frank Stumpt, and unknown; (third row) unknown, Warren Taylor, unknown, Enos Stanhope, unknown, unknown, Elsie Tornquist, Alan Kane, and Edna Conover (the kindergarten teacher); (back row) unknown, Beatrice Davison, Myrtle Copeland, ? Miner, Mary Stumpt, and ? Crowshaw. (Elizabeth Silvers)

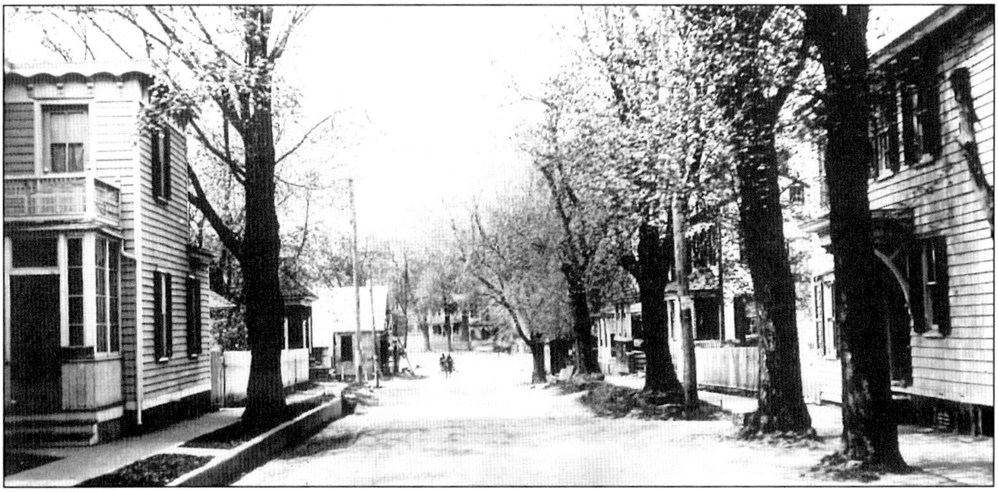

WEST WARD STREET (1910). At the time this photograph was taken, Elizabeth Grover (Silvers) lived in the house that has since been torn down at right on the corner of South Main Street. The house on the left was the office of Dr. Buchanan. Ward Street is shown running west toward Mercer Street. Elizabeth remembers that her mother often told her that if she wasn't good, she'd let the rag man have her. When the rag man came with his horse and wagon, Elizabeth would hide in the outhouse. (Elizabeth Silvers)

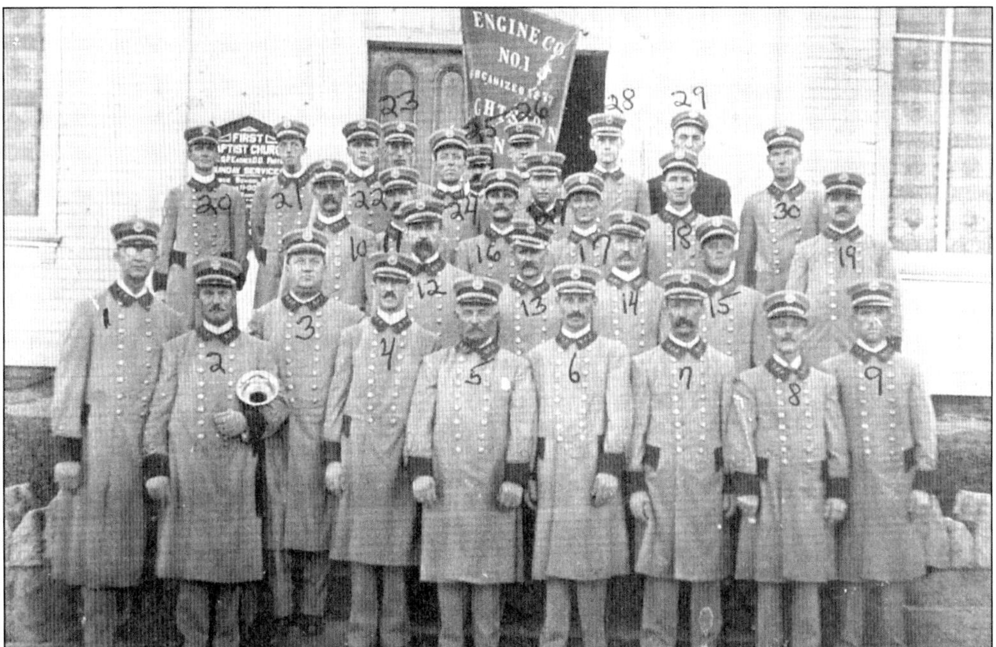

SHARPLY UNIFORMED FIREMEN (1910). A formal photograph of Hightstown's Engine Company No. 1 includes: (front row) unknown, F. Bodine, ? Chamberlin, ? Whitlock, C. Brandt, F.H. Wright, W.W. Scott, R. Lanning, and W. McCue; (second row) A. Norton, T. Ryart, C.C. Norris, C. Mortoti, and B. Weller; (third row) A. Early, J.C. Norris, Jacob Wetherill, ? Pierson, and C. Welch; (back row) J.B. Taylor, Al Hollenback, F.A. Doyle, S. Hulit, C. O'Hara, S. Wilson, W. Taylor, J. Mulvan, ? Van Doren, ? Hoff, and H. Taylor. (Hightstown-East Windsor Historical Society)

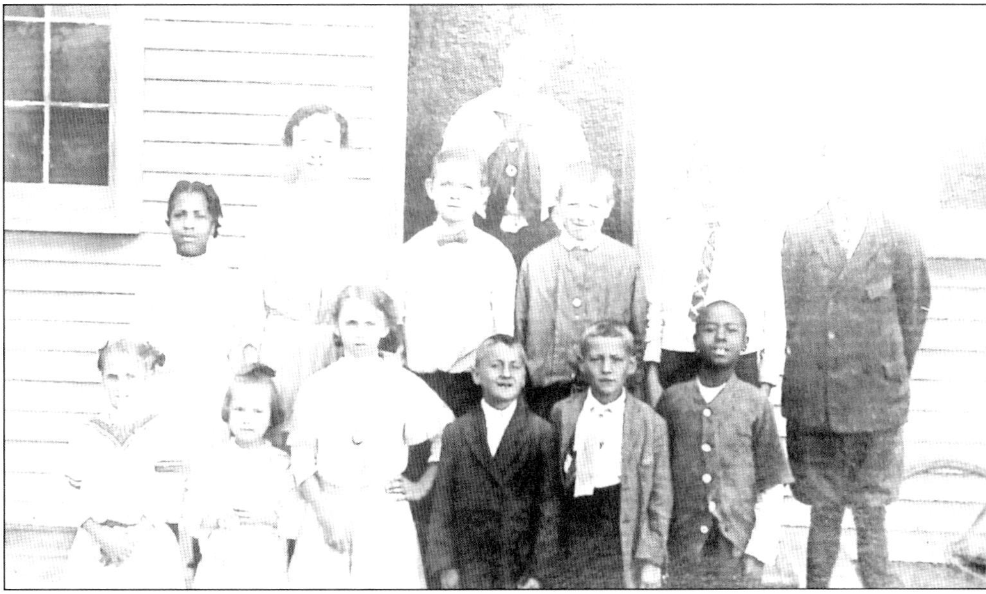

HICKORY CORNER SCHOOL (*c.* 1910). This rural school closed around this time and was razed in 1913. It was located where the little pavilion in Anker Park is situated today. The students shown here with their teacher, Miss Marian Hensch (later Mrs. James Dawes), are: (front row) Mabel Wilson, Lydia Groendyke, Bessie Wilson, Floyd Matthews, Philip Matthews, and Philip Coltrane; (back row) Lucy Coltrane, Ida Chenkin, Levi Lee, William Blizzard, Paul Bradner, and Albert Disborough. Albert traveled several miles to school each day by bicycle. Levi Lee recalls that the whole neighborhood learned to ride on Albert's bicycle (shown at far right). After this school closed, the younger students attended school above Cunningham's Drug Store in Hightstown and were transported by a school wagon. Around 1907, a teacher at Hickory Corner was paid $200 per year and the town received no assistance from the state since she was not a certified teacher. (Hightstown-East Windsor Historical Society)

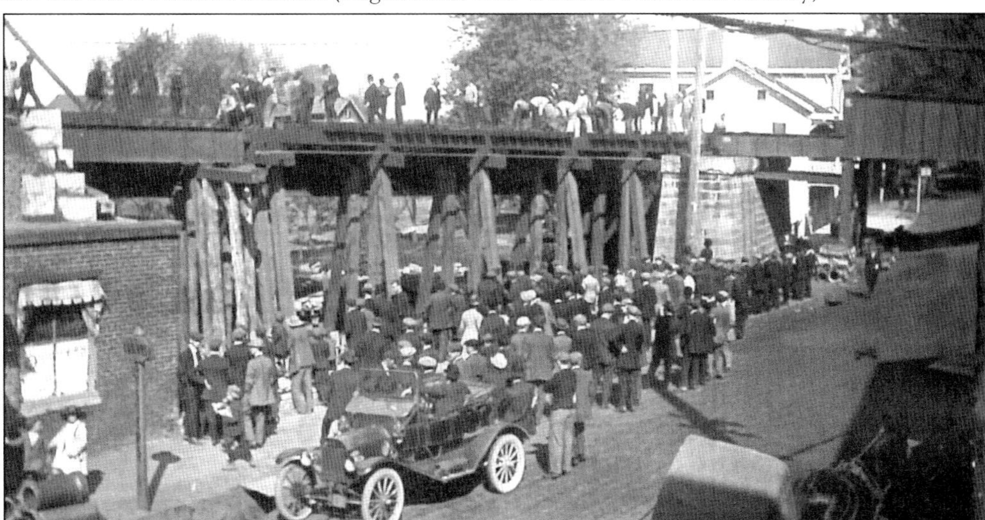

RAILROAD CONSTRUCTION (1911). Many spectators and a few workers assemble as a new railroad span is placed over Rocky Brook near Main Street. (Hightstown-East Windsor Historical Society)

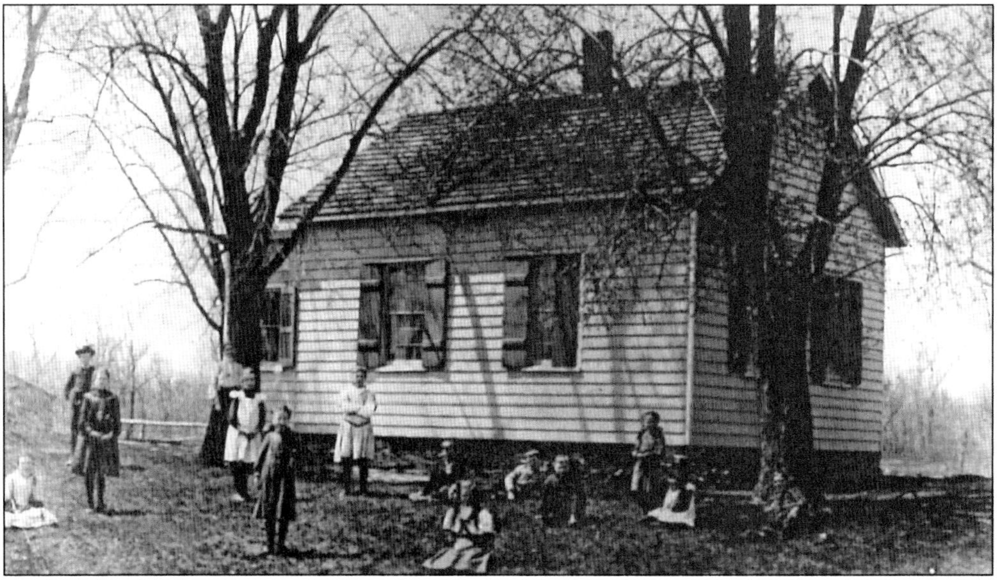

ETRA SCHOOL (1911). The teacher standing against the tree is enjoying a few moments of recess with her pupils. The girl in the foreground is Helen Peterson and the girl with her arms crossed is Edith Burroughs. Other students include: Emily, Verna, George, and Catherine Courtney, as well as Isabel Banker, Frank and Alva Norton, Milton Kerby, Isabel Damone, Anna Vote, and Albert Allen. Closed in 1913, the schoolhouse was razed in 1967. (Hightstown-East Windsor Historical Society)

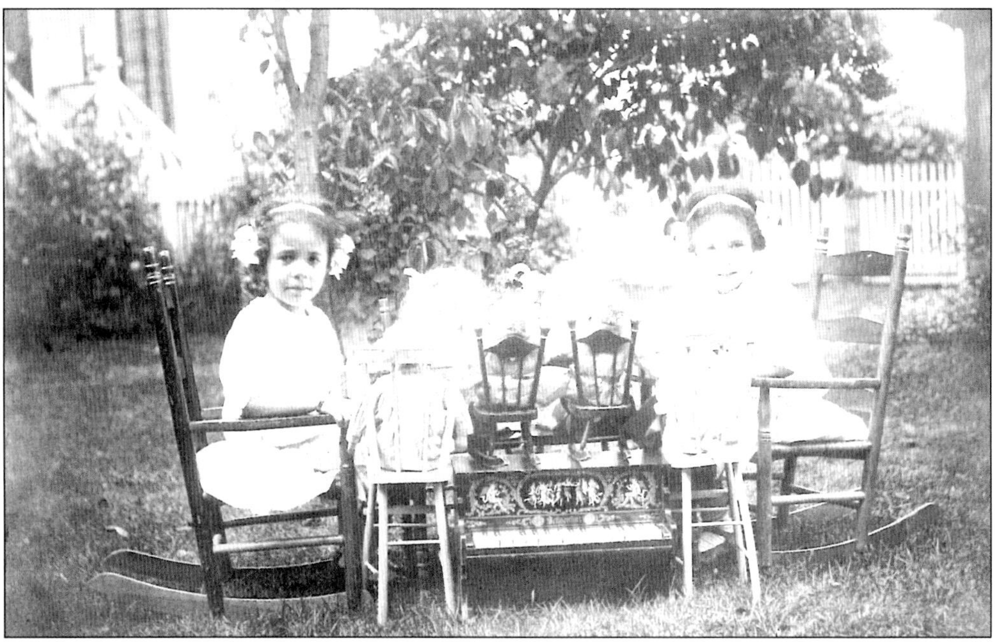

CHILDREN'S TEA PARTY (*c.* 1911). The Ashton twins, Grace and Dorothy, are seated in their rocking chairs having readied their dolls, doll high chairs, and their toy piano for a celebration in the yard of their 172 Stockton Street home. Years later, the sisters, who never married, gave piano and voice lessons to hundreds of area residents in their home. (Jim and Barbara Walker)

BAPTIST CHURCH FIRE (1911). On Sunday evening, June 12, 1911, while a Peddie Junior Prize Declamation Contest was in progress, a bolt of lightning struck the 168-foot steeple of the Baptist church. This photograph shows the resulting destruction. The bell in the steeple was damaged to such an extent that it had to be recast. Adelaide Mitchell's grandmother, Emma Eldridge, was in the church at the time and Aledaide remembers her telling of the fire. In 1857 the congregation decided to build a new church at a cost of $13,270 since the congregation had outgrown the capacity of the older building. (C. Stults Family-Allen & Stults Collection)

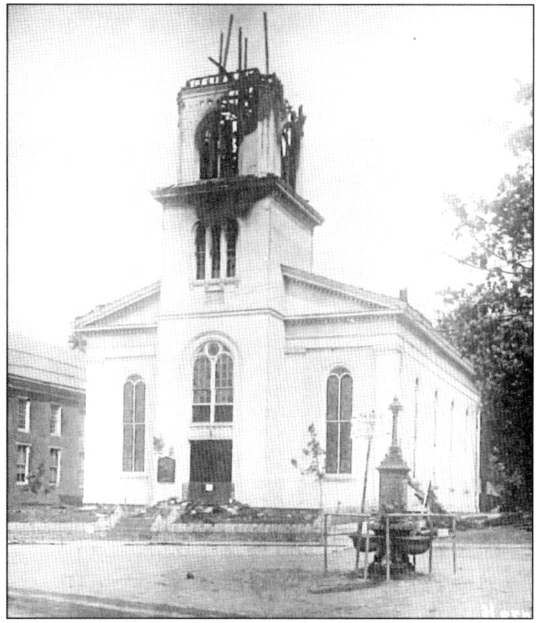

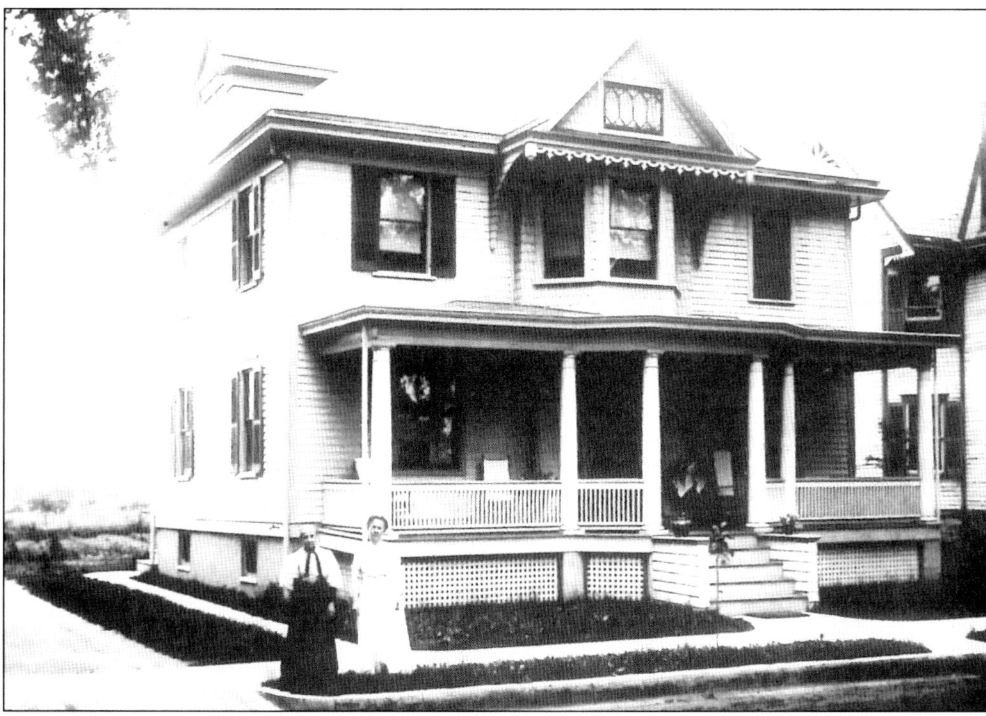

THE GROVERS' NEW HOME (1911). Emma Rogers and her daughter, Ella Rogers Grover, stand in front of the 410 North Main Street home belonging to Ella and her husband Frank. It had been built one or two years earlier for Frank Swinger. Frank Grover owned a haypress where the Hightstown Fuel Oil Company is located today. There were three fires in two years in his haystacks on Maxwell Avenue, two started by tramps who slept there and one by a spark from fireworks at Peddie. Grover later sold Studebaker cars where Kelty's Law Office is presently located. (Elizabeth Silvers)

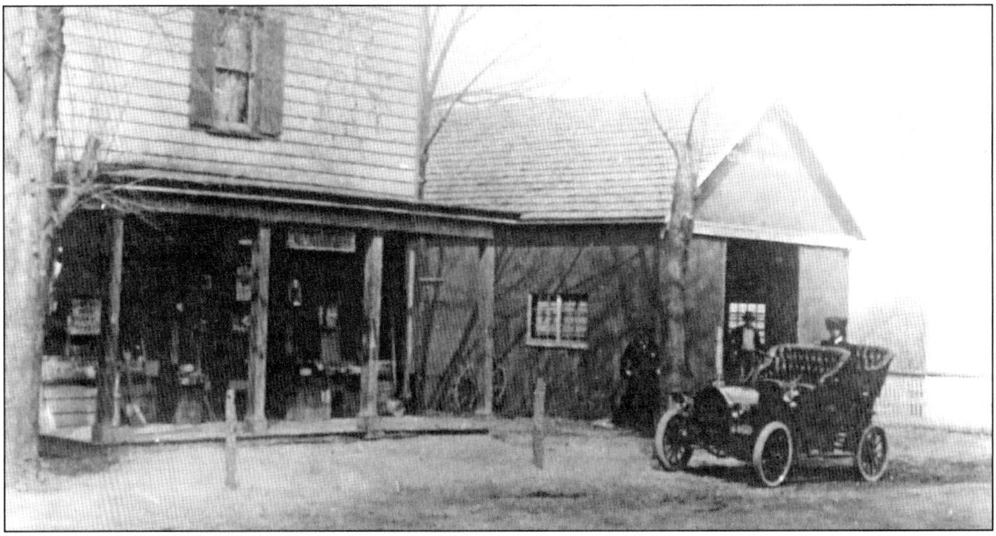

THE ETRA POST OFFICE AND GENERAL STORE (*c.* 1912). The building that housed the combined store and post office was built in 1880 by C.W. Mount. He was a member of the New Jersey Legislature and was appointed postmaster by United States Postmaster General John Wanamaker. Mount's son Syncllus was appointed to the same office in 1894. The post office closed in 1933. (Hightstown-East Windsor Historical Society)

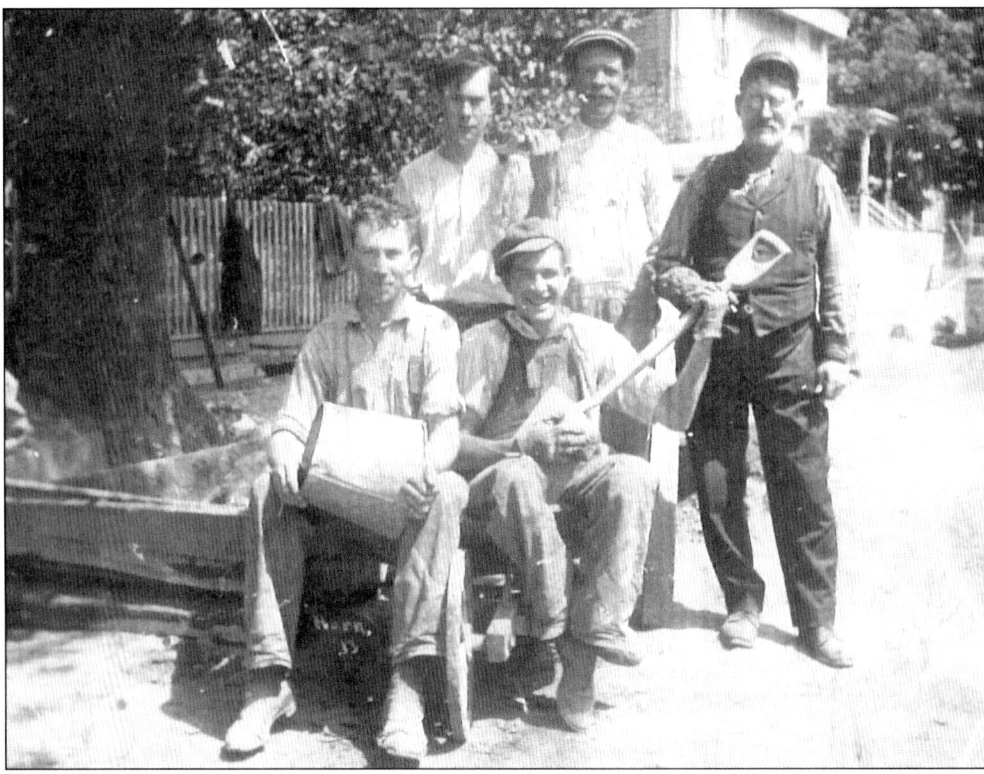

A BAND OF WORKERS (1913). While Bill Platt and an unknown friend ham it up with a pail and shovel, Sam Platt, Jr. (left), Sam Platt, Sr. (right), and an unknown worker look on. (The Al Peterson Family)

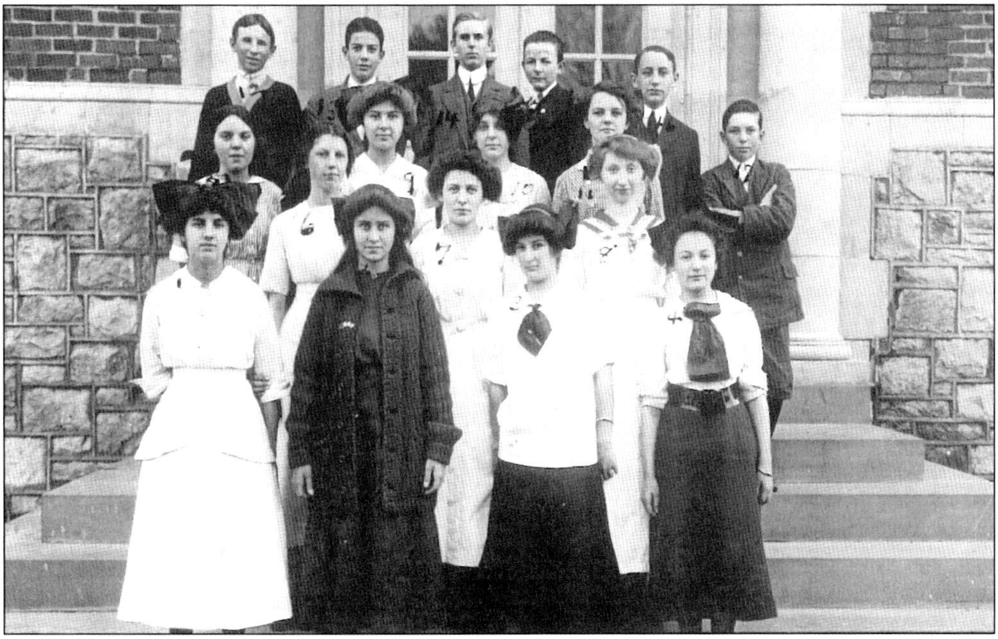

CLASS PICTURE (1913). Hightstown High School tenth graders pose on the steps of the new Stockton Street School. They are: (front row) Anna Robbins, Roberta Dey (Staley), Jule Dobson (Campbell), and Gertrude Rod; (second row) Helen Conover, Elma Black (Locke), Minnie Norcross (Howell), and Sadie Lingerman (Carson); (third row) Anna Updike (Chamberlin), Marion Bunting, and Isabelle Perrine (Eldridge); (back row) James C. Norris, Jr., Carlton Stults, Leon Dunbar, Lloyd Miller, Philip Chamberlin, and Malcolm Hutchinson. (Dorothy Petty Dey)

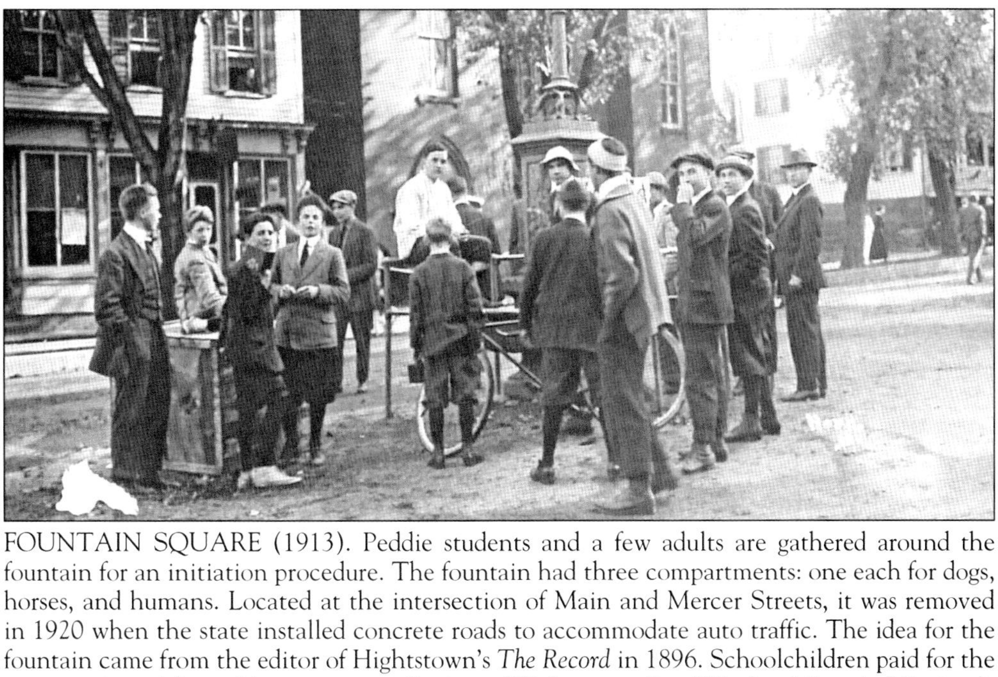

FOUNTAIN SQUARE (1913). Peddie students and a few adults are gathered around the fountain for an initiation procedure. The fountain had three compartments: one each for dogs, horses, and humans. Located at the intersection of Main and Mercer Streets, it was removed in 1920 when the state installed concrete roads to accommodate auto traffic. The idea for the fountain came from the editor of Hightstown's *The Record* in 1896. Schoolchildren paid for the construction with weekly penny contributions. (Hightstown-East Windsor Historical Society)

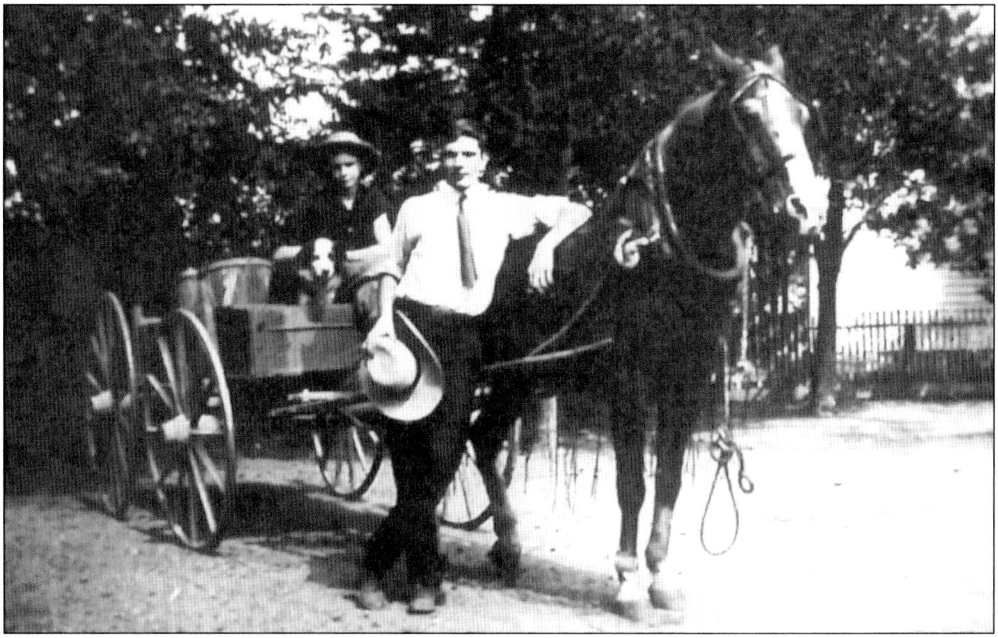

FARM WAGON (*c.* 1913). Levi Lee and his dog are seated on the wagon at the Lee farm while an unknown friend, with straw hat in hand, rests on the horse. Levi often drove the wagon when his mother sold cottage cheese and eggs door to door. He kept chickens on his father's farm, where apples were the specialty crop. Most of the farm produce was sold to small grocery stores in Trenton. (The Lee Family)

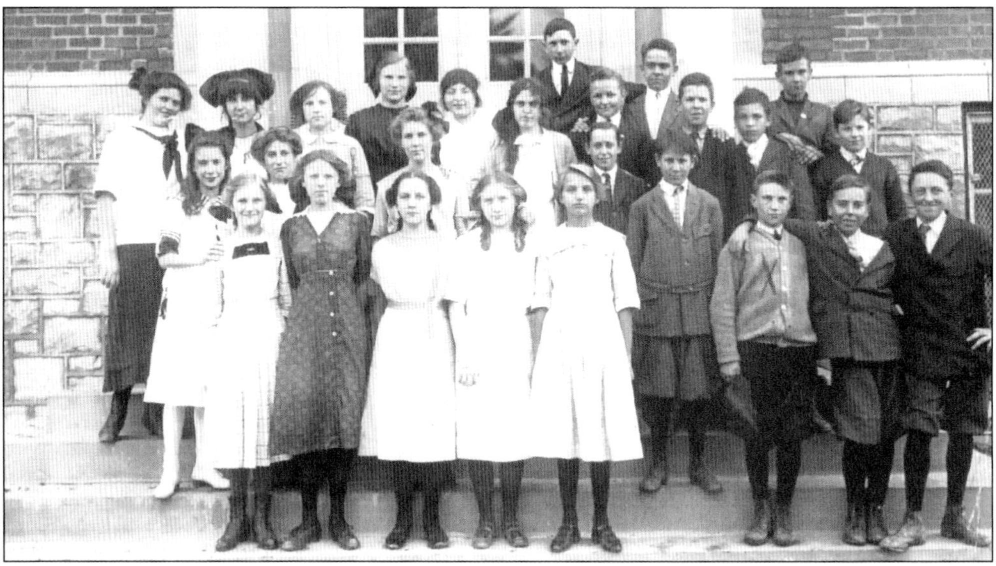

FIRST EIGHTH GRADE (1913). In September of 1913, these students were members of the first eighth grade to attend the Stockton Street School. Pictured are: (front row) Ginny Perrine, Julie Grover, Margaret Chamberlin Stults, Grace ?, Bertha Staudinger, Willard O'Phare, Hartzell F. Dubell, and Myron N?; (second row) Sue ?, Gladys ?, Grace Norton (Rogers), Merle ?, Harry Pullen, and Joe Dey; (third row) Mannie ?, Esther Dey, Sara Hutchinson, Esther Jones, Minnie Pieffer, John Chamberlin, Kirby ?, Cecil Dancer, and Thomas Assam; (back row) H. Eilers, Leroy West, and Ernest Reed. (Dorothy Petty Dey)

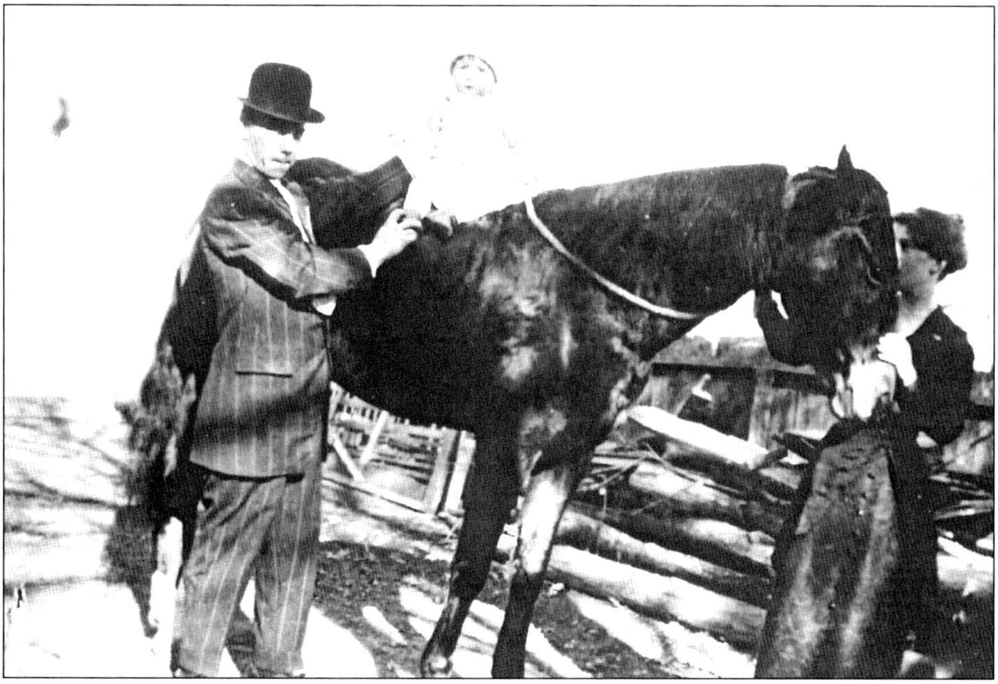

THE BABY AND THE BOWLER (1913). Edward Crowell Taylor Hutchinson, Jr. is steadied by his father, Edward, Sr., while his mother, Laura Mae (Stults) Hutchinson, calms the horse. Eddie, Jr., born in 1913, was killed in action in France on June 23, 1944. This photograph was taken on their farm at the corner of Old York and Airport Roads. (Richard S. Hutchinson)

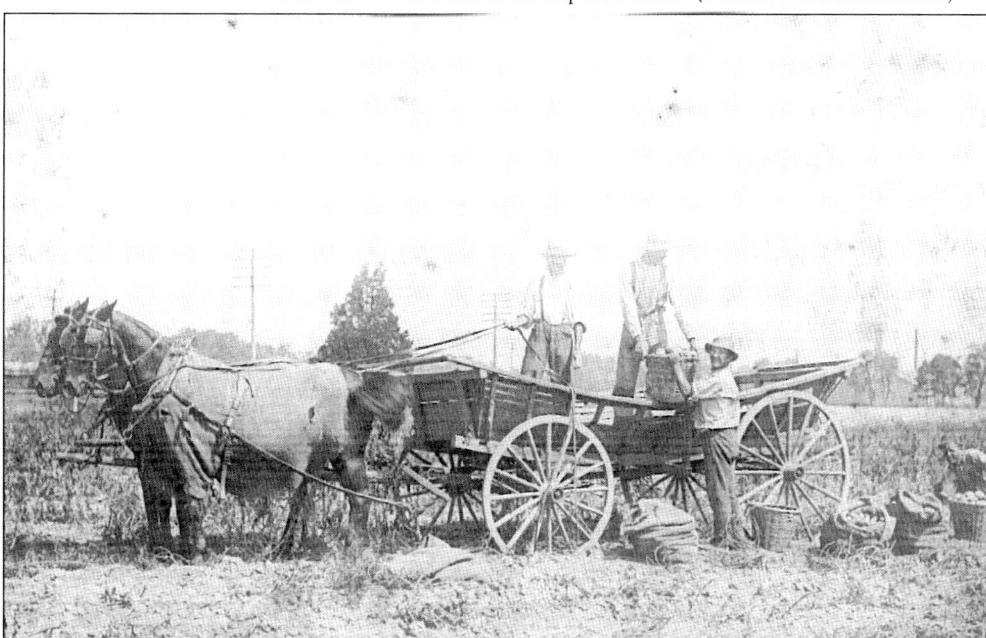

"SHOVELING" (*c.* 1915). Potatoes were dug in late summer and the process of picking them off the ground was called "shoveling." They were then placed in burlap bags or baskets and loaded on wagons. One of the three men standing here is Levi C. Updike. (The Lee Family)

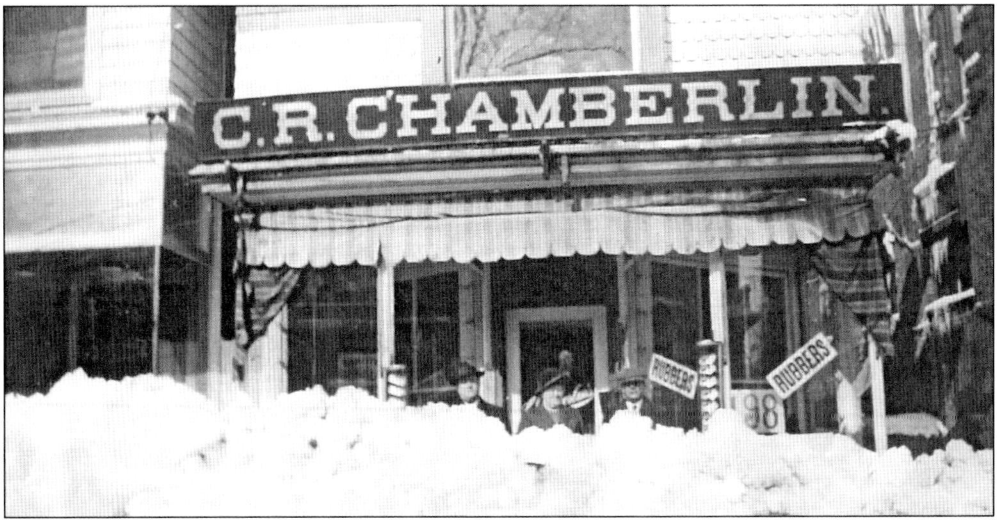

THE BLIZZARD OF 1914. The rubbers advertised at C.R. Chamberlin's Shoe Store on the west side of Main Street were of little help during the blizzard of March 3. Mrs. Chamberlin had a millinery department on the store's second floor. This building and others south of it were destroyed by fire on August 27, 1925. (C. Stults Family-Allen & Stults Collection)

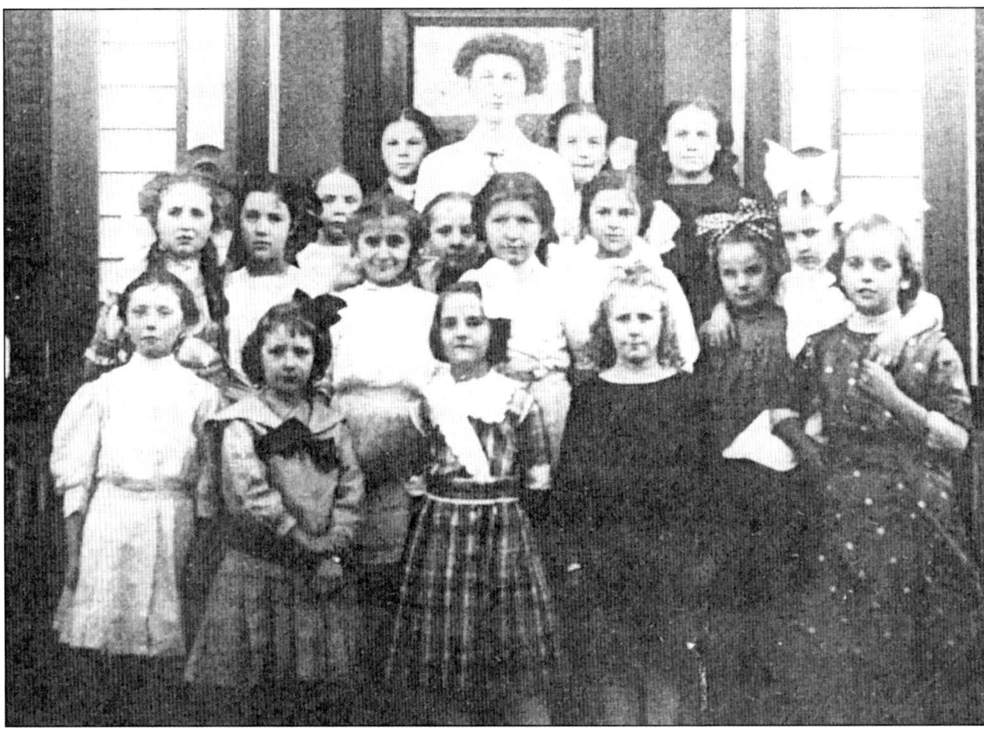

BAPTIST SUNDAY SCHOOL CLASS (c. 1914). Hannah Dey Hutchinson's Sunday school class at the First Baptist Church is having their photograph taken before a church picnic. They are: (front row) Edith Lingerman, Ruth Reed, Lucille Robinson, Adelaide Mitchell, and Leota Perrine; (middle row) Elsie Rogers, Edith Cole, Anna Lord, Lillian Wood, unknown, Maggie Hutton, Florence Updike, Jeannette Peterson, and Edna Hutchinson; (back row) Helen Jemison, Hannah Dey Hutchinson, Margaret Laird, and unknown. (First Baptist Church)

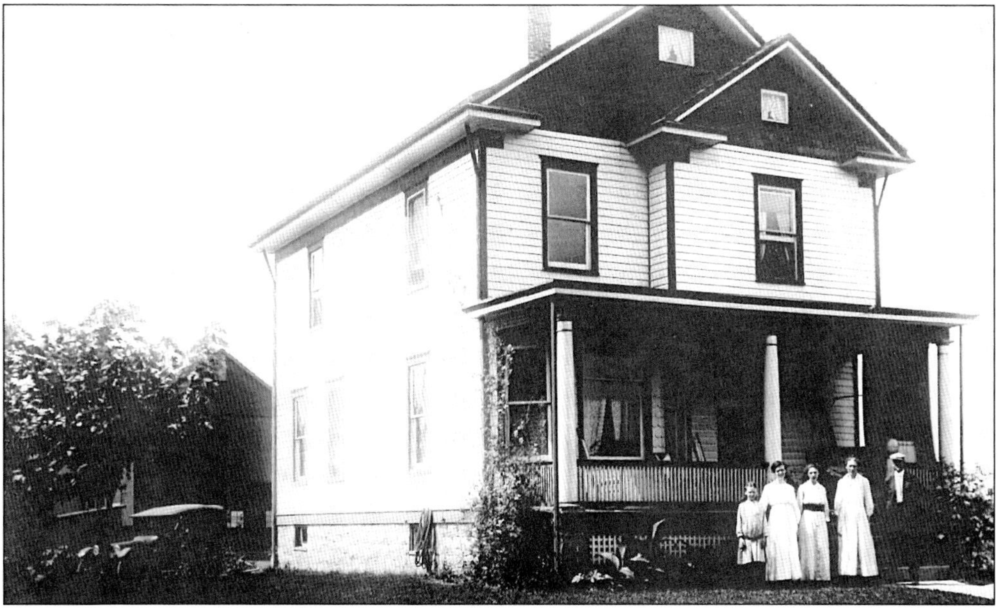

DURYEE HOUSE (*c.* 1915). The house and barn at the corner of Stockton and Summit Streets were built in 1912 by William McKnight and his brother at a cost of $2,500. Shown here are: Irene Duryee (Dey), Mrs. Bessie Tarbox, Gertrude L. Duryee (Mrs. Arthur), Mrs. Myrtle Tadt (Gertrude's sister), and Arthur Duryee. Arthur's Buick Touring Car can be seen near the barn. Ken Duryee remembers that, because he had been "bad," his parents would not allow him to pose with the others when this photograph was taken. (Kenneth Duryee)

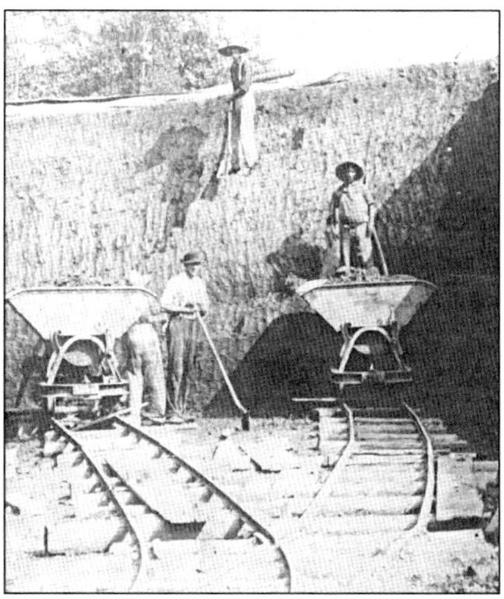

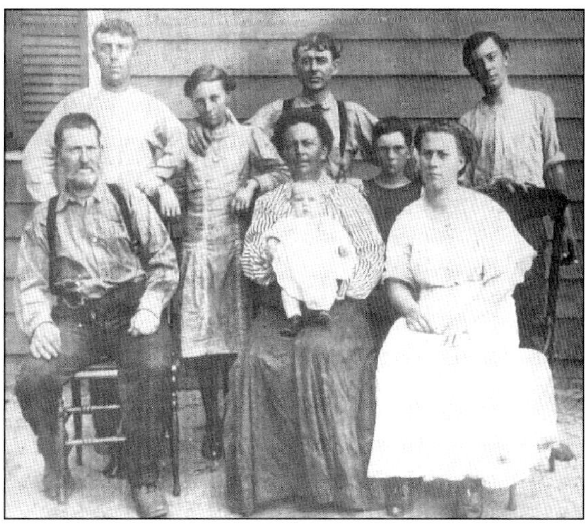

REED BRICK YARD (*c.* 1915). Workmen are digging at the Reed Brothers Brick Plant along the railroad on Brick Yard Road. Operated by brothers Benjamin, Olmstead, and Alberto Reed, at one time it was a major brick manufacturer in the state. In the year 1910, an output and shipment of 200,000 bricks was reported. Operations were discontinued in 1920. (Hightstown-East Windsor Historical Society)

THE PLATT FAMILY (*c.* 1915). Samuel T. Platt, Sr. and his wife, who lived at 108 Morrison Avenue, are showing off granddaughter Virginia McGovern. Virginia's mother Eva is at the right in the front row. In the rear are Bill Platt, Etta Platt (Rocco), George, Clifford, and Samuel, Jr. (The Al Peterson Family)

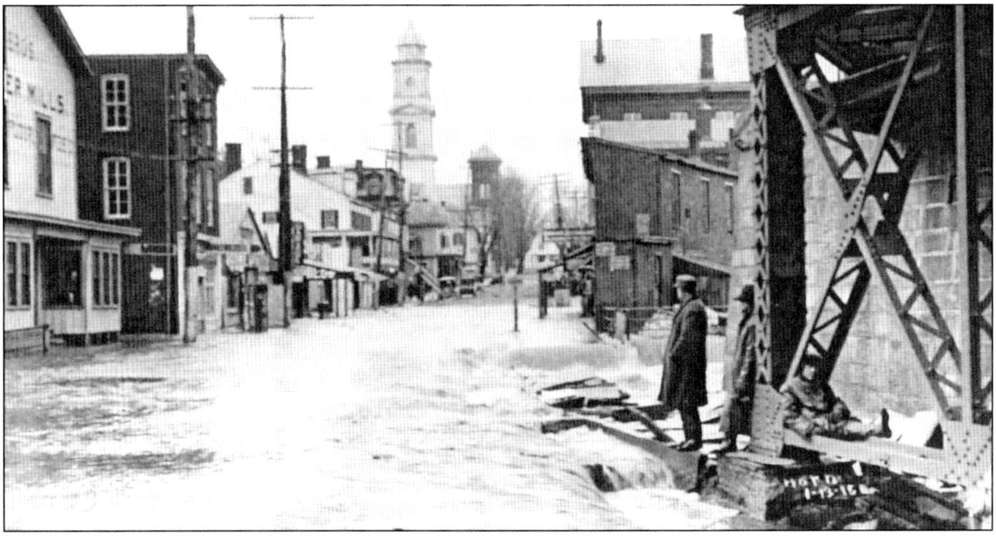

MAIN STREET—FLOOD OF 1915 (1915). Rocky Brook often overflowed, leaving Main Street knee deep in flood water as shown in this January photograph. The Cereal Roller Mills (at left) was built in 1906 by William R. Norton and was one of the largest and most complete mills in New Jersey, having a production capacity of two thousand barrels of flour per month. In 1909 Harry and David Gross bought the mill and operated it until it was destroyed by fire in 1920. Today it is the site of Memorial Park. (C. Stults Family-Allen & Stults Collection)

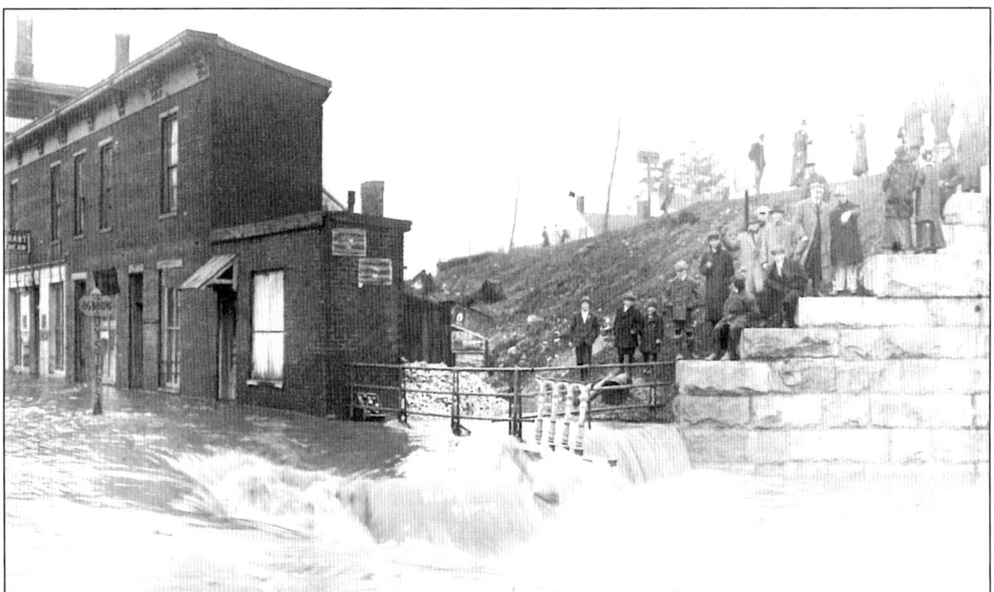

FLOODED OYSTER HOUSE (1915). Streams are inundating the Main Street section, known at the time as "The Bowery." Ogborn's Oyster House—shown here—was one of the unusual local businesses catering to both travelers and locals. It served only oysters and clams on the half shell and in stews, as well as good old-fashioned coffee. The oysters came from the Chesapeake Bay and were three times the size of New Jersey products. When located here, the restaurant was only large enough for three stools. It later moved to Mercer Street near Rogers Avenue. (Fred R. Tornquist, Jr.)

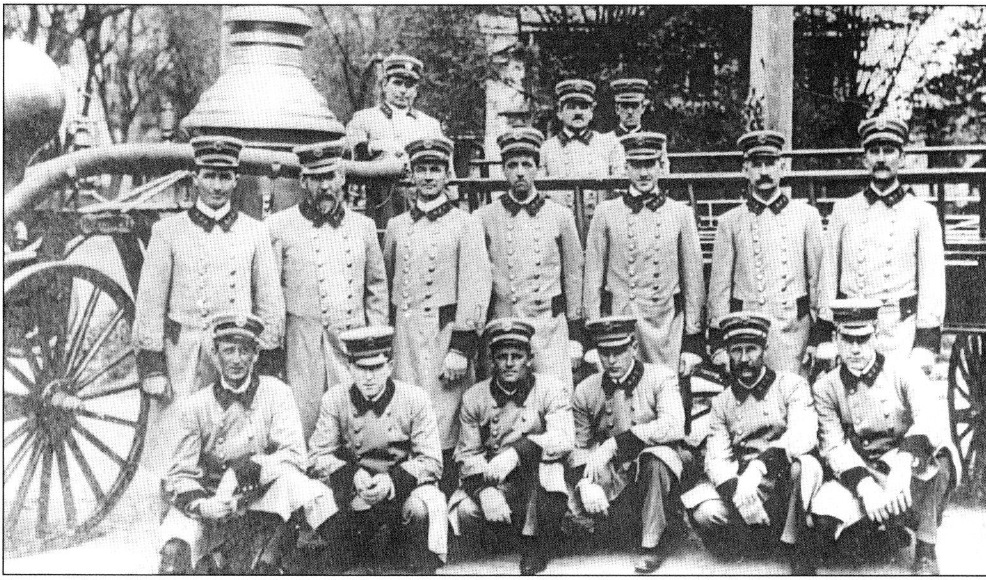

FIRE DEPARTMENT WITH HORSE-DRAWN STEAM ENGINE (1915). Members of the fire department are shown with the button steam engine, a horse-drawn model purchased in 1887 for $3,000. Hightstown's third fire engine, it was sold shortly after this photograph was taken. The firemen are: (front row) Alonzo Pierson, unknown, Charles Henry Morton, unknown, George Norris, and unknown; (middle row) unknown, unknown, James Taylor, and Al Hollenback; (back row) unknown, Frank Weller, and Walter McCue. (Thelma Babcock)

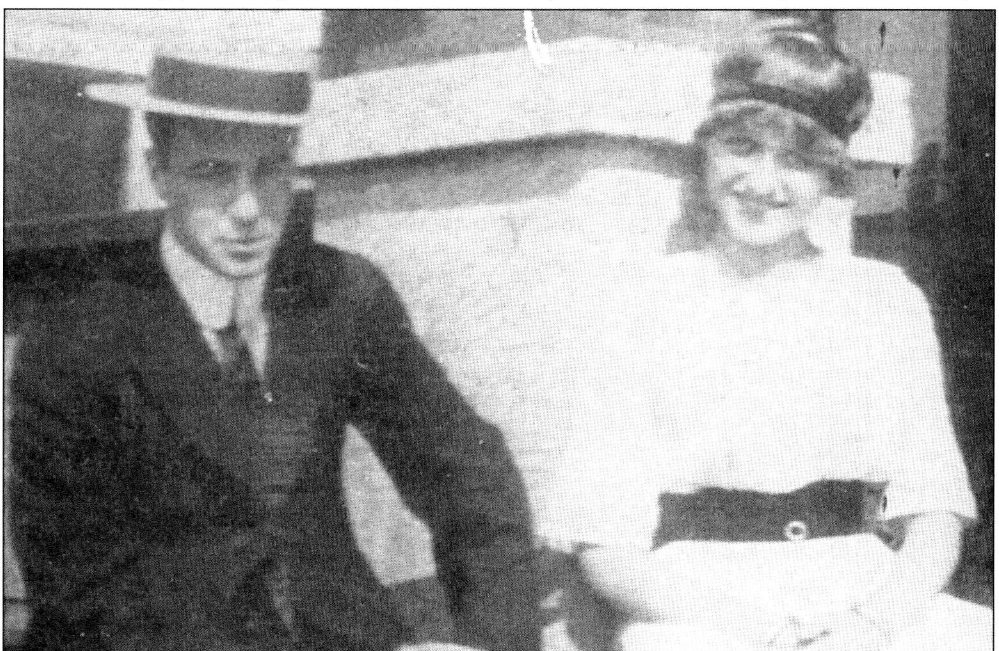

RECENT NEWLYWEDS (*c.* 1915). Ernest and Jane Thompson rest on the porch of their 175 South Street home. Having moved there after their marriage in August of 1914, they remained until 1928. A pharmacist, Ernest had bought Harvey Rue's drug store soon after arriving from England in 1905. (Ernest Thompson)

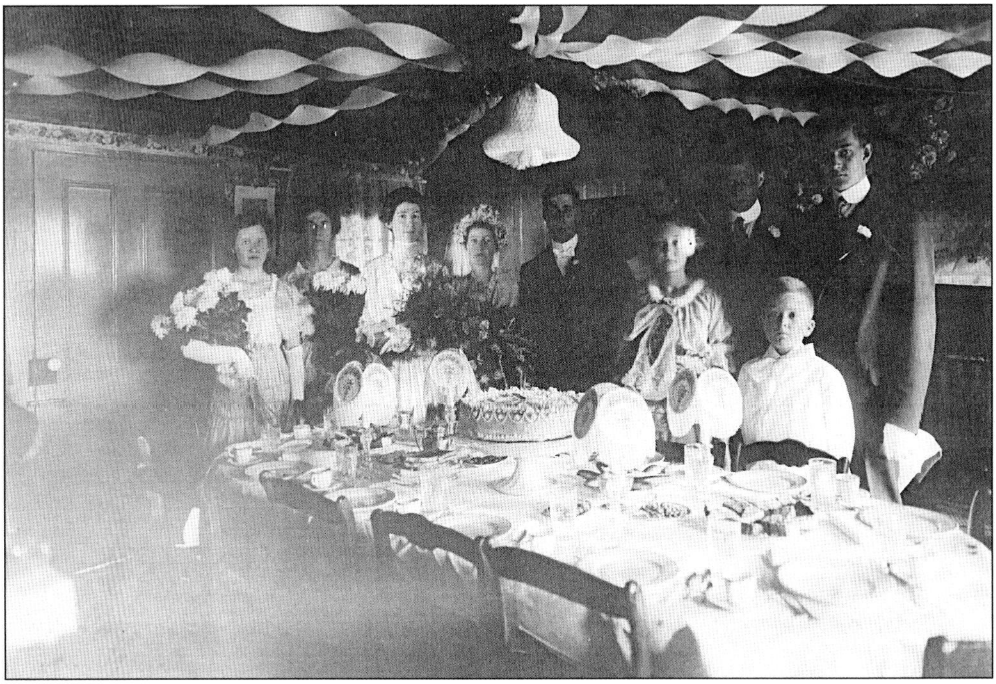

HOME WEDDING RECEPTION (1915). On September 29, Margaret Duncan Ely married J. Ely Dey at her parents' farmhouse near Etra. Her father was Joseph Addison Ely and her mother was Sara Fisher Segoine Ely. Her sister Grace is at her left. Before her marriage, Margaret, who died in 1966 at age eighty-three, had been a teacher in a one-room school on the road to Perrineville. (Hightstown-East Windsor Historical Society)

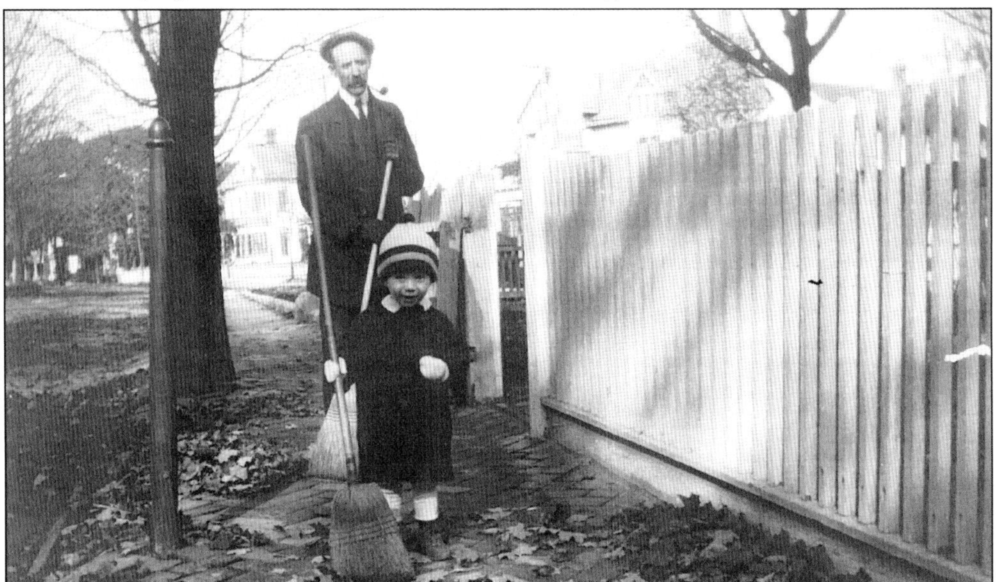

AUTUMN CHORES (*c.* 1916). Edward T. Jones and his son Jay are ready to sweep the leaves on the Rogers Avenue side of their Stockton Street home. The house is located just east of the Civil War Monument. (Dorothy Petty Dey)

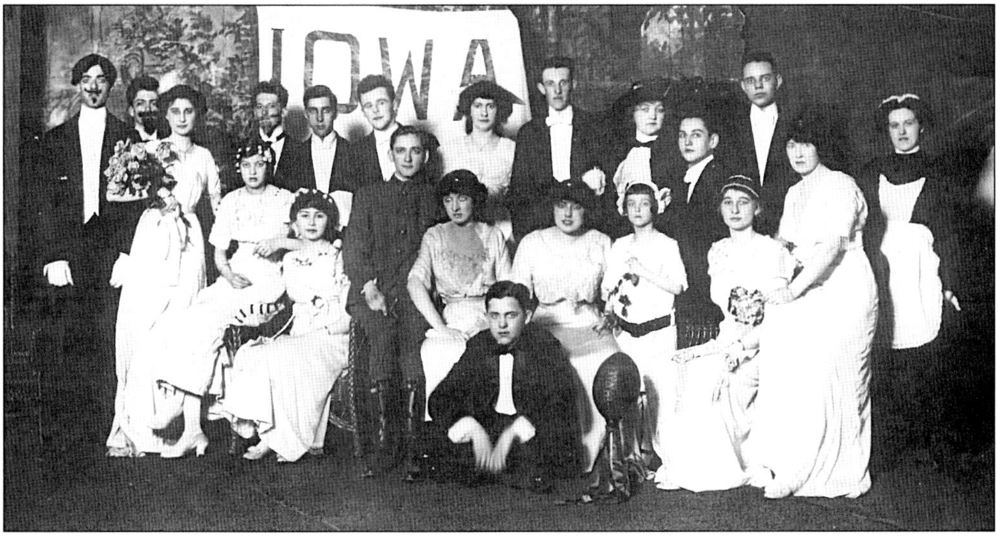

FIRST BAPTIST CHURCH DRAMA (*c.* 1916). These cast members of a play directed by Josephine Hutchinson for the First Baptist Church are: (sitting in front) Duncan Chamberlin; (front row) Lydia Dey, Mildred Stults, Anna Updike (Chamberlain), John Perrine, Eleanor Field, Isabella Mount, Josephine Dawes, Hannah Dey (Hutchinson), Marion Field, and Kathryn Burch; (back row) unknown, unknown, unknown, J. Ely Dey, George Burch, Helen Wilson, ? Jemison, unknown, ? Thomas, and Roger Stanton. (First Baptist Church)

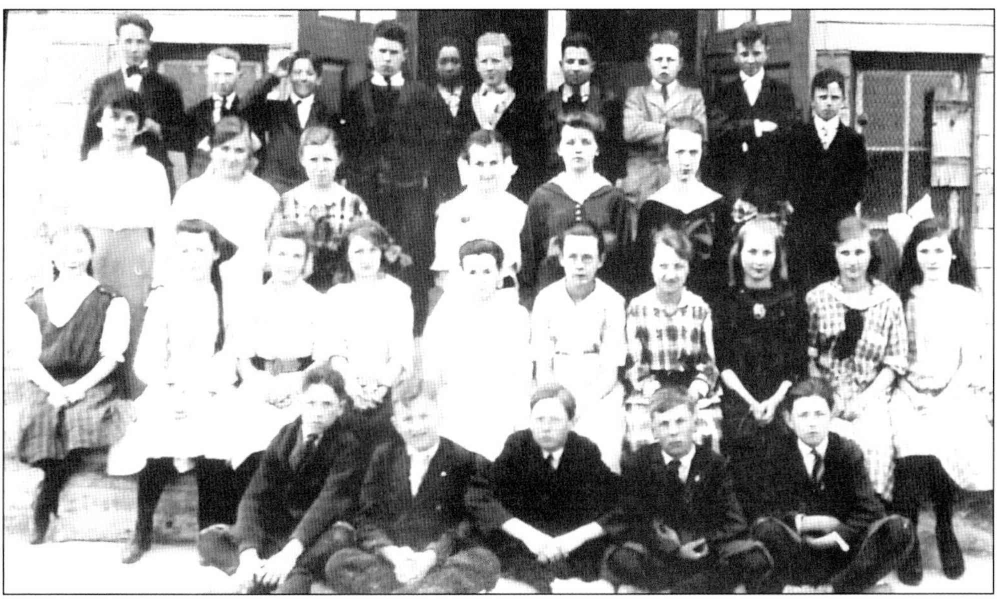

CLASS PHOTOGRAPH—STOCKTON STREET SCHOOL (*c.* 1916). Those appearing in this image are: (front row) Everett Pullen, Homer Thompson, Fred Huber, Louis Allen, and unknown; (second row) Edith Lingerman, Lottie Ralph, Jeannette Peterson, Ruth Reed, Anna Schlevogt, N. Wyckoff, Genevieve Wilson, Blanche Thompson, Delma Wilson, and Minnie Von Lieshout; (third row) Kathleen Reed (temporary teacher), Elsie Rogers, Ethel McKnight, Edna Hutchinson, Leota Perrine, and Cora Varian; (back row) Howard Campbell, Clayton Webb, Stuart Arnold, Leon Craig, John Blake, Mount Norris, James Damasco, Harold Riggs, Wilton Mount, and unknown. (Hightstown-East Windsor Historical Society)

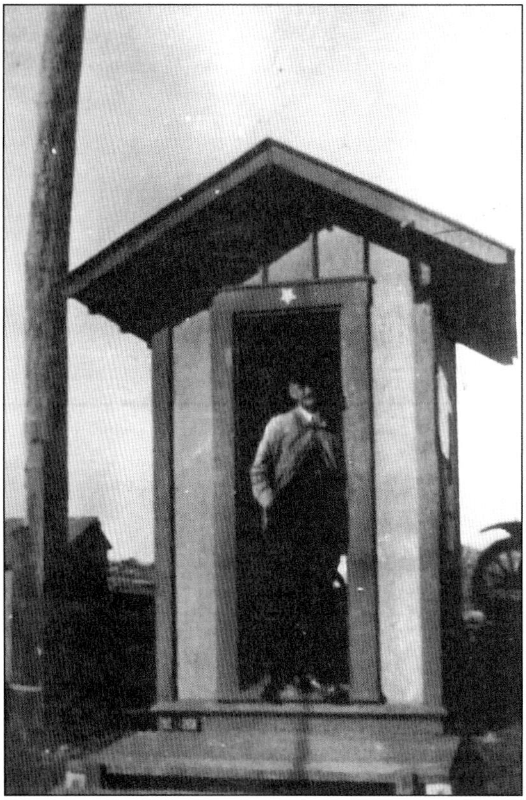

RAILROAD WATCHMAN (1917). Jasper "Jep" Laird was a flagman at the Summit Street railroad crossing after the freight station was moved to that location on January 14, 1917. "Jep," who resided at 122 Dey Street, lived to be ninety-four years old. (Hightstown-East Windsor Historical Society)

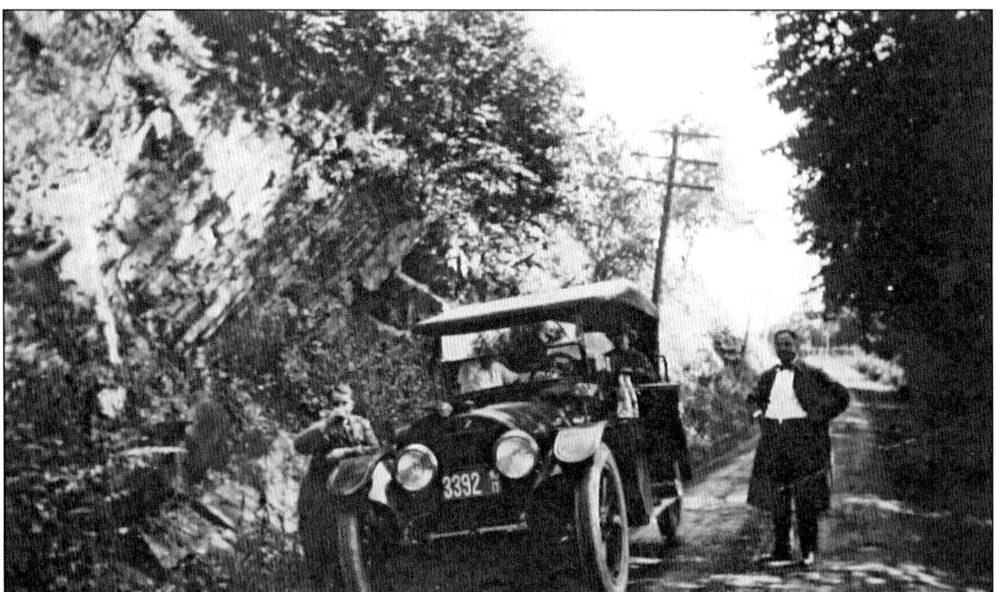

RESPITE (1917). Young Calvin L. Chamberlin and driver Frank P. Field stretch their legs while Mary Tindall Field remains in the rear seat. (Janet Field)

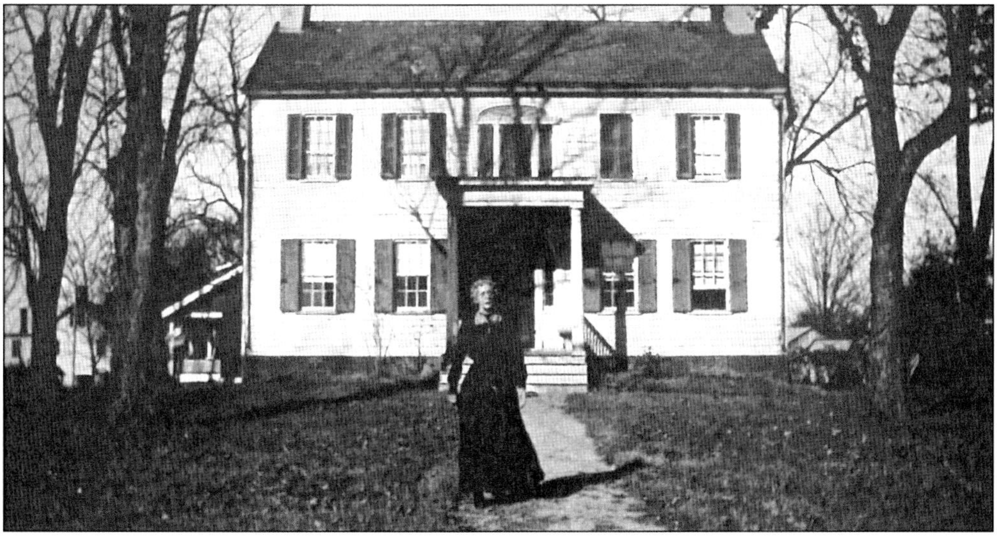

COMPOSER'S BIRTHPLACE (1917). This is the home of Robert Morrison Stults, who was born here in 1862. His father was Jacob Stults, a successful newspaper publisher, and his mother was Martha Jane Morrison Stults, who is shown here. Robert's first music lessons were given by his aunt, Margaret Swift Morrison, in this house. He wrote more than one thousand compositions—piano and organ pieces as well as numerous vocal works. In addition he wrote many sacred and secular cantatas and operettas. His most famous work, *The Sweetest Story Ever Told,* was published in 1898 and sold more than 750,000 copies in the United States alone. It enjoyed more than forty years of unbroken popularity. (*The Etude Music Magazine*)

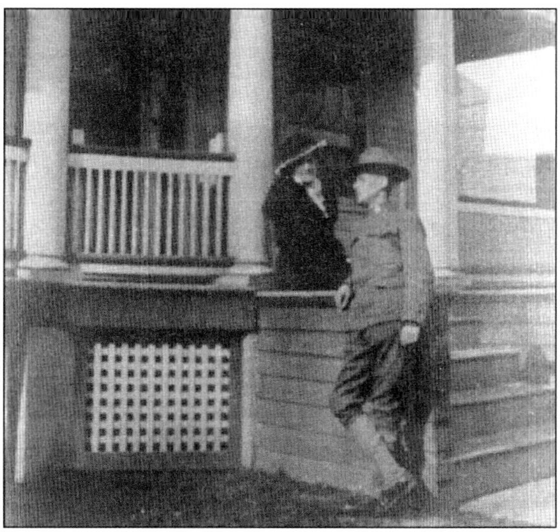

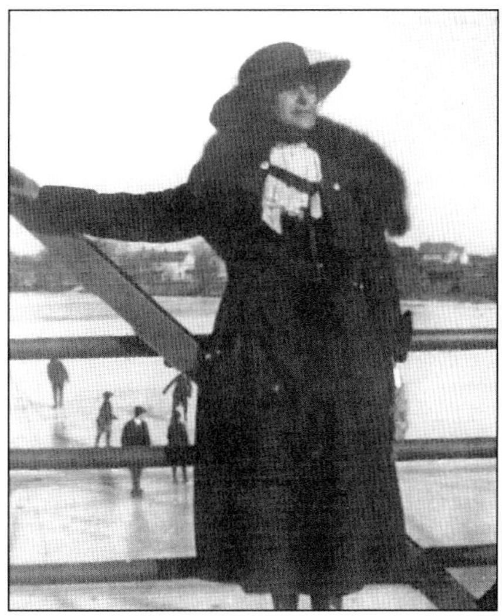

A VISIT WITH MAMA (1917). Stenson W. Rogers and his mother Lulu share a few moments of his military leave at their 410 North Main Street home. The photograph was taken on November 17 and by May of 1918 Stenson was in France as a private at the U.S. Army artillery headquarters. He was married in 1934 to Grace Norton, whom he met in 1921; Grace stated that his mother did not approve of the courtship. (Elizabeth Silvers)

LULU ROGERS (1917). Mrs. Rogers, stylishly dressed in her high-buttoned shoes, fur piece, lace jabot, and veiled hat has selected a spot on Peddie Bridge where she can watch the ice skaters. (Elizabeth Silvers)

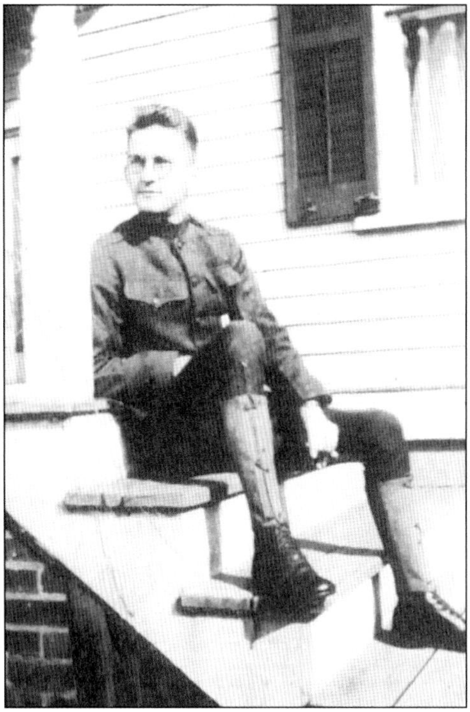

DOUGHBOY (c. 1918). Calvin Perrine, shown on the side porch of his home at 360 South Main Street, returned to Hightstown after service in World War I and lived to more than one hundred years of age. (The Lee Family)

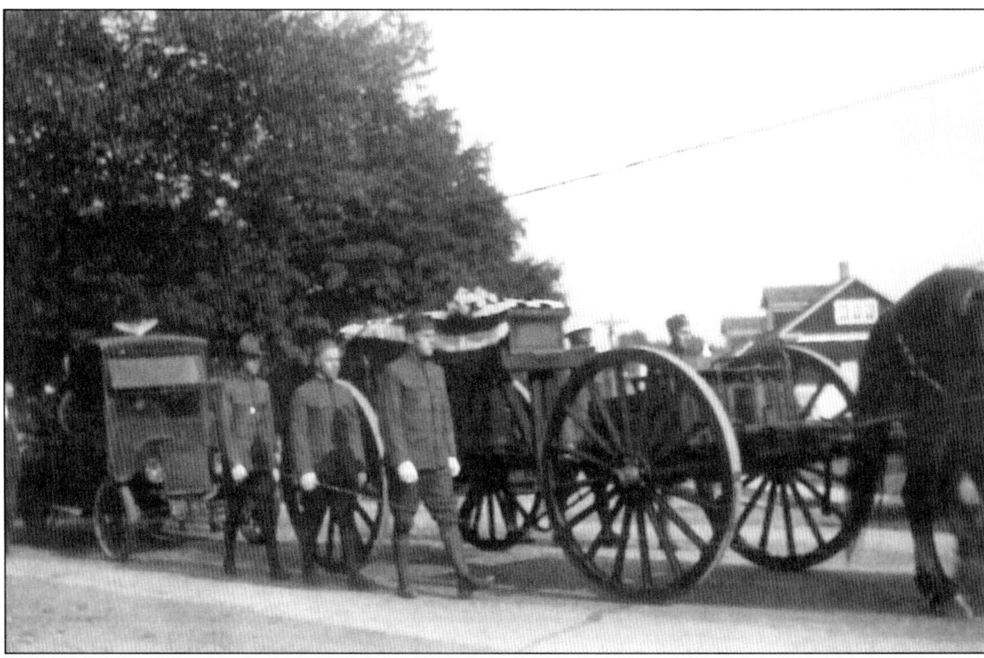

FUNERAL PROCESSION (1918). The first Hightstown soldier to fall on a European battlefield was Private Samuel T. Platt, Jr. of the 37th Division. Born in 1888, he was killed in action in France on September 25, 1918. The photograph shows a horse-drawn caisson bearing the casket through the streets of Hightstown. At the time he was called to service, Sam was a flagman at the Monmouth Street railroad crossing. (The Al Peterson Family and Kathryn Dennis)

VETERANS OF THREE WARS (1918). Men representing the armed services in the Spanish-American War, the Civil War, and World War I posed for this photograph most likely on Armistice Day, November 11, 1918. They are: Captain Tucker (left), William R. Riley (center), a private in Company G, 10th NJ Infantry, and Raymond Stonaker (right), who was born in Prospect Plains. Stonaker later lived in Hightstown, where he worked for Allen & Stults Company and was past master and past grand chaplain of Hightstown Apollo Lodge No. 41, Grand Accepted Masons. (The Hightstown Apollo Lodge No. 41 and C. Stults Family-Allen & Stults Collection)

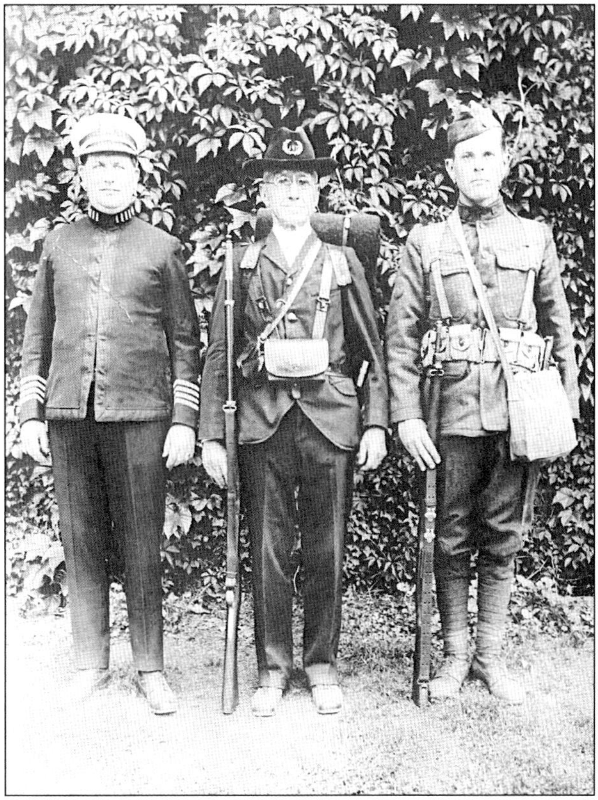

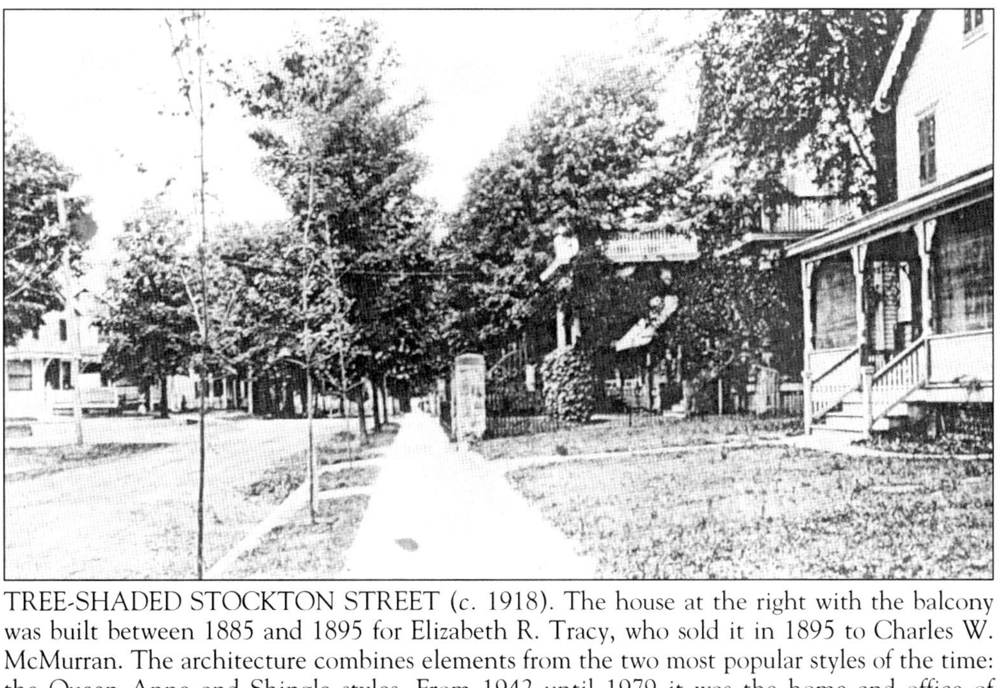

TREE-SHADED STOCKTON STREET (*c.* 1918). The house at the right with the balcony was built between 1885 and 1895 for Elizabeth R. Tracy, who sold it in 1895 to Charles W. McMurran. The architecture combines elements from the two most popular styles of the time: the Queen Anne and Shingle styles. From 1942 until 1979 it was the home and office of Dr. John D. Barlow and his family. (Dr. and Mrs. John D. Barlow)

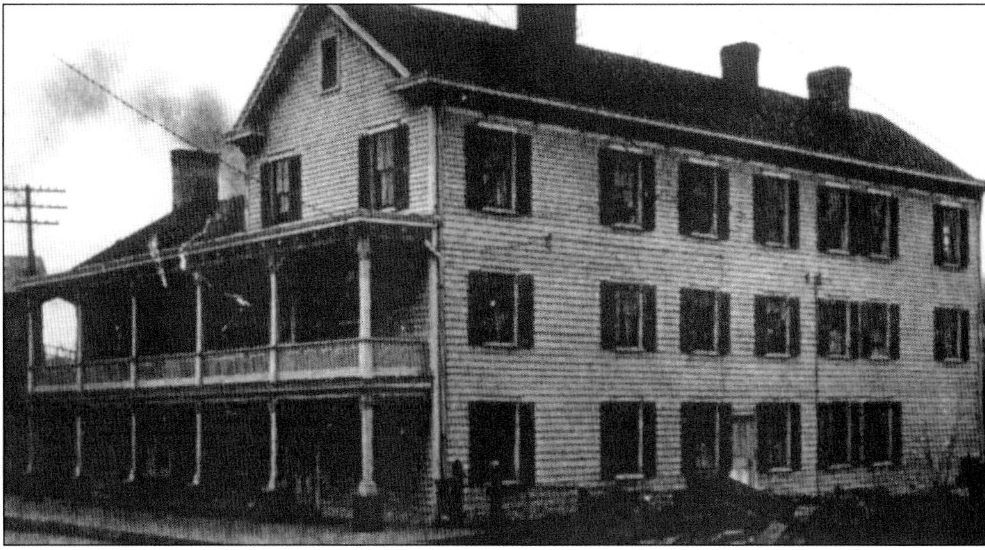

VIEW OF THE LELAND HOUSE (c. 1919). Situated on the bank of Rocky Brook, this building was said to occupy the exact spot where the first log cabin in Hightstown was erected, that of John and Mary Hight, who reportedly settled here in 1721. The original part of the structure was built in the 1820s or earlier and served as a tavern managed by Higbee Applegate during the stagecoach era when Hightstown was the half-way point between New York and Philadelphia. In 1850 additions were made, and in the 1860s A.P. Van Kirk was the tavern owner. Later the building became Lantz's Hotel, operated by "Aunt Fannie" Lantz. After she lost her boarding house license the establishment was used during World War I by the Peddie School as a dormitory for older boys and was called Leland House. In 1926 it was razed to make way for construction of a firehouse. (Norris Robbins Collection)

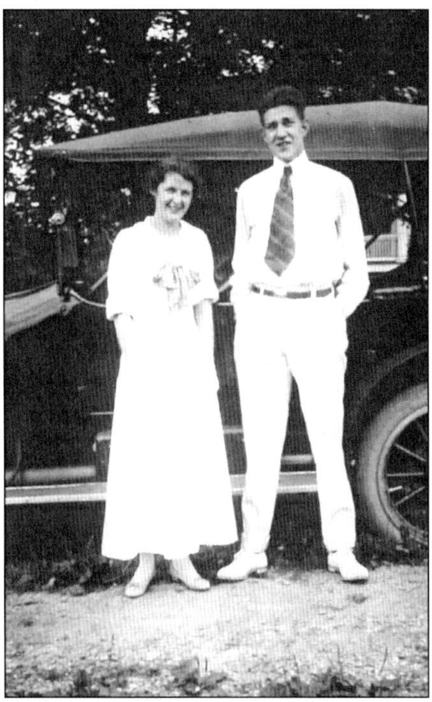

NETTIE AND C. STANLEY STULTS (1918). The young couple pose at the side of their 201 Stockton Street home. This photograph was taken after he became president of Allen & Stults Company in 1917. In the ensuing years, he was the chief executive officer of the Hightstown Savings and Loan Association and served as the president of the Independent Insurance Agents of New Jersey and Mercer County, the Mercer County Real Estate Board, and the Society of Residential Appraisers. Mr. Stults was a founding director of The Hightstown Trust Company, now the New Jersey National/CoreStates Bank. He served in the New Jersey Assembly from 1946 to 1948. An outstanding leader in local religious and community activities, he was a charter member of the Lions Club, treasurer and trustee of the First Baptist church and the YMCA, and received the highest award given to a New Jersey Mason—the Daniel Cox Medal. (C. Stults Family-Allen & Stults Collection)

Five

1920 to 1929

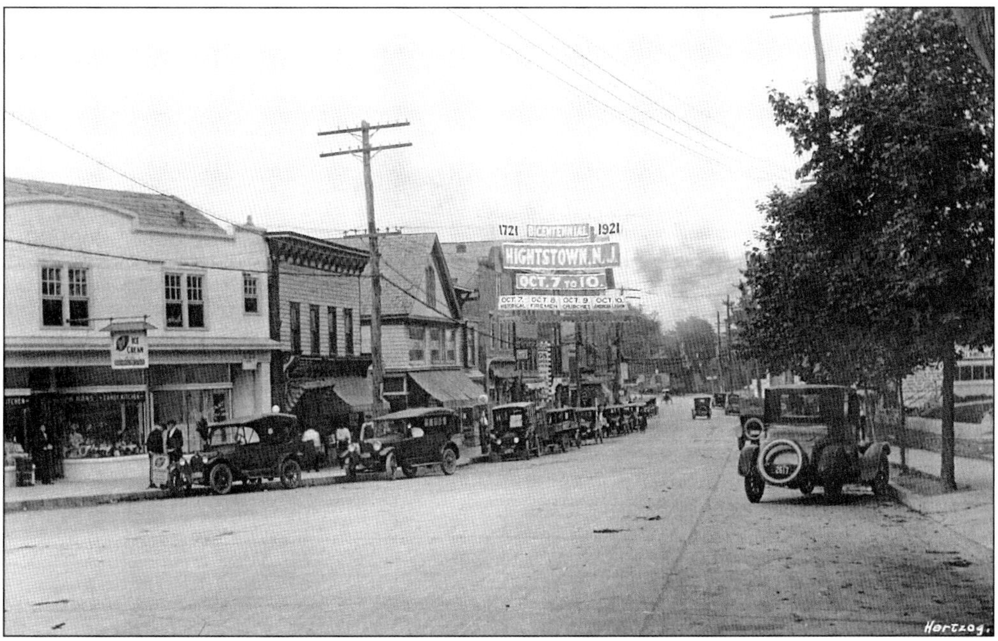

BICENTENNIAL CELEBRATION (1921). Main Street is prepared for Hightstown's four-day bicentennial festivities. Probably the two Breyers signs in front of the Candy Kitchen will help to sell lots of ice cream. Parades were held on each of four days: October 7 was the date of the historical parade; on October 8 the firemen's parade was held; on October 9, the churches'; and on October 10, the American Legion's. On the last day, three thousand people gathered in a large Chautauqua tent on the Peddie campus to hear an address by Thomas R. Marshall, Vice President of the United States during the two terms of President Woodrow Wilson. *The State Gazette* of Trenton reported that a "magnovox," or sound amplifier, was used to "distribute the expressions of the talkers and make their voices more audible. However, Mr. Marshall explained that he proposed to make himself heard without speaking into the "magnovox" and thereby proved to his audience that although he was a former Vice President, he was not a machine man." (C. Stults Family-Allen & Stults Collection)

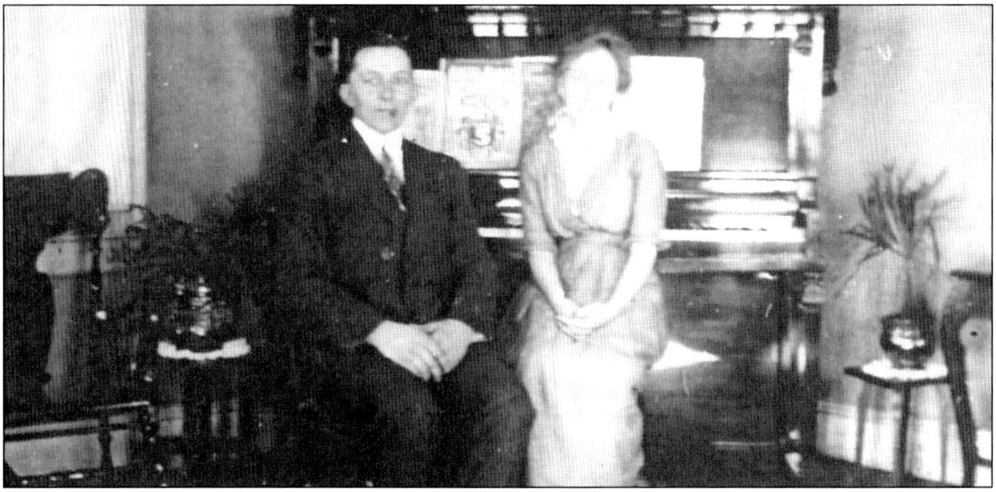

A PARLOR OF THE 1920s (*c.* 1920). Ernest W. (1886–1981) and Mary Conover Hancock (1891–1984) sit in the parlor of their East Windsor home. They were married on January 7, 1913, and spent their honeymoon in Washington, DC. The room decorations are typical of the early twentieth century: oak furniture, potted plants, and an upright piano. (Lois Groendyke)

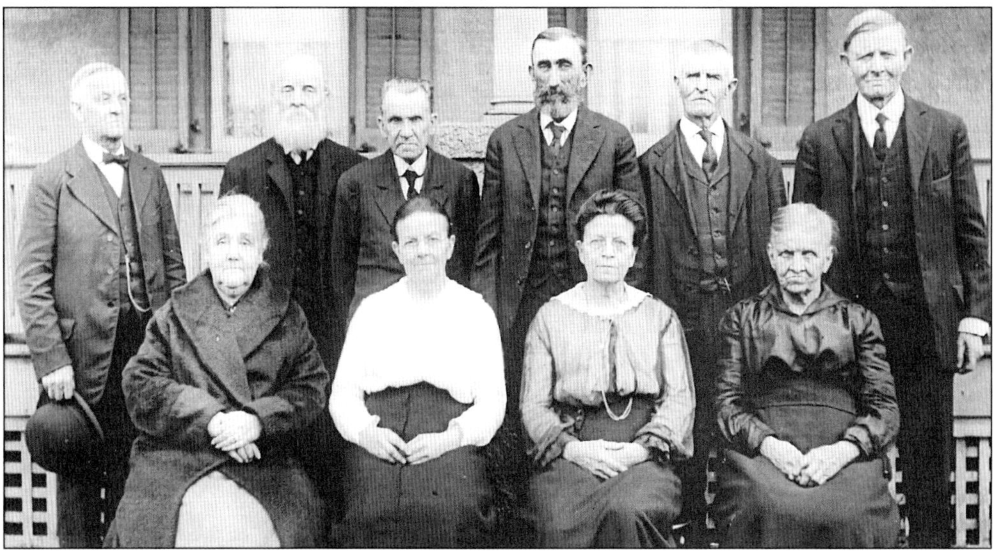

UNSMILING FAMILY (*c.* 1920). William I. Davison and his wife, Ann Maria Herbert Davison, were the parents of ten children, three of whom died before 1870. The remaining children and some of their spouses sit for this photograph. They are: (front row) Rebecca D. Mount (1856–193?), Lydia D. Robbins (1860–1940), unknown, and Mary Ann D. Dey (1846–1926); (back row) Isaac B. Davison (1841–1924), James M. Davison (1848–1935), Ed Mount, William Robbins, John W. Davison (1844–1926), and Joseph Van Doren Davison (1845–1923). Lydia married William Robbins in November 1893 and that year they built a large home at 198 Stockton Street, which they sold to the Chamberlin family in 1909. The Robbins' son Milton was born in 1894 and graduated from Peddie School and Princeton University. Joseph Davison ran Davison's General Store on Main Street for many years before purchasing the controlling interest in the Hightstown Smyrna Rug Company in 1907. One of Joseph's children, C. Herbert Davison, continued to run the rug mill after his father retired. (Hightstown-East Windsor Historical Society)

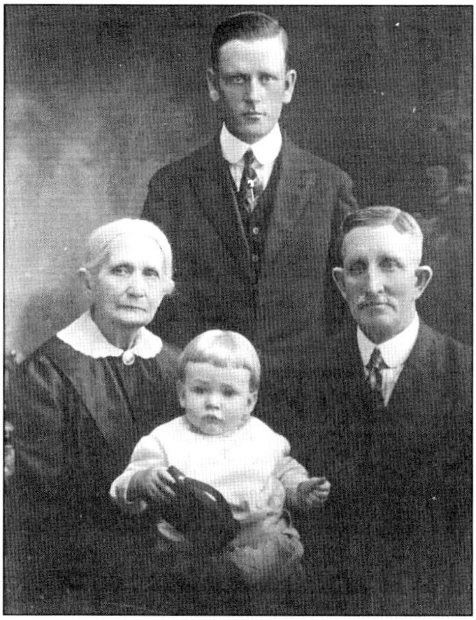

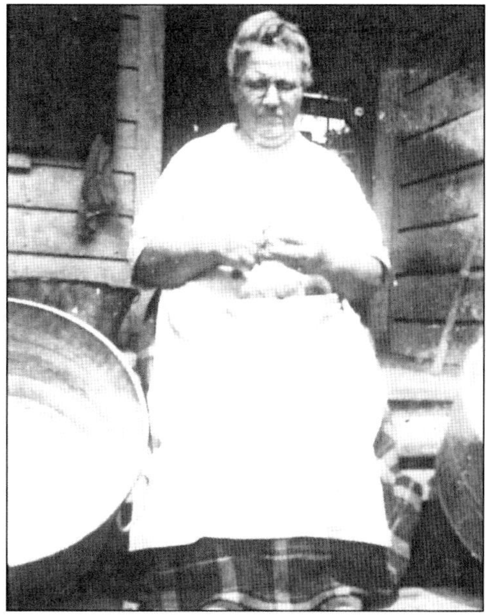

FOUR GENERATIONS (1920). Elizabeth Vancleaf Roszel (1840–1923) is shown here with her son Eugene (1860–1946, at right), her grandson William E. (d. 1956), and great-grandson Malcolm (b. 1919). (Lillian Roszel Black)

MARTHA JANE PEELING POTATOES (1920s). Wearing a large apron, Martha Jane (Gordon) Hutchinson (1863–1940) is peeling a potato on the porch of the family's farmhouse at the corner of York and Airport Roads. In 1886 she married John Tindall Hutchinson (1855–1938) and they had seven children. (Richard S. Hutchinson)

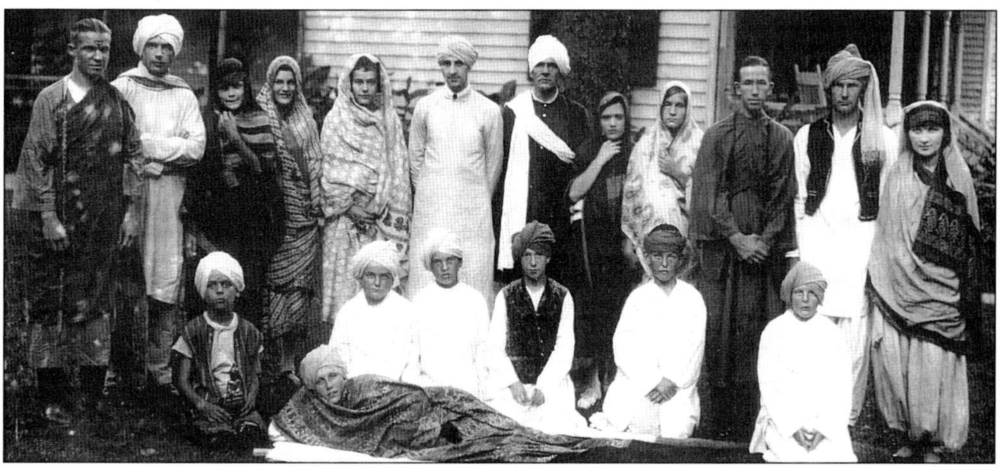

METHODIST CHURCH PLAY (*c.* 1920). Against the background of the Methodist parsonage is the cast of a play performed by the church group in the early 1920s. Irene Duryee Dey remembers that she was "dying to be in the performance," but there was no part for her. Her brother, Ken Duryee, reclines on a stretcher in the foreground. The young boys kneeling in the front are: Edward Fenton, Calvin Hughes, Charles Donnell, Charles Clark, Earl Compton, and Richard Ewart. The actors in the back row are: Lawrence (Babe) Ivins, Edward Van Dorn, Letitia Fenton, Esther Hess, Esther Schanck (Hoyt), unknown, unknown, Florence Wooley (Eldridge), Dorothy Hunt Young, David "Sonny" Horne, Leonard Norcross, and Lillian Cain. This parsonage was torn down and replaced by a newer one on the same site. (Kenneth Duryee)

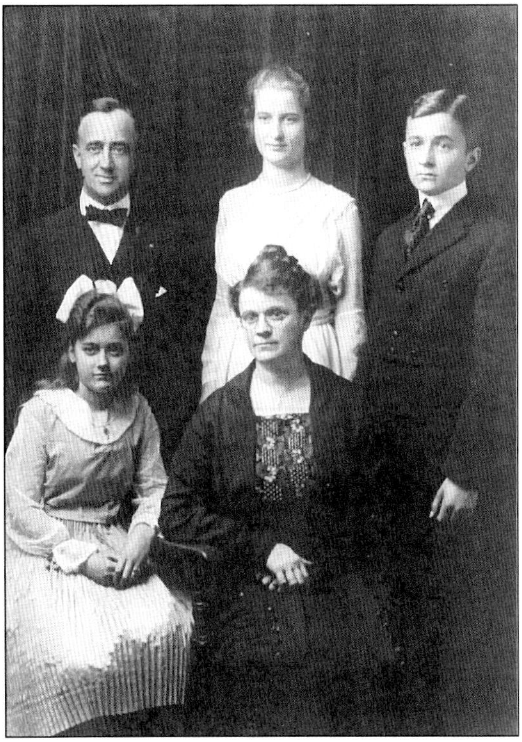

THE THOMPSONS (c. 1920). William Homer Thompson, Sr. and Ada Keeler were married on October 31, 1902, at the Universalist church on Main Street. They are shown here with their children: Kathryn (front), Blanche, and William Homer, Jr. (rear). (Beth Wham)

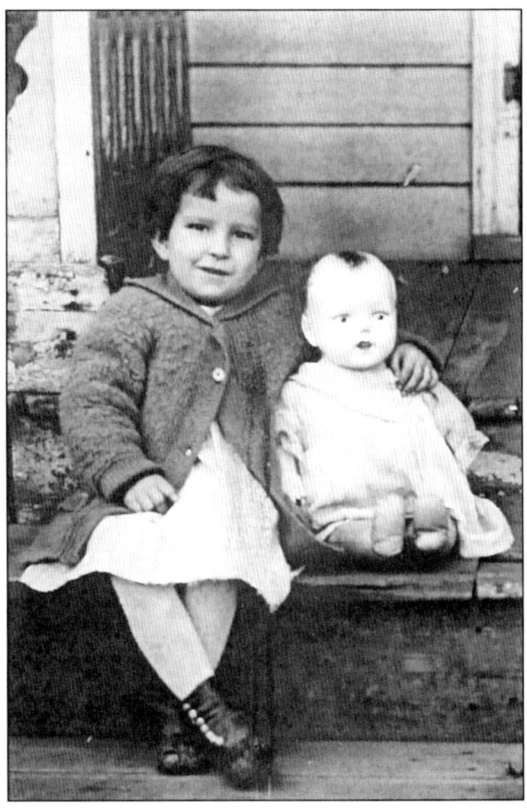

LITTLE GIRL AND DOLL (1921). Mary Florence Silvers (Hutchinson) and her most cherished possession—a life-sized doll—sit together on the porch of her Liberty Street home. The daughter of William R. and Evelyn Jane Leming Silvers, Mary was born in 1919. As an adult, Mary graduated from the St. Francis Hospital School of Nursing, became a registered nurse, and in 1941 married Stanley Stults Hutchinson, a Hightstown plumber. (Richard S. Hutchinson)

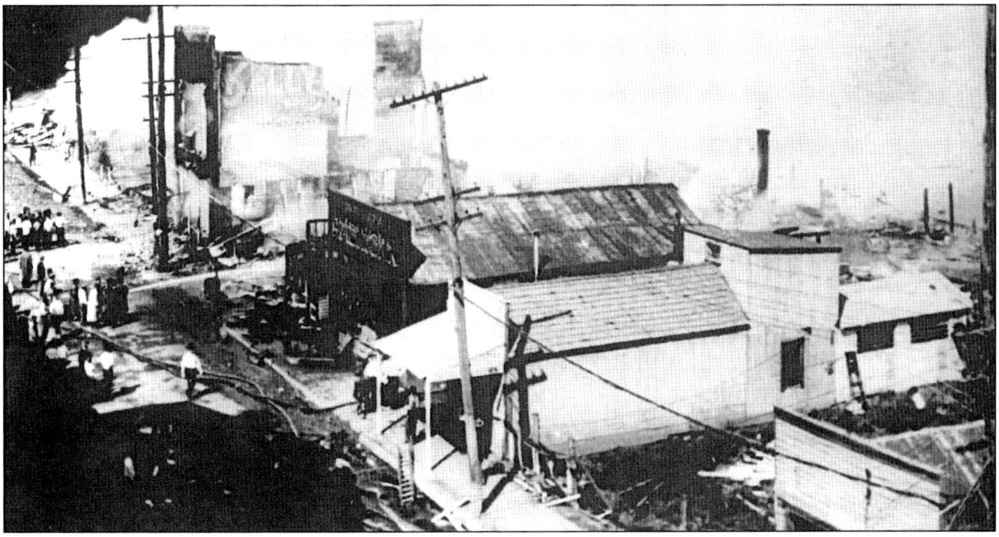

DESTRUCTIVE CONFLAGRATION (1920). The largest fire in local history occurred on May 29, 1920. The blaze started at the Gross Brothers Flour and Feed Mills (at left) on the east side of Main Street, the site of Memorial Park today. It would have wiped out the entire business district were it not for outside assistance from volunteer fire companies from as far away as Princeton and Trenton. Many old landmarks, including the A.S. Voorhees Furniture Store, as well as more modern structures, became skeletons or piles of rubble as the flames consumed building after building. The loss of property totaled $250,000 and supported the need for a new pumper, which was later purchased by the fire company. (C. Stults Family-Allen & Stults Collection)

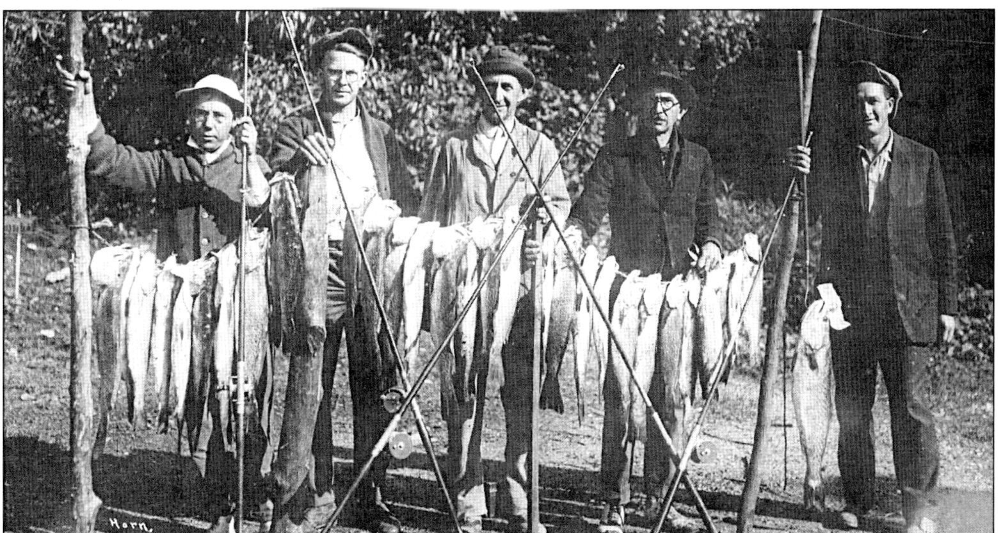

WHAT A CATCH ! (1921). Five veteran anglers display the fantastic catch of weakfish that they made in Barnegat Bay on August 21. They are: Ed Hutchinson (a Hightstown butcher), Monte Norcross (an East Windsor farmer), Charlie "Tote" Weller (a cigar store owner), Ed Kothe (operator of a barber shop on Stockton Street), and Charlie Welch (operator of the borough pumping station on Bank Street). The dollar in the mouth of the fish hanging in front of Charlie indicates that his fish, the largest caught, won the pool. (Richard S. Hutchinson)

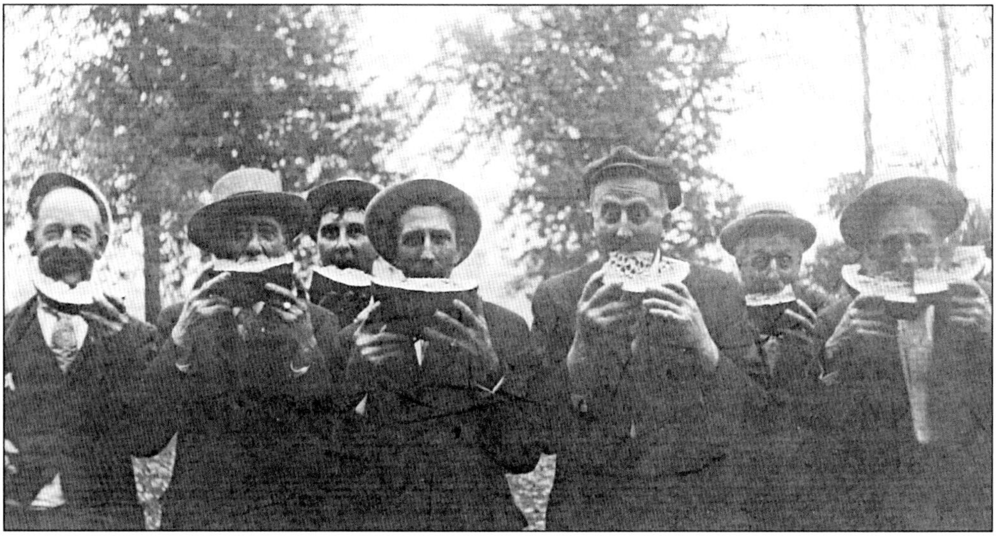

SWEET COMPETITION (*c.* 1920). What appears to be a watermelon-eating contest at the First Baptist Church includes the following participants: Joseph Smith, William Riley, Bert Thomas, William Hutchinson, Dr. Roger W. Swetland (Peddie headmaster), Henry Chamberlain, and unknown. (The First Baptist Church and Peddie School Archives)

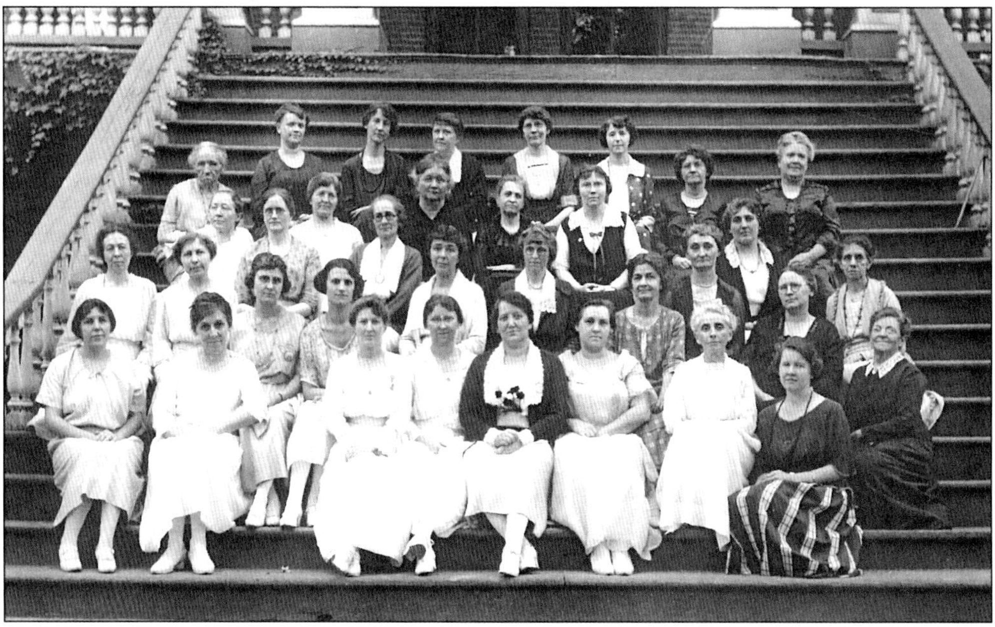

WOMEN'S BICENTENNIAL COMMITTEE (1921). Responsible for much of the planning and implementation of the bicentennial celebration were: (front row) Estella B. Waite, Sarah Norris, Margaret Dey, Georgia M. Riley, Jane B. Donnell, Marion Dawes, Ella West, Evalyn Ely, and Hattie Cunningham; (second row) Grace Ashton, Edna Conover, Edith Dey, Hazel Waite, Maude Davison, Nellie Totten, Jennie Hutchinson, Mary Mount, Maude Jones, and ? Mount; (third row) Edna Wyckoff, Bessie Keeler, Margaret Franklin, ? Brearley, Carrie Swetland, Hannah Smith, Alice Davison, Helen Polhenus, and Marion Rivenberger; (back row) ? Simpson, Ada Thompson, Bette Reeves, Mabel McCarnes, Honorine Grover, and Anna Updike. (C. Stults Family-Allen & Stults Collection)

BICENTENNIAL FLAG RAISING (1921). On the first day of Hightstown's four-day celebration, a large flag is raised during morning ceremonies near the lake. The reviewing stand trimmed with bunting is in the center. In 1921 the town had two lumber yards, three haypresses, three coal yards, a movie theater, three hotels, nine churches, and shirt, lace, and rug factories. (Hightstown-East Windsor Historical Society)

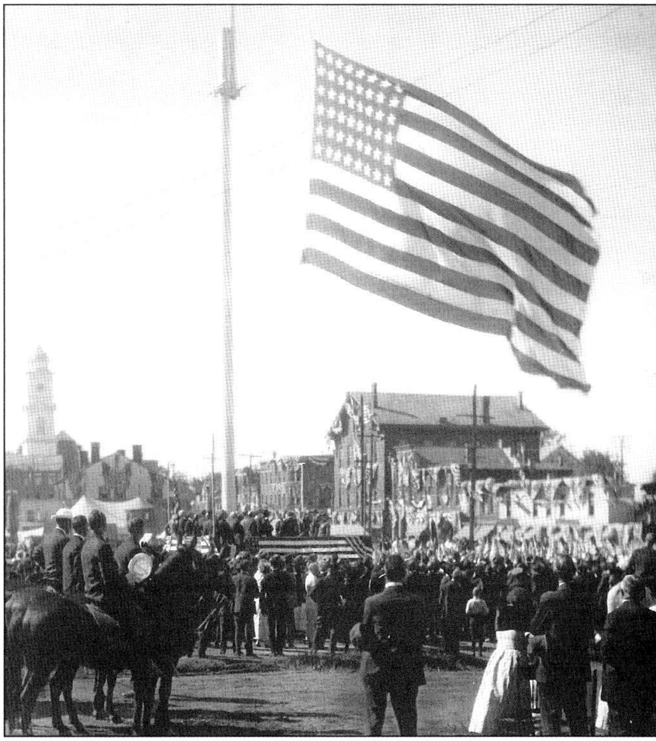

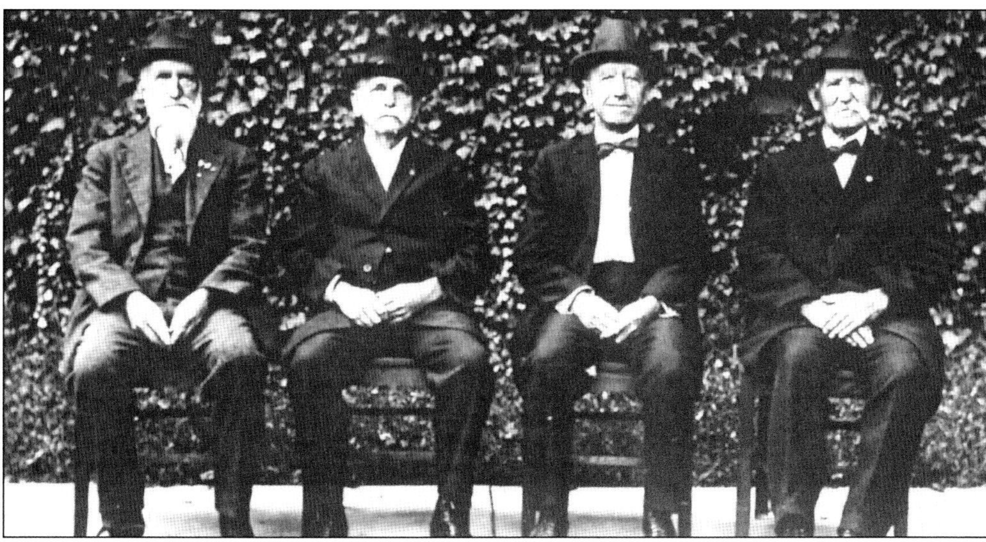

HIGHTSTOWN'S CIVIL WAR VETERANS (1921). At the time of the bicentennial, these four men were all that remained of the Hightstown veterans who fought in the Civil War. They are: Private George M. Dey, Company A, 38th NJ Infantry; Corporal George Washington Conover, Company K, 40th NJ Infantry; Private William G. Riley, Company G, 10th NJ Infantry; and Private Thomas Thompson, Company I, 2nd NJ Infantry. At least seventeen local men gave their lives in the war. A few died on the battlefield but a number perished from disease and in Confederate prison camps (three in Andersonville and one at Libby Prison in Richmond), and another—Charles A. Coward—was "murdered" in the rebel prison at Lynchburg, Virginia, by a brutal guard. (Hightstown-East Windsor Historical Society)

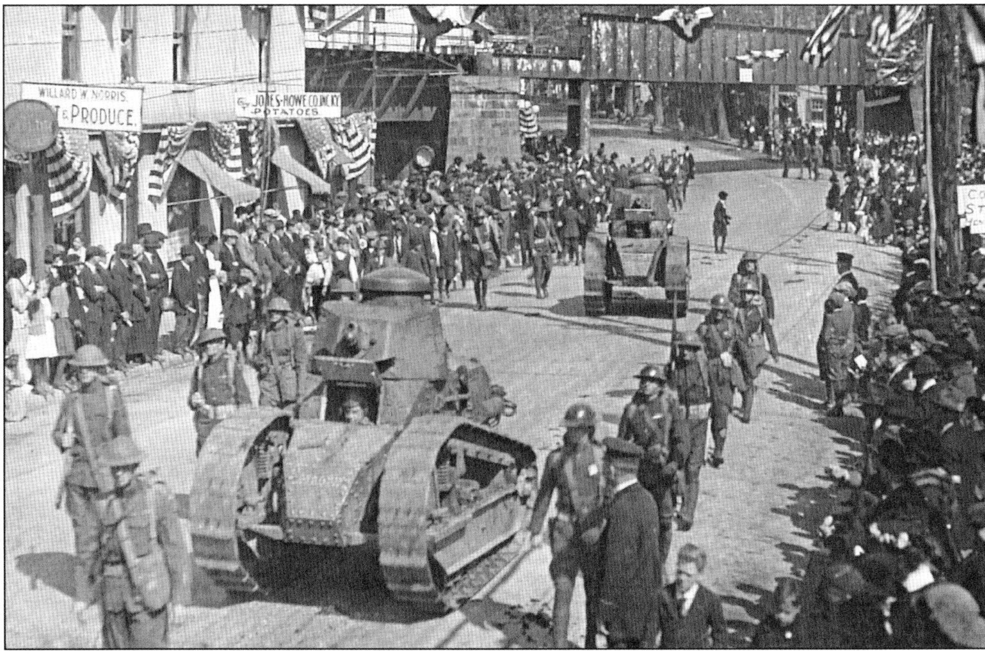

ARMOR AND INFANTRY CHEERED BY THE CROWD (1921). Tanks accompanied by doughboys from Fort Dix roll on North Main Street during the last day of the bicentennial celebration. The day's activities were sponsored by the American Legion. Onlookers dressed in their Sunday best lined the parade route, offering encouragement to the marchers. (Hightstown-East Windsor Historical Society)

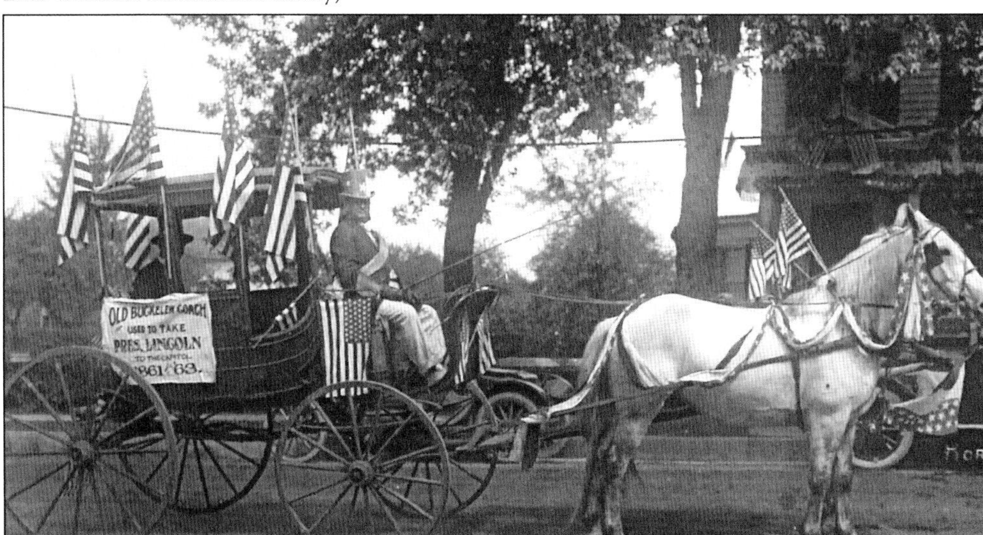

THE LINCOLN COACH (1921). This coach in February of 1861 was used by Abraham Lincoln during his visit to Trenton. The coach belonged to Mr. James Buckelew, founding father and namesake of the Borough of Jamesburg; it is currently owned by the historical society in that borough. In March of that year, Lincoln entered Washington, DC, secretly, and on March 4 he was inaugurated president. The occupant of the coach is dressed in a top hat similar to that worn frequently by Lincoln. (Hightstown-East Windsor Historical Society)

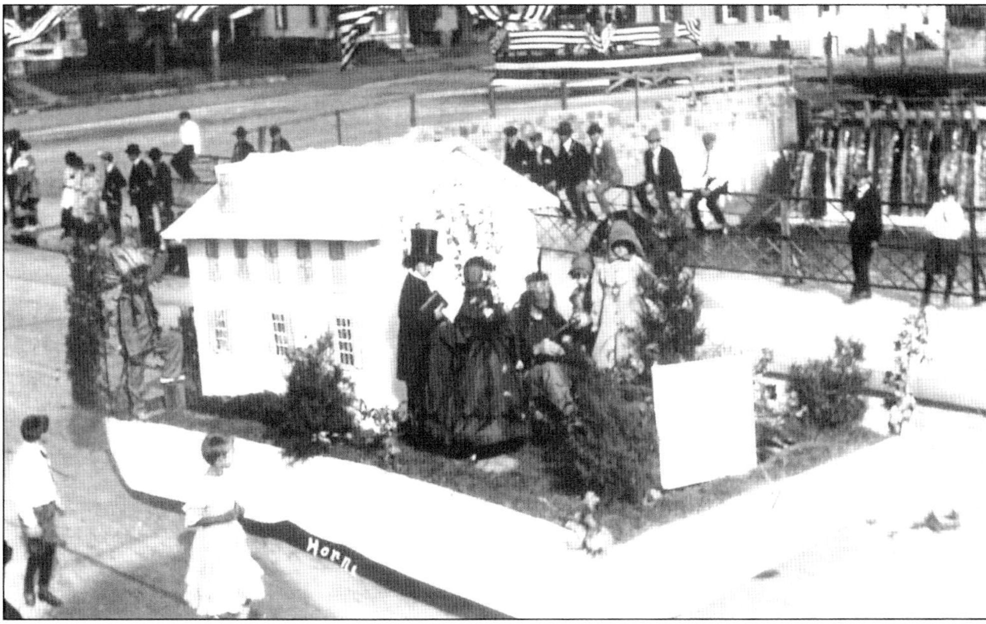

FIRST BAPTIST CHURCH FLOAT (1921). The float transports a model of the First Baptist Meeting House, built in 1785. In this Thanksgiving Day scene, Alvin Dey wears a top hat; at his right is Bertha Grover Bennett. (Elizabeth Silvers)

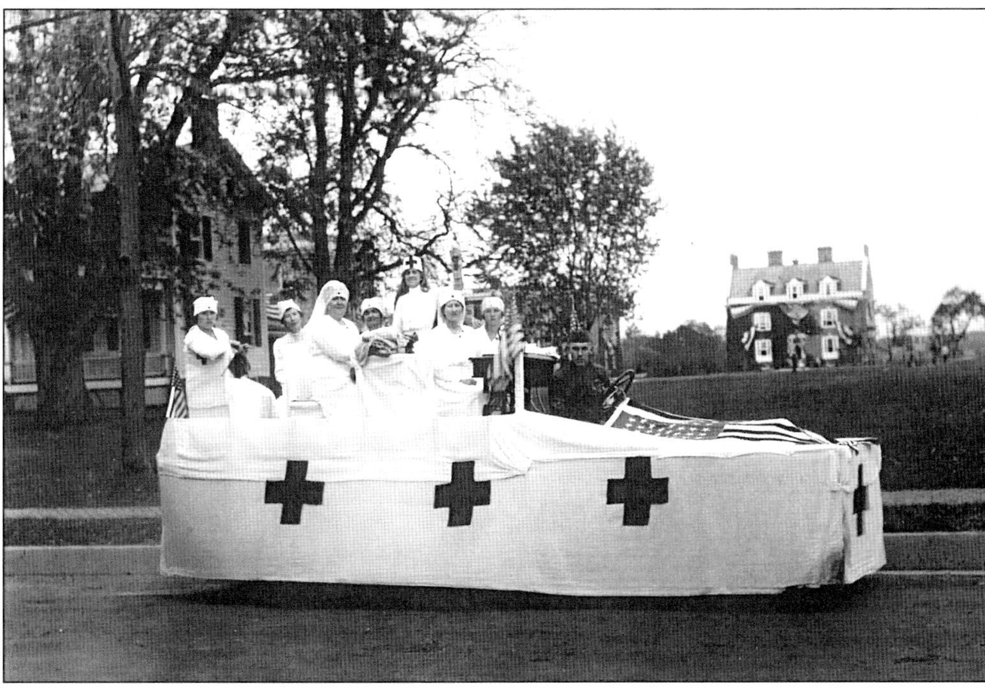

AMERICAN RED CROSS (1921). With Trask Hall on the Peddie campus in the background, this float with women dressed as Red Cross workers is driven by Joseph Ely. The women are: Mary Ewart English, Grace Ely, Margaret Ely Dey, Dorothy Ewart Howell, Mrs. Albert Rogers (standing), Marianna Hutchinson, and Mrs. R.H. Rivenburg. (C. Stults Family-Allen & Stults Collection)

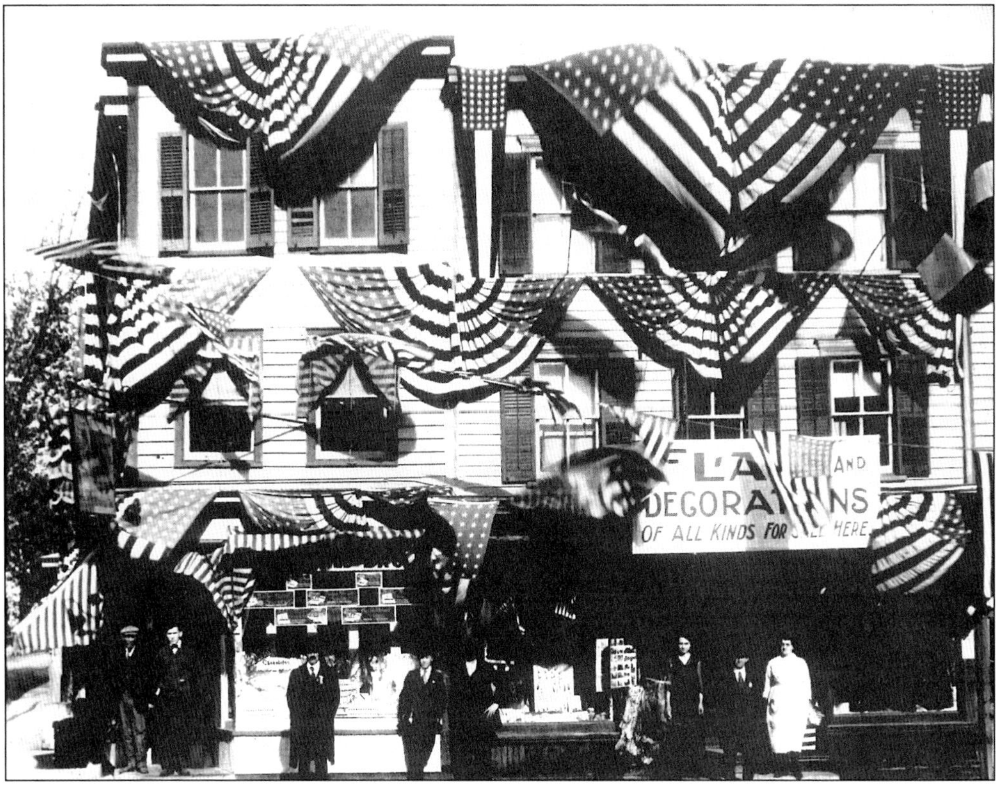

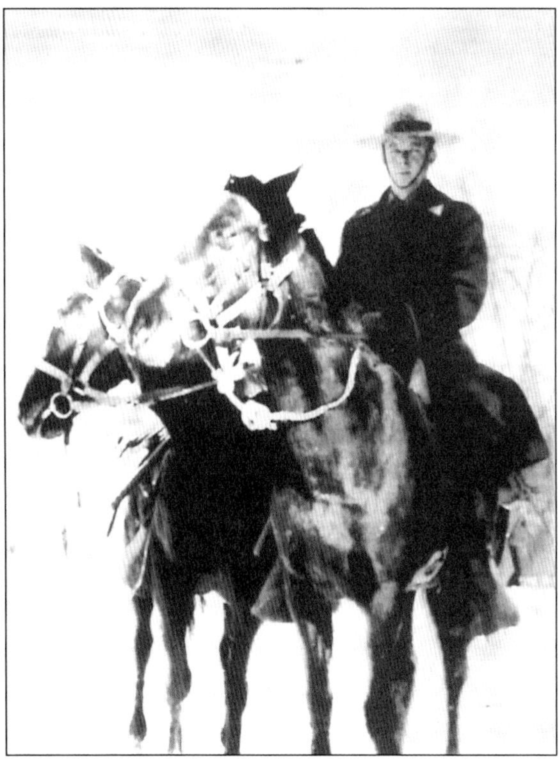

ELABORATE PATRIOTIC DECORATIONS (1921). Rothchild's Ice Cream Store, located on the corner of Main Street and Rogers Avenue, and Sam Ford's 5-10 Store are definitely prepared to celebrate Hightstown's 200th anniversary. In late 1919, Rothchild's became a successor to Fiestal's, a candy, fruit, and ice cream store. (Norris Robbins Collection)

MOUNTED TROOPER (c. 1923). Lieutenant Joseph Hoch was a graduate of the first class of the New Jersey State Police. The first contingent of eighty-one troopers went on duty on December 5, 1921, and patrolled on horseback. Hoch served under its first superintendent, H. Norman Schwarzkopf, who was twenty-five years old when he was appointed to that position in July 1921. (Hightstown-East Windsor Historical Society)

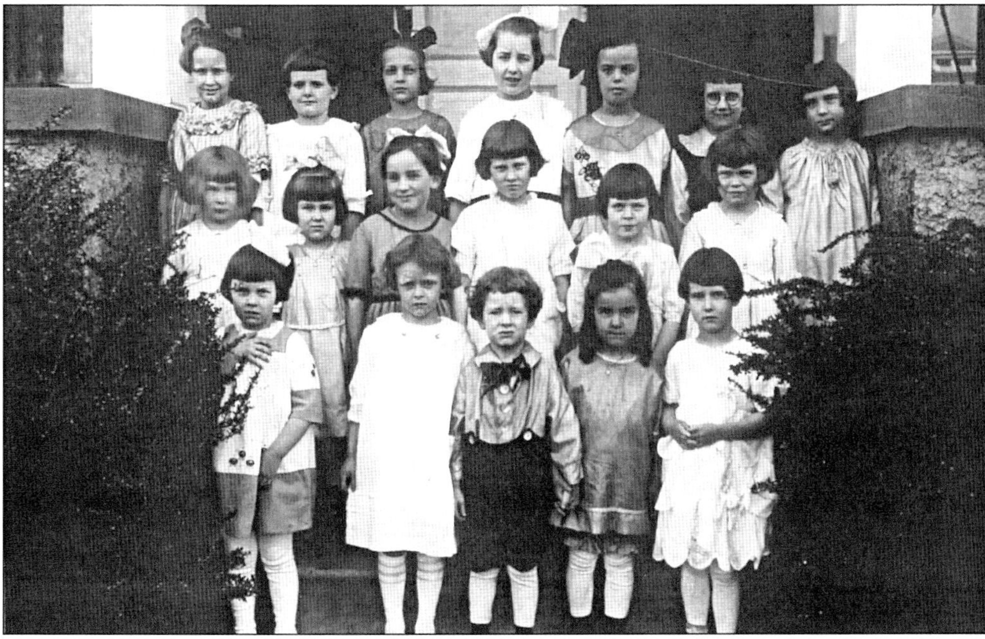

SURROUNDED BY YOUNG GIRLS (*c.* 1923). Alphaeus Albert, Jr. is the only boy attending a birthday party probably given for Margaret Davison. The youngsters are gathered on the front porch of 444 South Main Street, the home Margaret's father C. Herbert Davison had built *c.* 1910. They are: (front row) Bernice Davison, Mary Alice Shangle (Bedell), Alphaeus Albert, Jr., Jane Puglin (Perrine), and Betty Reeves (Klank); (middle row) Janet Davison (Dyle), Catherine Grover (Hernwall), Esther Conover (Robbins), Romelyn Rivenburg, Elizabeth MacArthur, and Dorothy Davison; (back row) Evelyn Conover (Danser), Mary Ann Messler, unknown, Erma Dilatush, Margaret Davison (Chubet), Dorothy Franklin (Simpson), and Marie Thompson (Dawes). (Alva "Bud" Perrine)

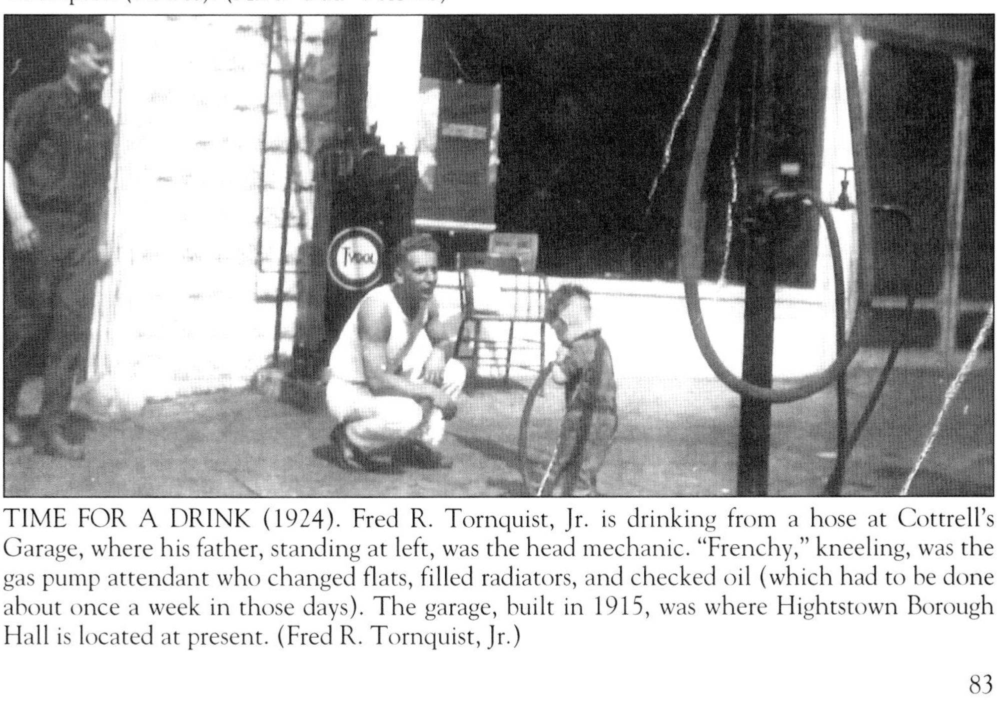

TIME FOR A DRINK (1924). Fred R. Tornquist, Jr. is drinking from a hose at Cottrell's Garage, where his father, standing at left, was the head mechanic. "Frenchy," kneeling, was the gas pump attendant who changed flats, filled radiators, and checked oil (which had to be done about once a week in those days). The garage, built in 1915, was where Hightstown Borough Hall is located at present. (Fred R. Tornquist, Jr.)

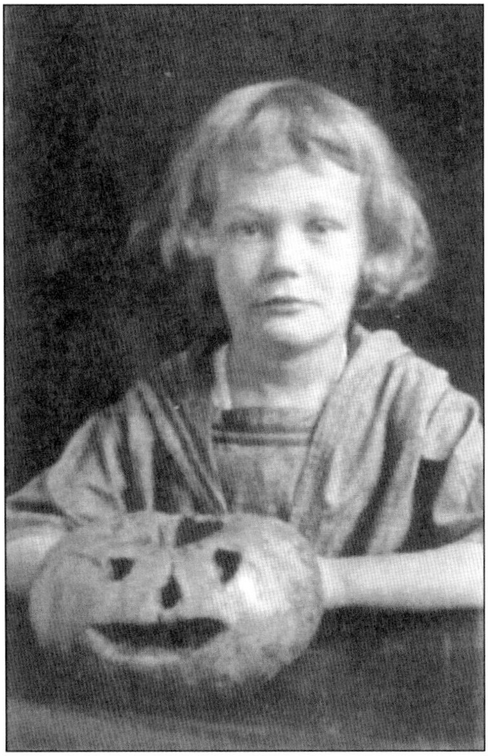

FUTURE NEWSPAPER EDITOR (*c.* 1924). With a jack-o'-lantern on his desk, Walton Palmer Dennis, present editor and co-publisher of *The Hightstown Gazette*, donned a sailor suit for this photograph taken at the Mercer Street School. (Kathryn Dennis of *The Hightstown Gazette*)

GEORGE WASHINGTON CONOVER (*c.* 1924). This Civil War veteran died just before Decoration Day in 1926. The photograph shows him at age eighty-one standing at the front of his 307 Stockton Street home. The father of two daughters, Maud Conover Jones and Edna Conover, George spent many years in the real estate and insurance businesses. (Dorothy Petty Dey)

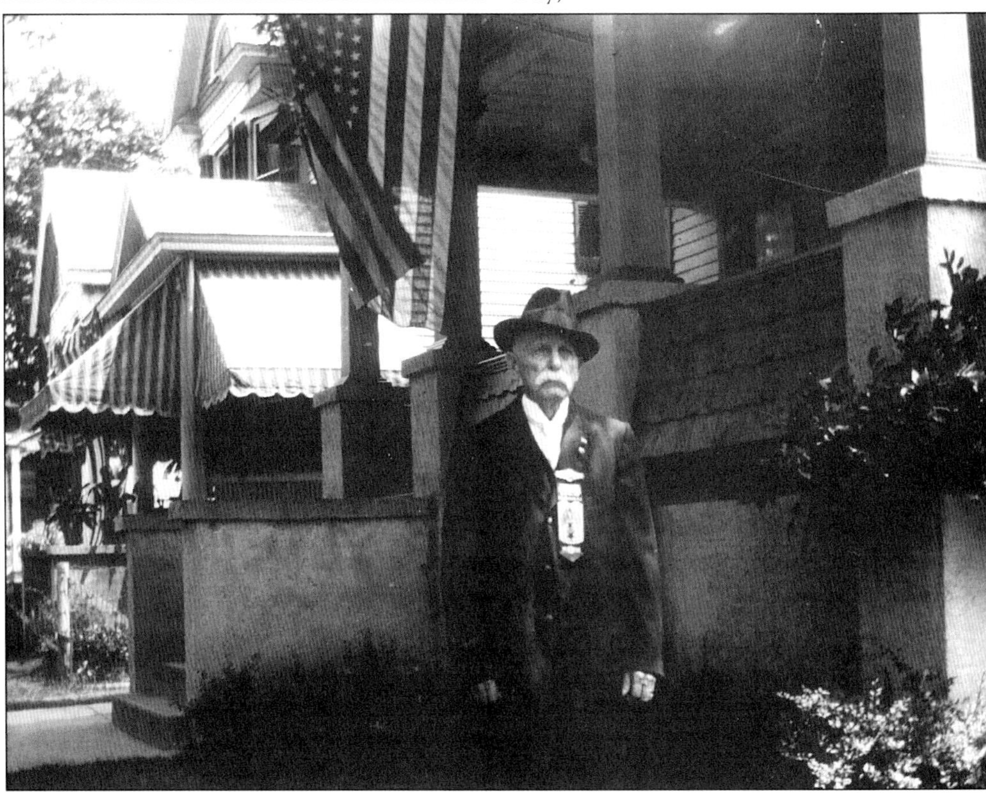

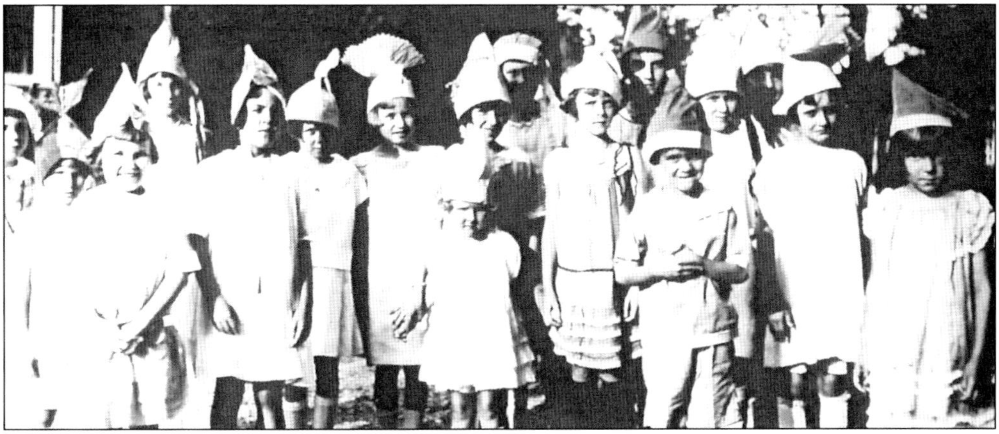

PARTY HAT COLLECTION (1925). These children attending Mary I. Field's sixth birthday party at her home on South Main Street are: Barbara Waite (Ticknor), Marion Thompson (McQueen), Ruth Waite (Hendrik), Marie Thompson (Dawes), Jane Puglin (Perrine), Florence Norcross (Fielder), Doris Norcross (Slover), Ruth Shangle (Pierce), Edith Field (Ely), Dorothy Franklin (Simpson), Mary Alice Shangle (Bedell), Florence Holman, Stuart C. Mitchell, unknown, unknown, Josephine Silver (Webb), and Mary I. Field. (Janet Field)

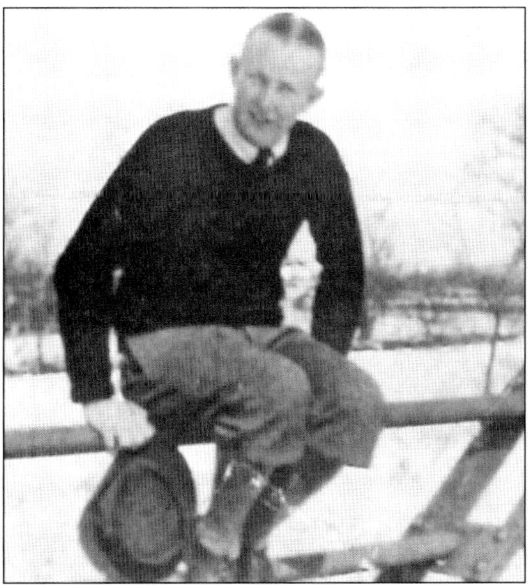

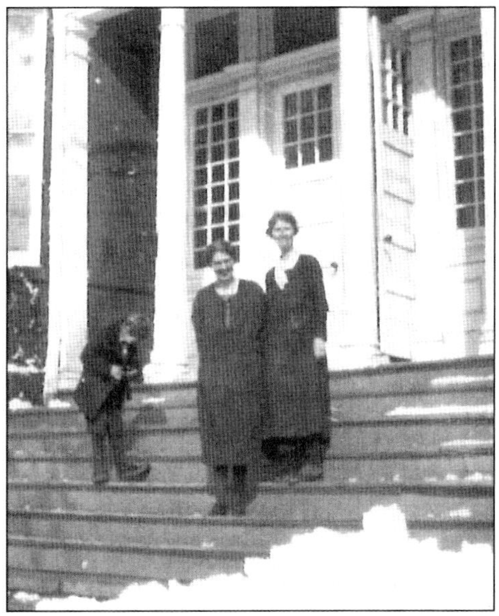

PERCHED ON PEDDIE BRIDGE (1920s). On a winter day with a frozen Peddie Lake in the background, Alfred Leland "Lee" Hutchinson (1902–1956) shows the style of the era in his knickers, crew neck sweater, and center-parted hair. Lee was born in a house at the corner of South Main and Ward Streets that was later torn down. The law firm of Turp, Coates, Essl and Driggers is presently located on that site. (Bob Hutchinson)

WELL-KNOWN EDUCATORS (1924). Grace Norton (Rogers) and Luella Dey stand on the steps of the Mercer Street School on April Fools' Day. These cousins were teachers in local schools for much of the century. Luella retired in 1950 at the age of seventy-one after teaching fifty-five years in Hightstown and East Windsor. Grace retired in 1965 at the age of sixty-six; in 1980 a school on Stockton Street was named in her honor. The school in the photograph was built in 1894 and had eight classrooms. It was in use as a public school for forty-seven years. (Brenda Dey MacMurray and Dorothy Petty Dey)

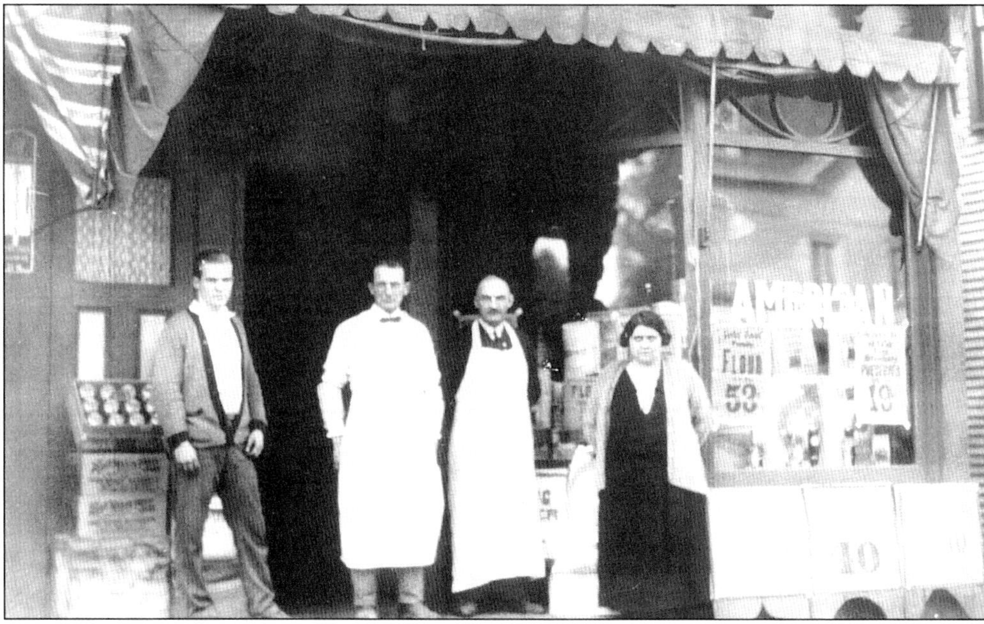

AMERICAN STORE STAFF (*c.* 1924). Store employees stand at the entrance of the American Store, located at 128 Stockton Street across the street from the Smith House. They are: Lawrence Ivins (clerk), Charles Rogers (produce manager), Daniel Webster Ivins (manager), and Edna Ralph (clerk). (Norris Robbins Collection)

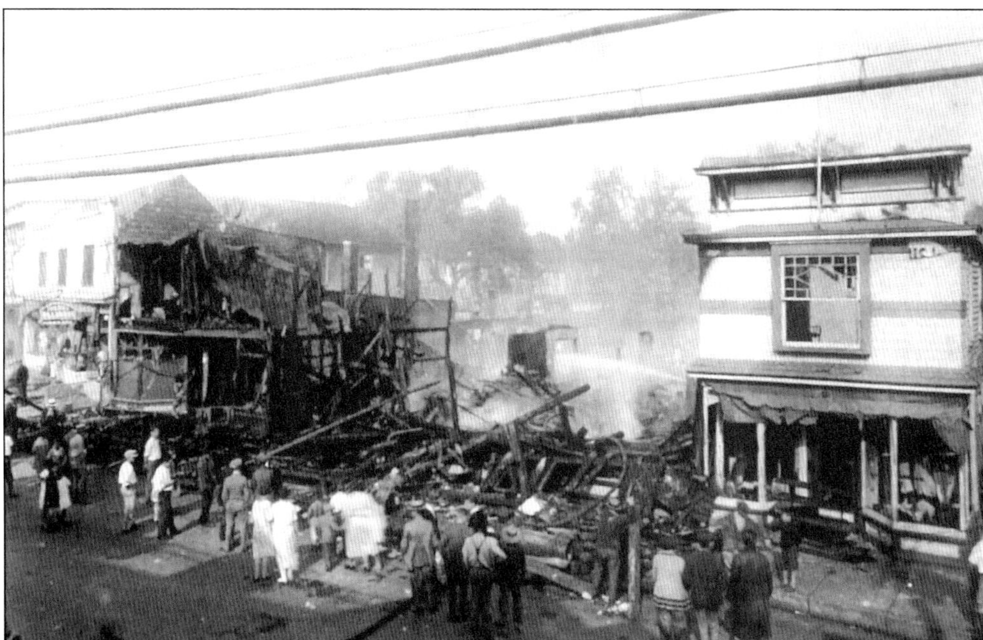

DEVASTATING DOWNTOWN FIRE (1925). An August 27 fire on the west side of Main Street destroyed the Hightstown Hardware Company and gutted the American Store and Candy Kitchen. The brick walls of the Hightstown Trust Company prevented the fire, which began in the hardware store, from spreading northward. The loss was $200,000. (Fred R. Tornquist, Jr.)

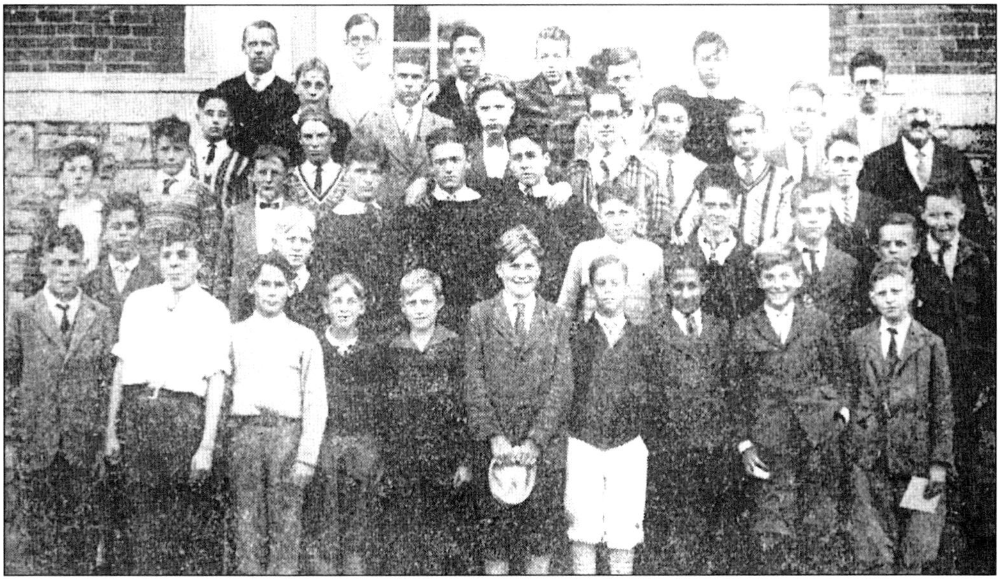

YMCA (mid-1920s). These YMCA members standing in front of the Stockton Street School are: (front row) Fred Allen, George Beely, Billy Riehl, Wes Howard, Earl Pullen, Bill ?, Jim Dawes, Joe Eufemia, Russ Ashby, and Jay Jones; (second row) Ed Fenton, Ely Hutchinson, Ken Duryee, Jack Babcock, George Peacock, Jimmy Archer, and Francis Larkin; (third row) Sam McGovern, Dave Greene, Dick Ewart, Bill Peacock, Ham Ewart, Bob Eldridge, and Lawton Pearsall; (fourth row) Happy Rue, Roy Pullen, Phil Burtis, Ken Berrien, Earl Davison, Calvin Hughes, Lloyd Rogers, and E. Shropshire; (back row) Cyril Davison, Edward Dennis, Leon Walker, Elmer Mount, Pete Van Sciver, Russ Mulvan, Herb Lutcken, Joe Morevec, and Paul Jones. (Ken Duryee)

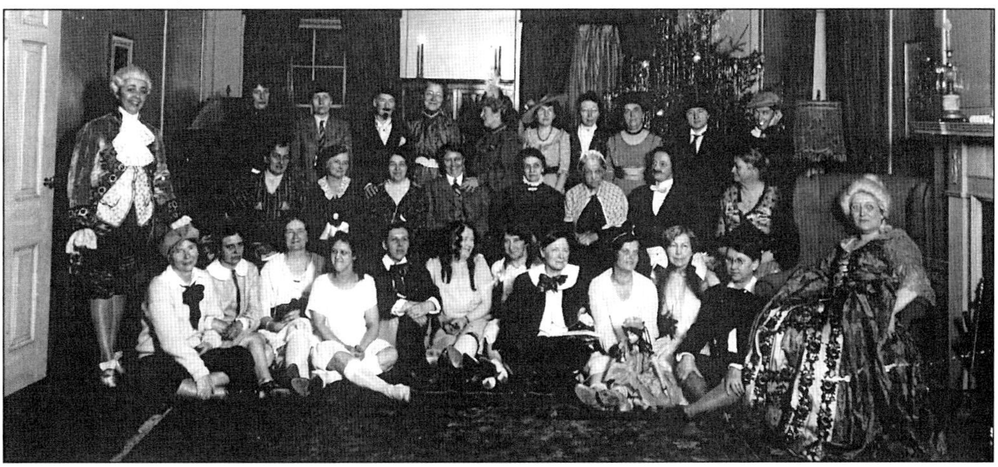

A CHRISTMAS GATHERING (1926). Members of the Friday Club, founded in 1896, are dressed as famous historical characters for a holiday meeting. They are: (front row) Alice Davison, Edna Norton, Bessie Keeler, Nell Shangle, Mrs. ? Judd, Mabel McCarnes, Maude Jones, Justine Messler, Edna Conover, Georgia Riley, and Jane Donnell; (middle row) Maude Davison, Beatrice Tyack, Irma Franklin, Carlotta Davison, Elsie Franklin, Mrs. Henry Mount, Maude Stevens, and Carrie Swetland; (back row) Josephine Cunningham, Mildred Davenport, Elizabeth Reeves, Virginia Wyckoff, Myrta Priory, Elinor MacArthur, Grace Ashton, Sarah Black, Lillian Albert, and Estelle Waite. (Hightstown-East Windsor Historical Society)

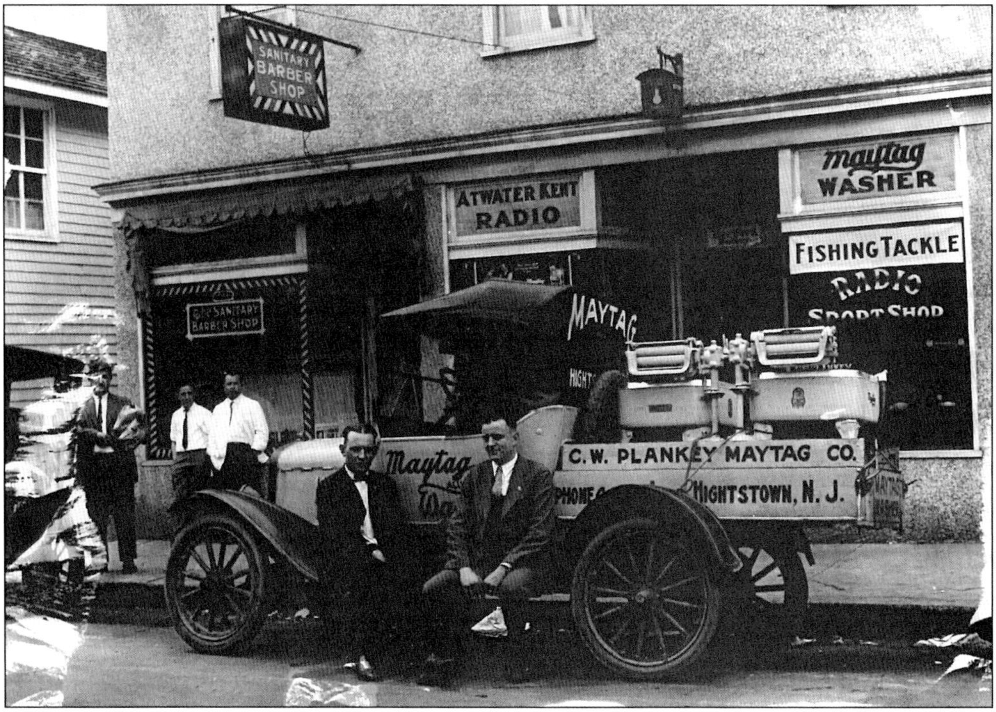

NEW MAYTAGS (1920s). C.W. Plankey, seated at right on the running board, is ready to deliver wringer washers to area homes. The Sanitary Barber Shop and Radio Sport Shop were located on Mercer Street. (Hightstown-East Windsor Historical Society)

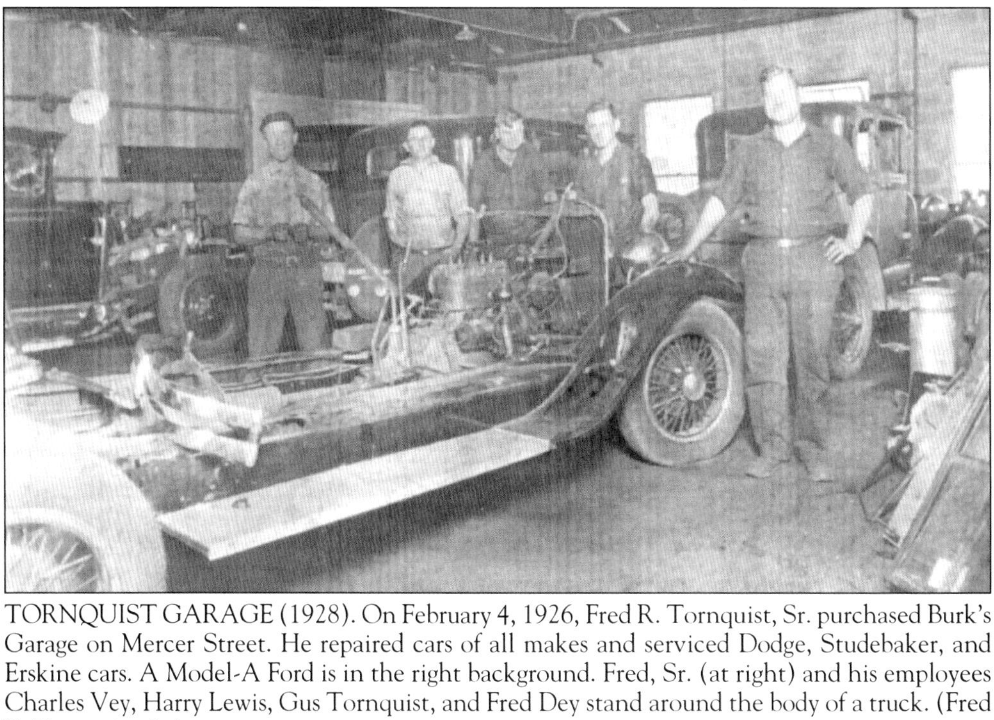

TORNQUIST GARAGE (1928). On February 4, 1926, Fred R. Tornquist, Sr. purchased Burk's Garage on Mercer Street. He repaired cars of all makes and serviced Dodge, Studebaker, and Erskine cars. A Model-A Ford is in the right background. Fred, Sr. (at right) and his employees Charles Vey, Harry Lewis, Gus Tornquist, and Fred Dey stand around the body of a truck. (Fred R. Tornquist, Jr.)

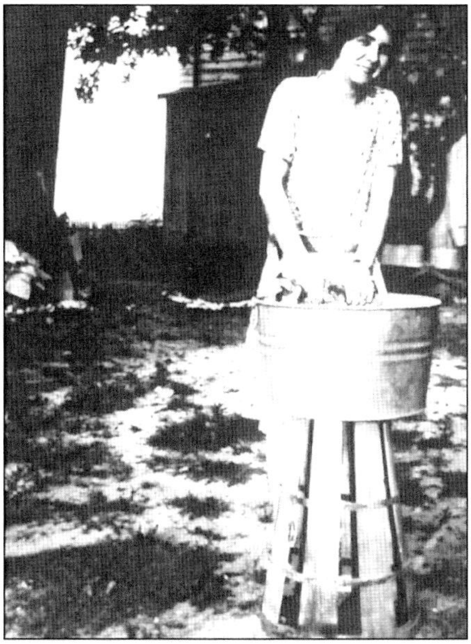

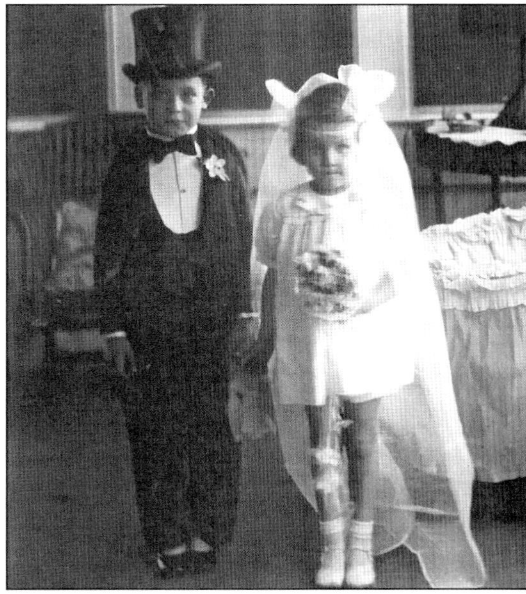

WASH DAY (c. 1929). It must be Monday, since Katherine Salzer is scrubbing clothes on a washboard in the yard of her home. (Hightstown-East Windsor Historical Society)

BRIDAL SHOWER (1929). Ernie Thompson and Beth Keeler (Wham) pull a wagon loaded with gifts for the upcoming weddings of sisters Blanche and Kathryn Thompson. (Beth Wham)

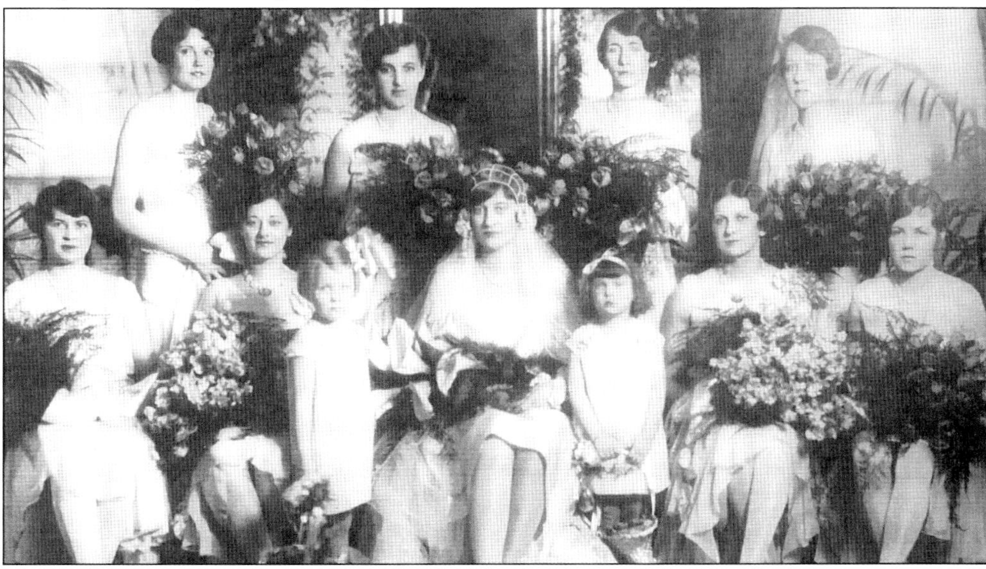

FASHIONABLE WEDDING (1929). Mrs. Thomas Duffield Hann, Jr., daughter of Mayor and Mrs. William Homer Thompson, is the bride at center. This photograph appeared in the Rotogravure Picture Section of the *New York Times* on Sunday, March 31. The wedding took place at the First Baptist Church and the reception was held at Carlton Villa, the bride's home, which is now the guest house at Meadow Lakes. From left to right are: (front row) Kathryn Thompson (Parker) and Gladys Ely; (middle row) Florence Updike (Chamberlin), Anita Beth Keeler (Wham), the bride (Blanche Thompson), Gloria Davison, and Mrs. Howard Hoffman (Orr); (back row) Mrs. Eugene Dawson, Mrs. Vete Davis, Miss Helen Fenton, and Mrs. Marian Baird. (Beth Wham)

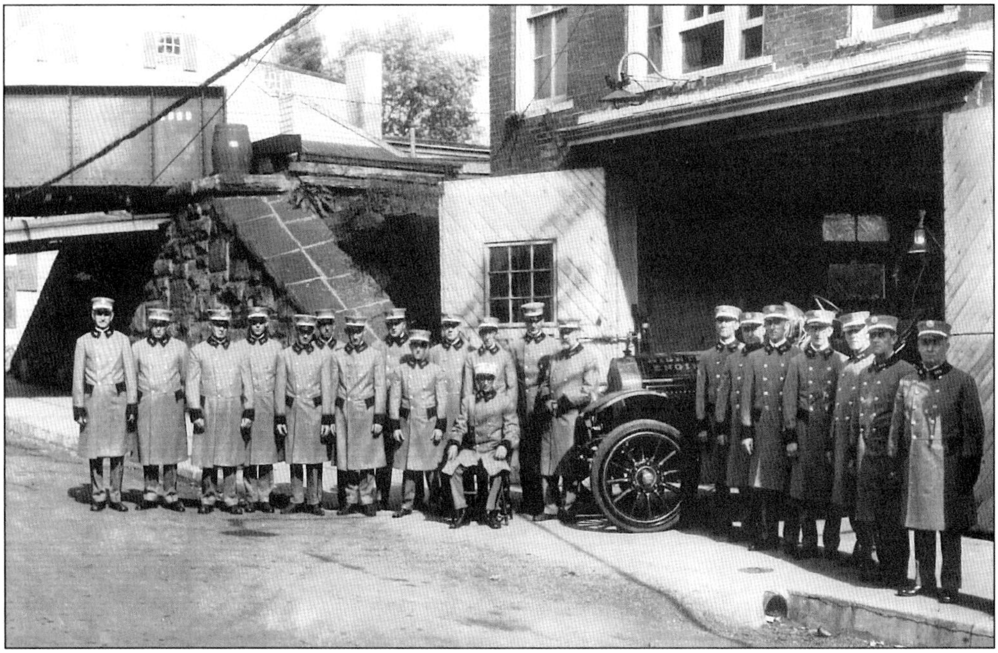

UNIFORMED FIREMEN (1920s). In their tan uniforms with maroon trim, Hightstown firemen stand on either side of a 1920 American La France pumper. The picture was taken in front of the Stockton Street firehouse. The firemen pictured are: unknown, John Mulvan, Edward F. Tabler, Horace Embley, Fred R. Tornquist, Sr., Al Hollenback, Claude Tabler, Lloyd Hulick, Walter McCue, unknown, Fred (Skeet) Martin, Chief Alonzo Pierson (seated), Ellis Cottrell, R.D. Norton, John A. Taylor, Elmer Tabler, Charles Templeton, Willard W. Norris, Willard L. Davison, unknown, and Charles L. Barsuglia. (Fred R. Tornquist, Jr.)

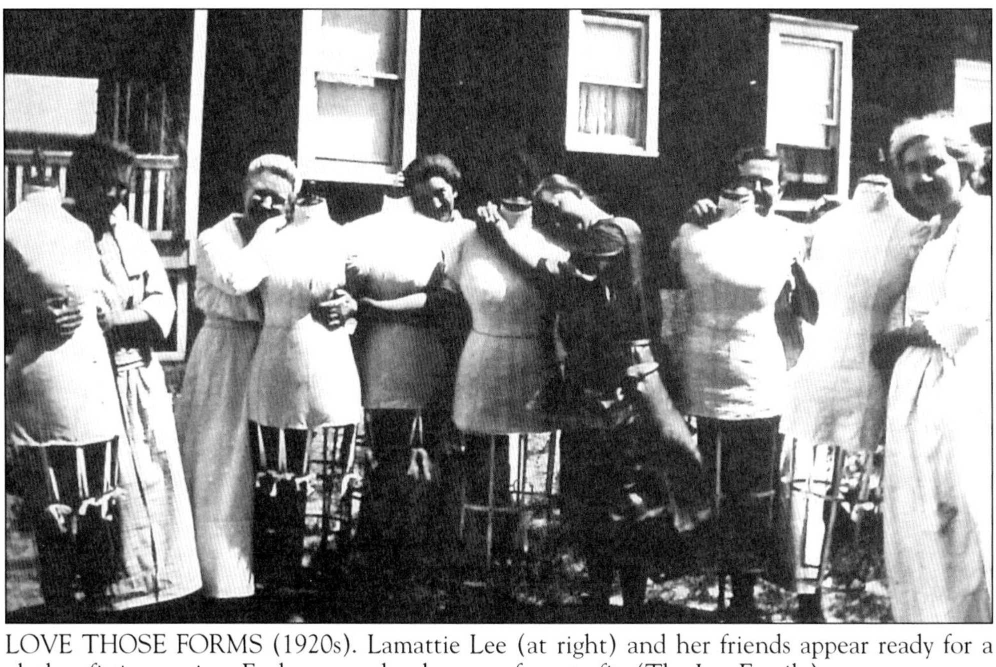

LOVE THOSE FORMS (1920s). Lamattie Lee (at right) and her friends appear ready for a clothes-fitting session. Each woman has her own form to fit. (The Lee Family)

Six

1930 to 1939

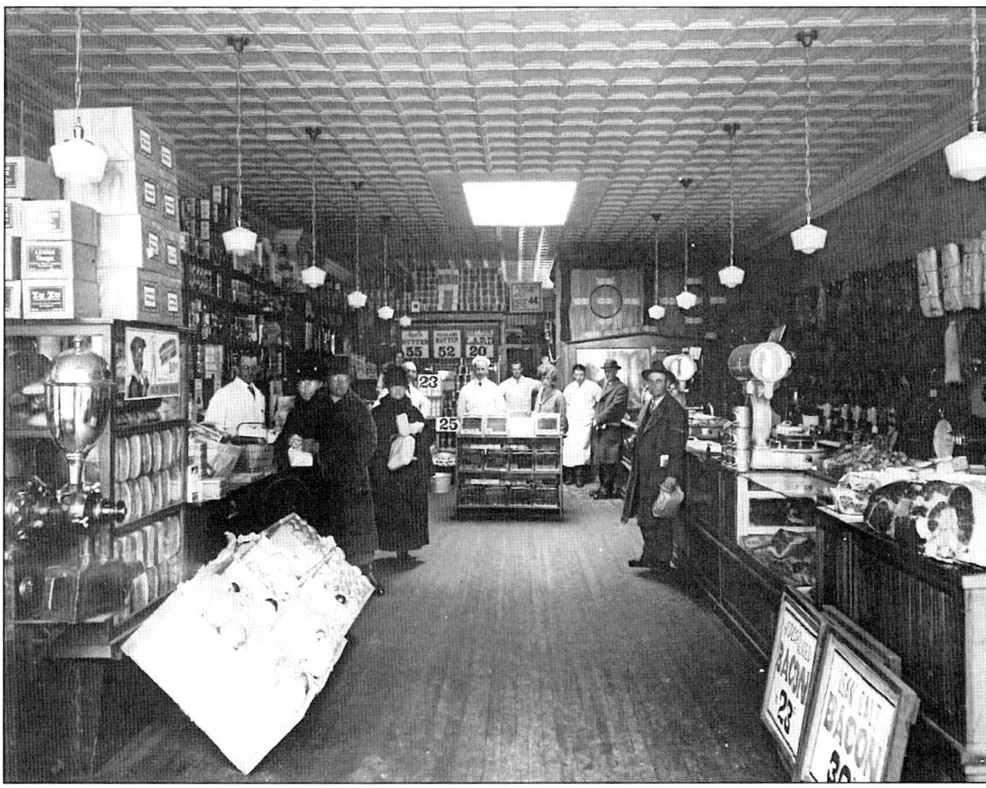

SHOPPING DURING THE DEPRESSION (mid-1930s). The employees' white jackets and aprons sharply contrast with the dark clothing of the customers in the American Store on Main Street across from the First Baptist Church. On the left is a coffee grinder; a sign opposite it advertises regular bacon for 23¢ per pound. Louella butter was selling for 55¢ per pound. The store manager was Daniel Webster "Web" Ivins, and Charlie Rogers was the clerk behind the counter on the left. Mrs. Emerson, who lived two doors down from the First Presbyterian Church, was one of the customers on the left. (Hightstown-East Windsor Historical Society)

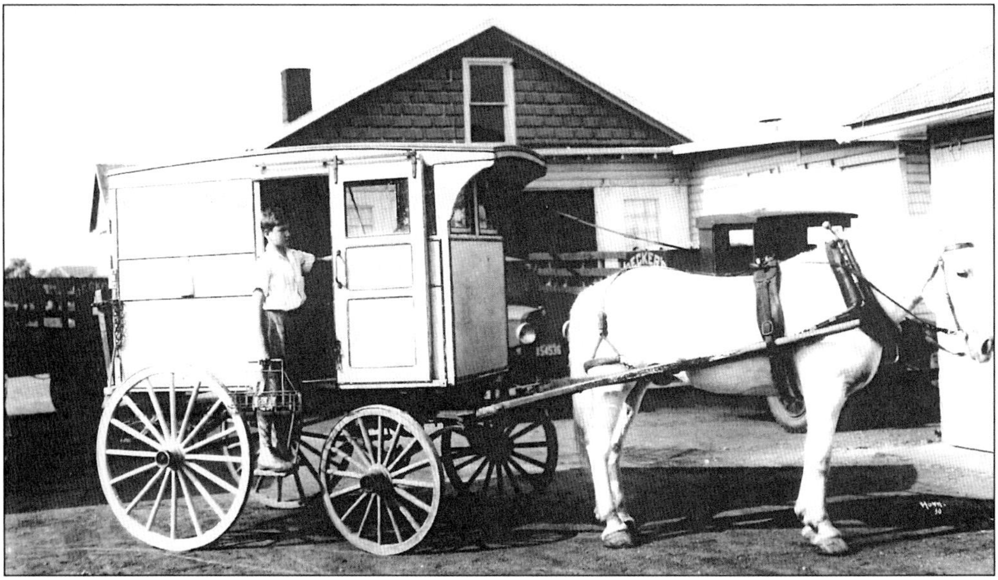

DAIRY DELIVERY WAGON (1930). Decker's Diary was founded in 1926 by Conrad Decker, Sr. At that time the delivery fleet consisted of the horse and wagon and three trucks in this photograph. Conrad Decker, Jr., later to become vice president and treasurer, is holding the customary wire basket used for milk bottles on home deliveries. (Hightstown-East Windsor Historical Society)

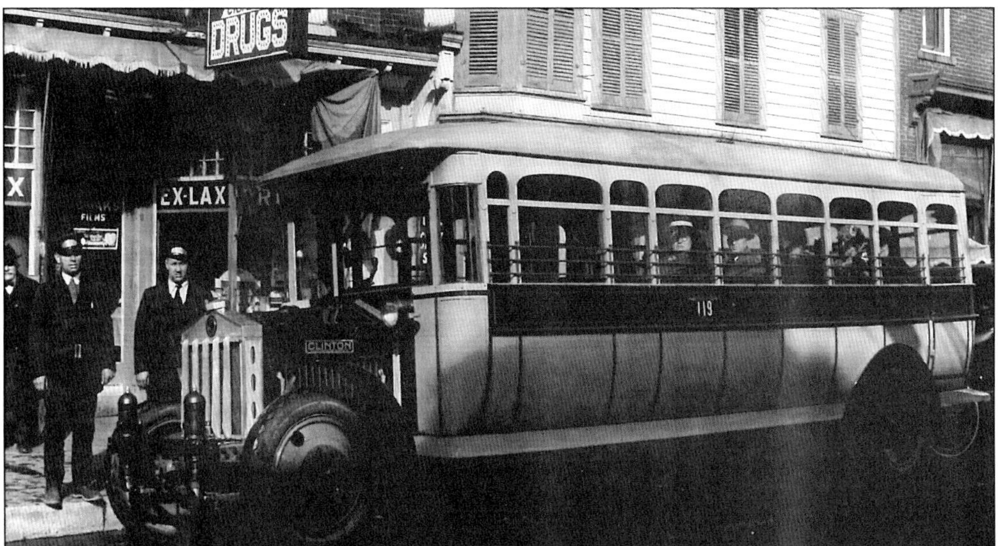

EARLY BUS TRANSPORTATION (*c.* 1930). After the railroad suspended passenger service, the city bus line provided transportation from Hightstown to Trenton and other destinations. The pick-up point was Burch's Drug Store on the west side of Main Street. Prior to this time, the building had served a number of purposes. It had been a bank that failed, a clothing store, a post office, and Harvey Rue's drug store. When the building was used as a post office, letter boxes were placed against the windows so that box holders could determine if they had mail without entering the building. Business increased, and the post office was moved to the lunch room at Scheible's Hotel across the street. (Hightstown-East Windsor Historical Society)

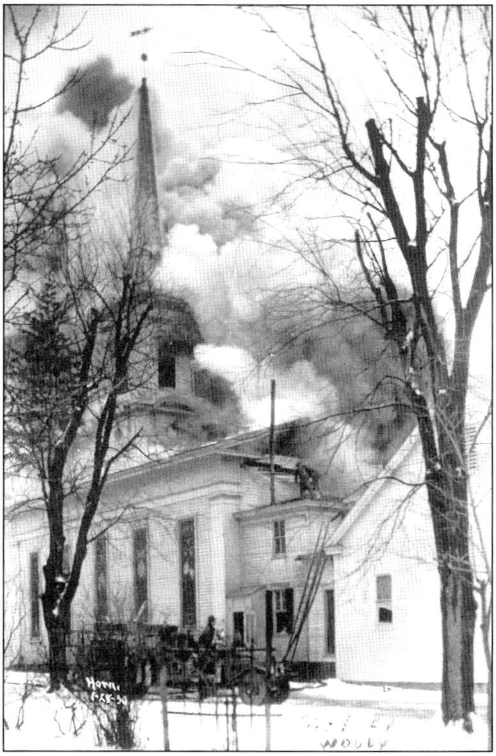
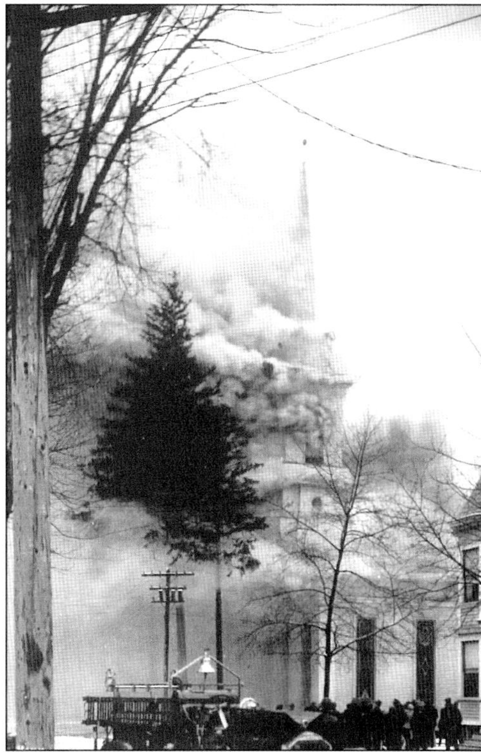

FIREMEN ATTACKING THE BLAZE (1930). Unfortunately, despite the best efforts of the fire department, the blaze soon consumed the structure. (Fred. R. Tornquist, Jr.)

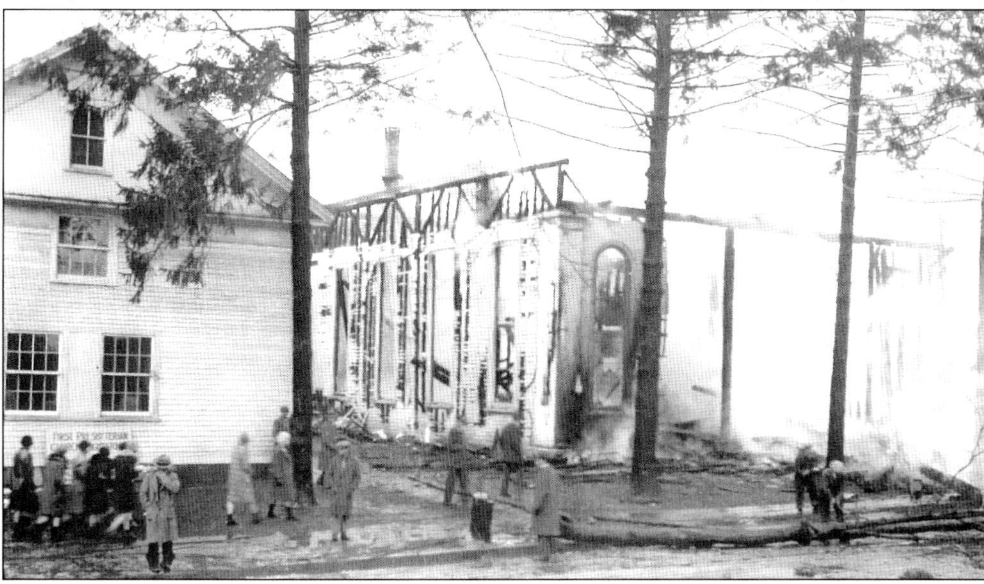

A SKELETON REMAINS (1930). The First Presbyterian Church burned down on January 28. It was rebuilt soon afterwards, and stood for decades before it was destroyed by a fire on Palm Sunday 1969. Each time it was rebuilt an effort was made to copy the design of the original steeple. The First Presbyterian Church in Hightstown was erected in 1857 on the current site. Prior to that time, worshippers attended church in Cranbury. (Fred R. Tornquist, Jr.)

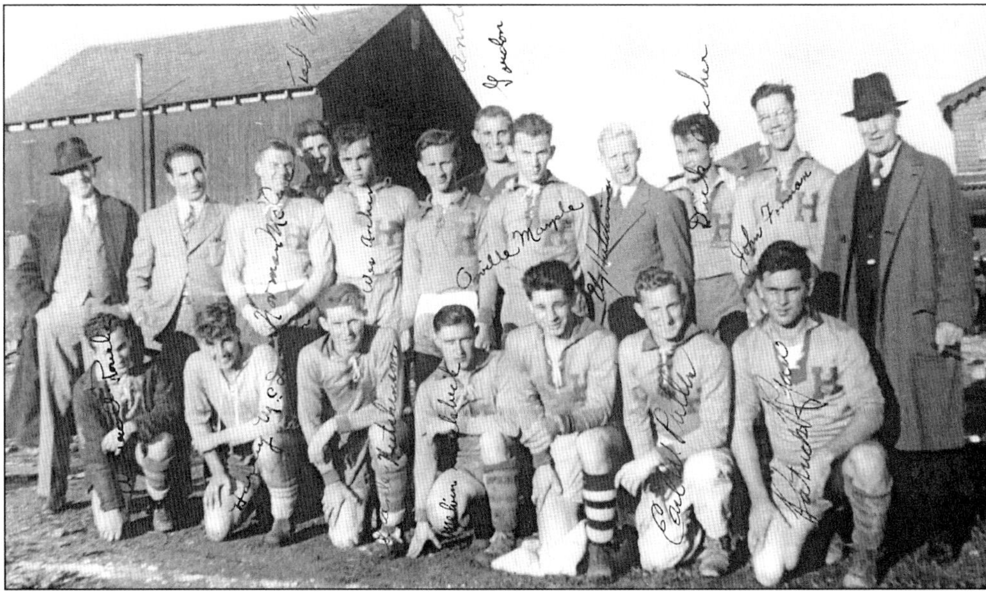

HIGH SCHOOL SOCCER TEAM (*c.* 1930). For many years soccer was the number one interscholastic sport of Hightstown High School. Members of this team are: (front row) W. O'Rourke, H. ?, Stanley Hutchinson, Melvin Denelsbeck, unknown, Earl W. Pullen, and Patrick Ryan; (back row) Norman McCue, Ted Matloz, Wes Archer, ? Anderson, Gordon Dorshay, Orville Marple, Ely Hutchinson, Dick Archer, and John Forman. The coaches in jackets and ties are unidentified. (Hightstown-East Windsor Historical Society)

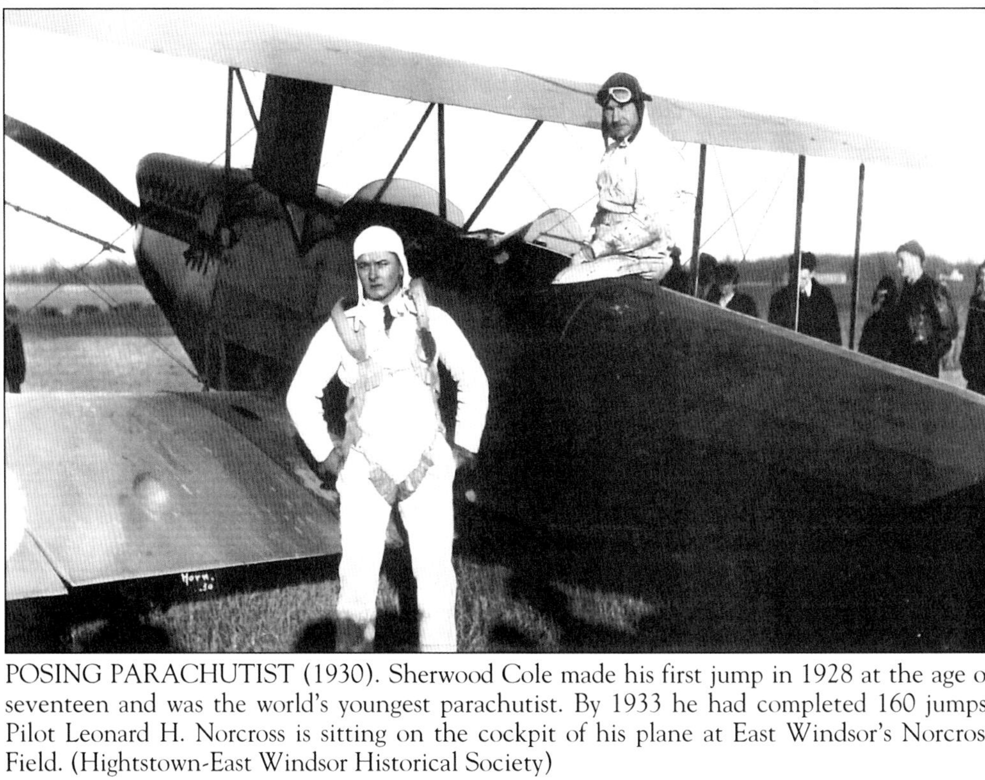

POSING PARACHUTIST (1930). Sherwood Cole made his first jump in 1928 at the age of seventeen and was the world's youngest parachutist. By 1933 he had completed 160 jumps. Pilot Leonard H. Norcross is sitting on the cockpit of his plane at East Windsor's Norcross Field. (Hightstown-East Windsor Historical Society)

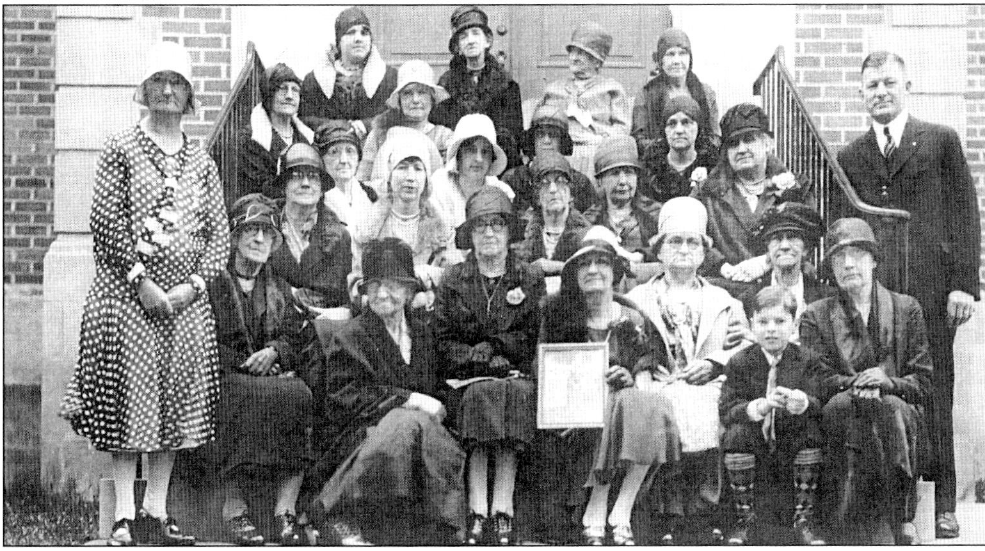

"THE HARMONY SUNDAY SCHOOL CLASS" (1930). This First Baptist Church Sunday School class consisted of the following: (standing) Mrs. Charles Mount and Mr. R.E. Harmon; (front row) Mrs. William Hutchinson, Miss Mary Simpson, Mrs. Hiram Van Nest, Miss Mary A. Hutchinson, Mrs. Eugene Roszel, Mrs. ? Dennis, William Rue, and Mrs. Clarence Grover; (middle row) Mrs. Lydia Applegate, Mrs. Edna Hoffman, Mrs. William Field, Mrs. John Dorrance, Mrs. Kate Field, Miss Grace Ely, Mrs. Sara Jane Hulick, Mrs. Randolph Chamberlin, and Mrs. Anthony Wilson; (back row) Miss Alberta Grover, Mrs. Samuel Mount, Miss Abbie Pennington, Miss Minnie Huckstep, Mrs. A.C. Grover, and Miss Sylvia Rogers. Mrs. Roszel is holding a framed photograph of Charity Thein. The cloche hats, popular in the 1920s and early 1930s and worn by most of the women, supposedly helped to give them the "boyish look." Pulled down low onto the forehead, the hats drew attention to the eyes. (First Baptist Church Archives)

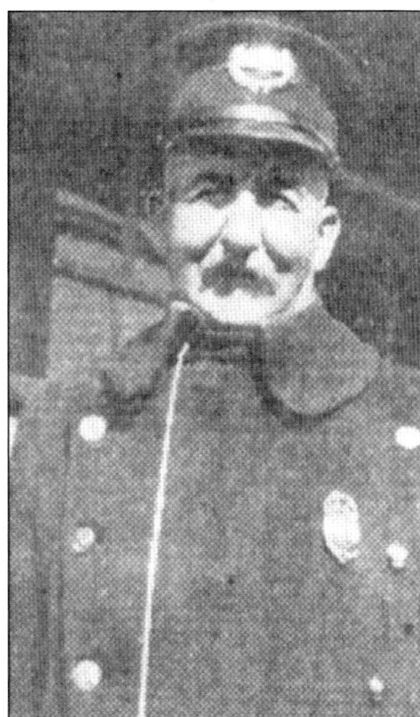

POLICE CHIEF (c. 1930). Charles W. Howard (1870–1933) was Hightstown's police chief from 1928 until his death. In 1913, after twenty-one-and-a-half years as a New York City police officer, he retired on pension and returned to Hightstown with his family. He and his wife Sadie had two sons, Charles J. and Harry, and lived on Oak Lane. (Charlotte Conover)

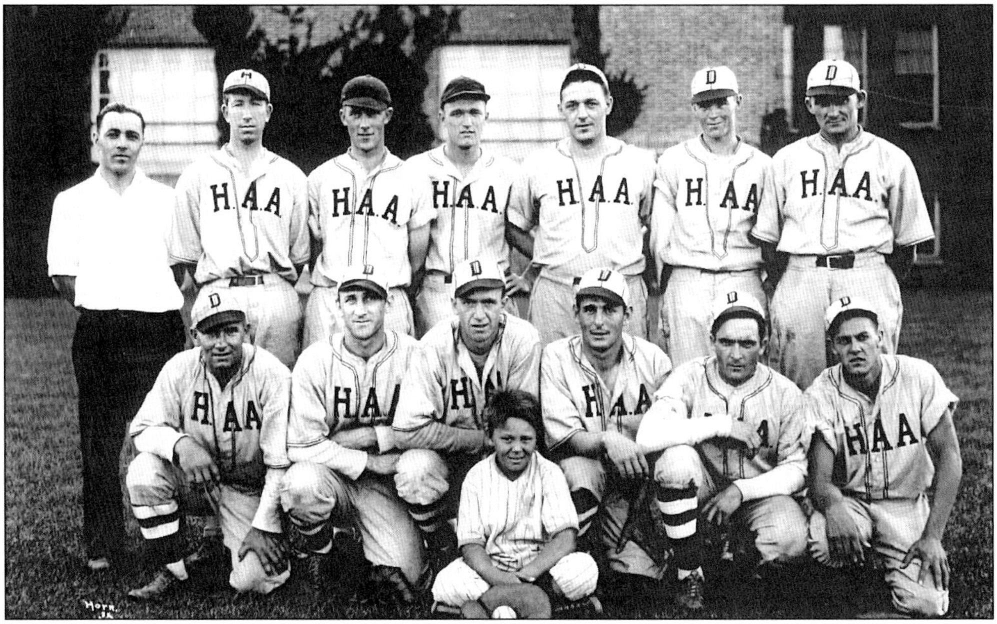

DECKER'S DAIRY BASEBALL SQUAD (1932). Bud Hopkins is the mascot and members of the team are: (front row) Lee White, Harry Lloyd, Steve Radische, Lem Wiley, Dick Morris, and Tit Cronce; (back row) Fred Paladino, Sonny Horn, Dave Farr, Ham Ewart, Yankee Freitag, Jack Nichols, and Tim Kelty. (Hightstown-East Windsor Historical Society)

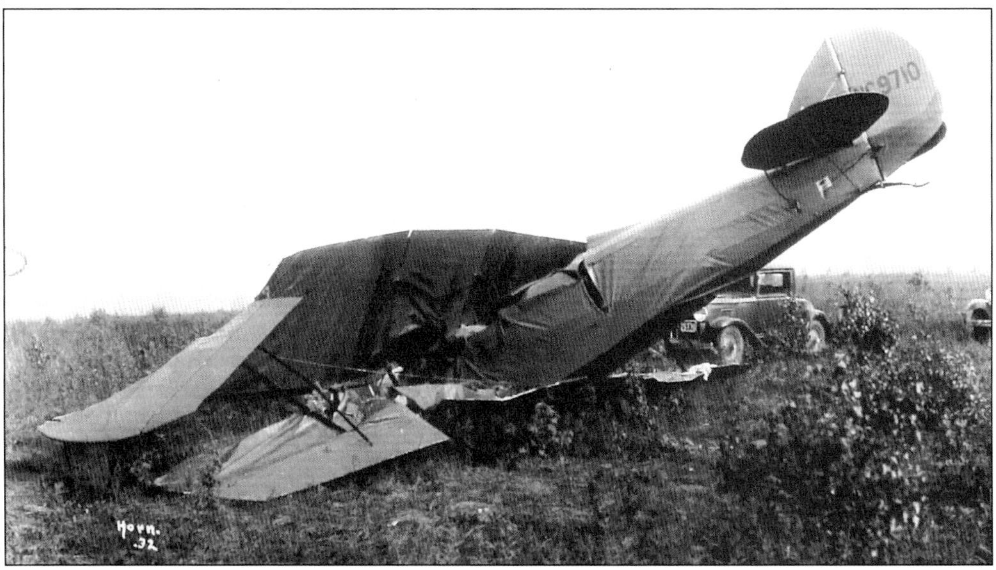

CRASH SCENE (1932). On Sunday, June 26, thirty-nine-year-old Leonard H. Norcross was killed in this local crash when the plane went into a tailspin and nose-dived into a field on the John R. Ewart farm. The plane fell with such force that the engine was buried in the ground. A graduate of Peddie and Brown University, Norcross was the operator of the Hightstown Airport and ran a poultry business. At the time of the crash, Norcross was giving flight instruction to William F. Thompson, who was seriously injured. Thompson, who lived at 156 North Main Street and was a garage mechanic, owned the Dual Waco biplane with two other men. (Hightstown-East Windsor Historical Society)

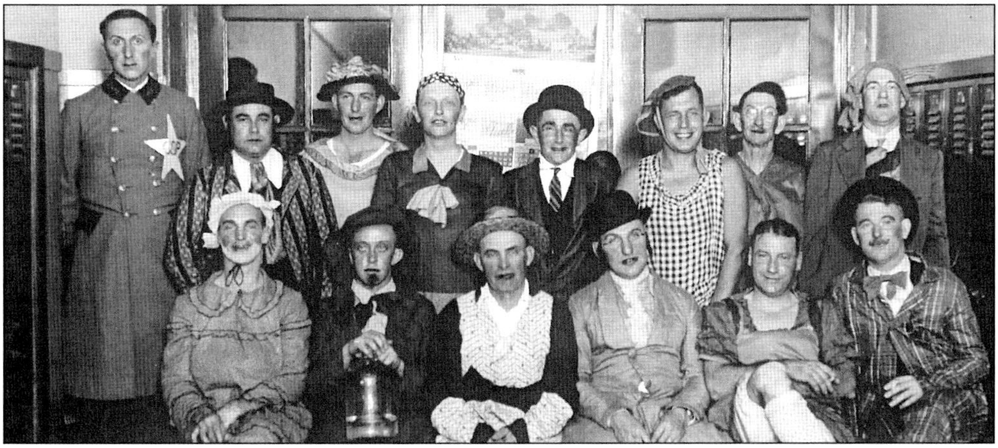

MALE REVUE (1933). This group of Little Theater enthusiasts, started in 1923, staged many plays of outstanding merit and entered tournaments in Trenton and New York City. These members posing in a hallway of Hightstown High School are: (front row) unknown, Albert Disbrow, William Horne, Leon Wetherill, Nelson Campbell, and unknown; (back row) William Heyer, James Turp, Clarence Conover, unknown, Henry Baers, unknown, Al Whitlock, and unknown. (Hightstown-East Windsor Historical Society)

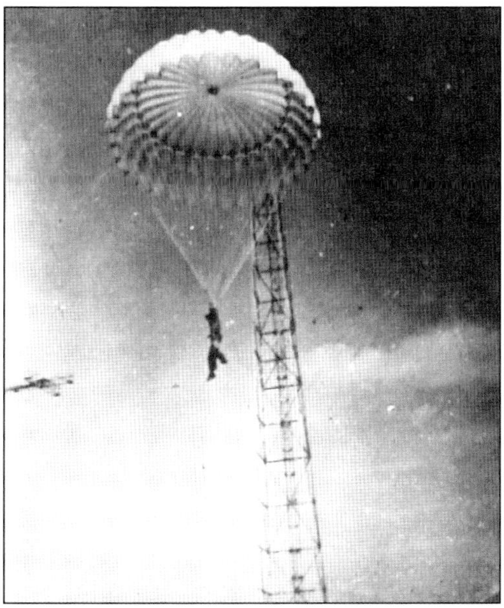

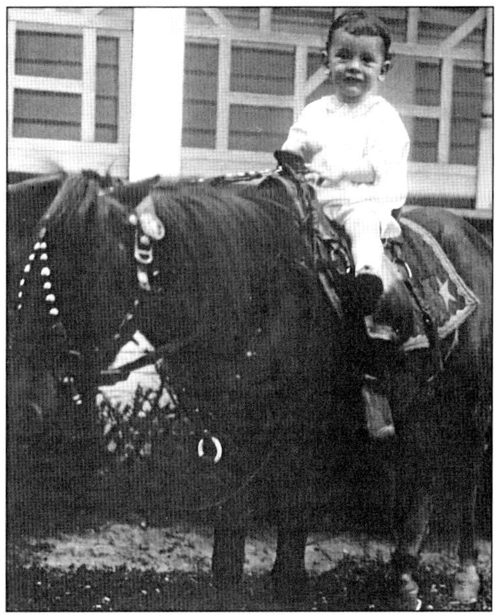

HIGHTSTOWN PARACHUTE TOWER (1930s). Located in a field near the corner of Route 25 (now 130) and Voelbel Road, this tower was built by the Switlik Parachute Company of Trenton. Amelia Earhart gave Switlik the idea for the structure, which was patterned after one that she had seen in the U.S.S.R. At one time The Hightstown Tower was used for U.S. Marine Corps training. (Hightstown-East Windsor Historical Society)

COWBOY "SKIP" (1933). At an early age, Dr. Harold C. Cox, Jr. is sitting on a pony in front of his 208 Stockton Street home. In later years, he worked as teacher and administrator for the East Windsor Regional Schools for thirty-six years and served as borough mayor from 1979 to 1982. Cox has also been active in the civic and religious life of the community, serving as an elder of the First Presbyterian Church, deacon of the First Baptist Church, and president of the Hightstown-East Windsor Historical Society. (Harold "Skip" Cox)

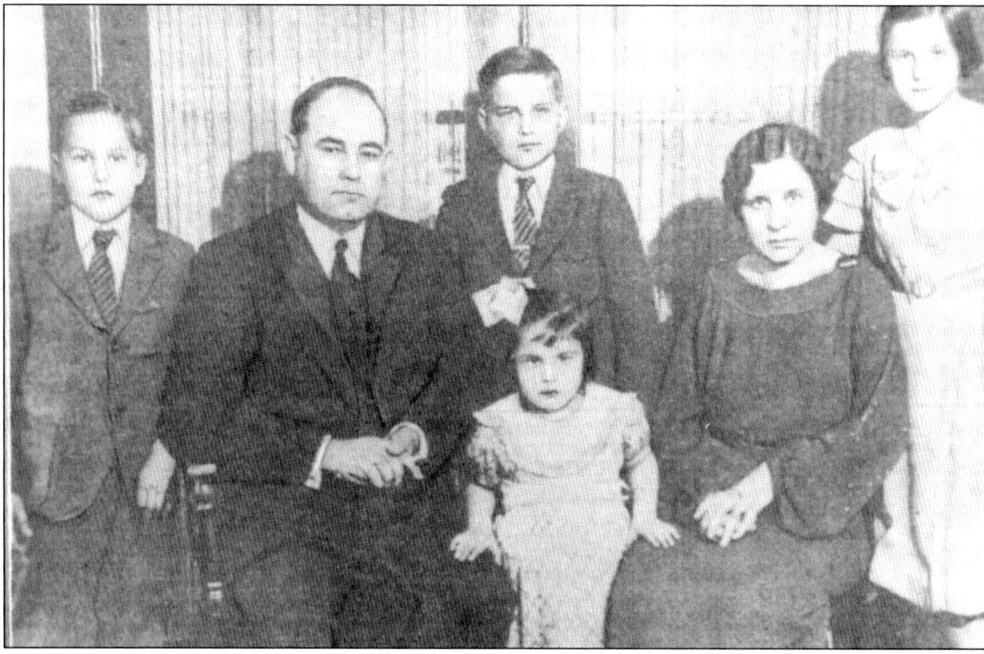

JUDGE TURP AND FAMILY (1935). James S. Turp, who became a Mercer County common pleas judge on April 1, 1935, is shown here in his home with his family. They are: Ernest, David, four-year-old Virginia Lois, his wife Anna P., and Maribelle. The Turp's oldest son Donald was attending school out of town when this picture was taken. A local attorney, Judge Turp served as mayor of Hightstown for two years, was superintendent of the First Presbyterian Church Sunday School, and was a prominent worker in the Mercer County YMCA as well as the Grange. (Maribelle T. Taylor and Ernest Turp)

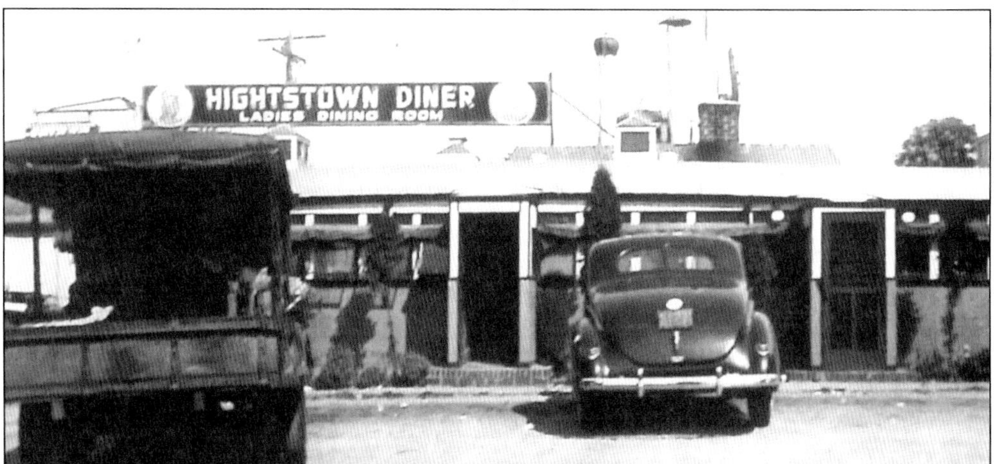

HIGHTSTOWN DINER (c. 1934). In 1927, the Corcodilos family came to Hightstown from Perth Amboy and started the Hightstown Diner. The owner was Nick Corcodilos. The building cost approximately $7,000 and came complete with a counter, twelve stools, a kitchen, glasses, dishes, cutlery, and cookware. It was calculated that the average customer occupied his stool for about eight minutes and spent 28¢. Service was provided by male waiters and cooks who wore white aprons and white starched hats. In 1936 a new diner replaced the earlier one on the same site. (Mary Mastoris)

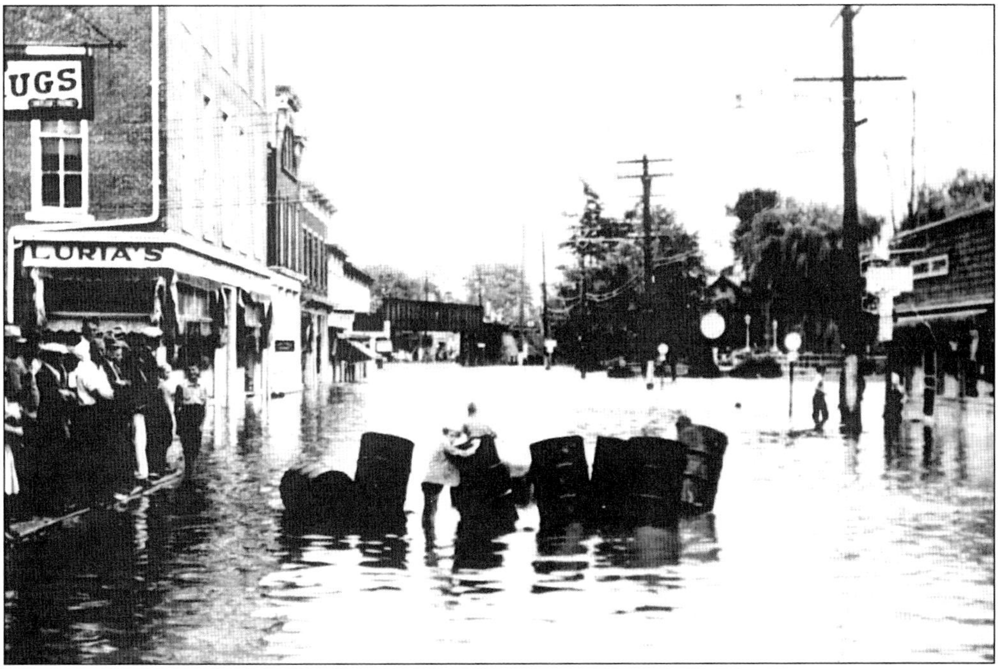

A FLOOD IN 1934. Taken at the corner of Stockton and Main Streets, this photograph shows the extent of the downtown flooding in September of 1934. According to *The Hightstown Gazette*, at times the water was 2 feet deep on Main Street and the cellar of Allen & Stults Company was filled. The high water mark was reached at 6 pm when water covered about 600 feet of the roadway. (C. Stults Family-Allen & Stults Collection)

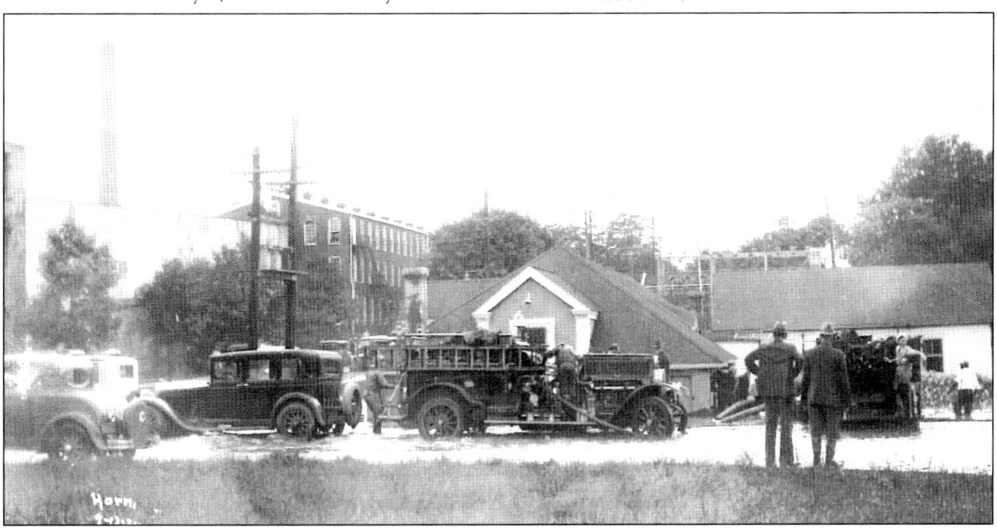

PUMPING OUT THE WATER PLANT (1934). O.T. Fenton and Charlie Ely in the foreground are observing the work being done by borough firemen at the water plant on Bank Street. Ely was Hightstown's superintendent of public works. Fred R. Tornquist, Jr. is standing on the back of the firetruck on the right. His father, Fred, Sr., is in the front seat of the firetruck on the left. The Hightstown Rug Mill is in the background to the left. Overflow waters caused the rug company to remove thousands of rugs from one of its storage buildings. Six inches of water covered the broad loom building and machine shop. (Fred R. Tornquist, Jr.)

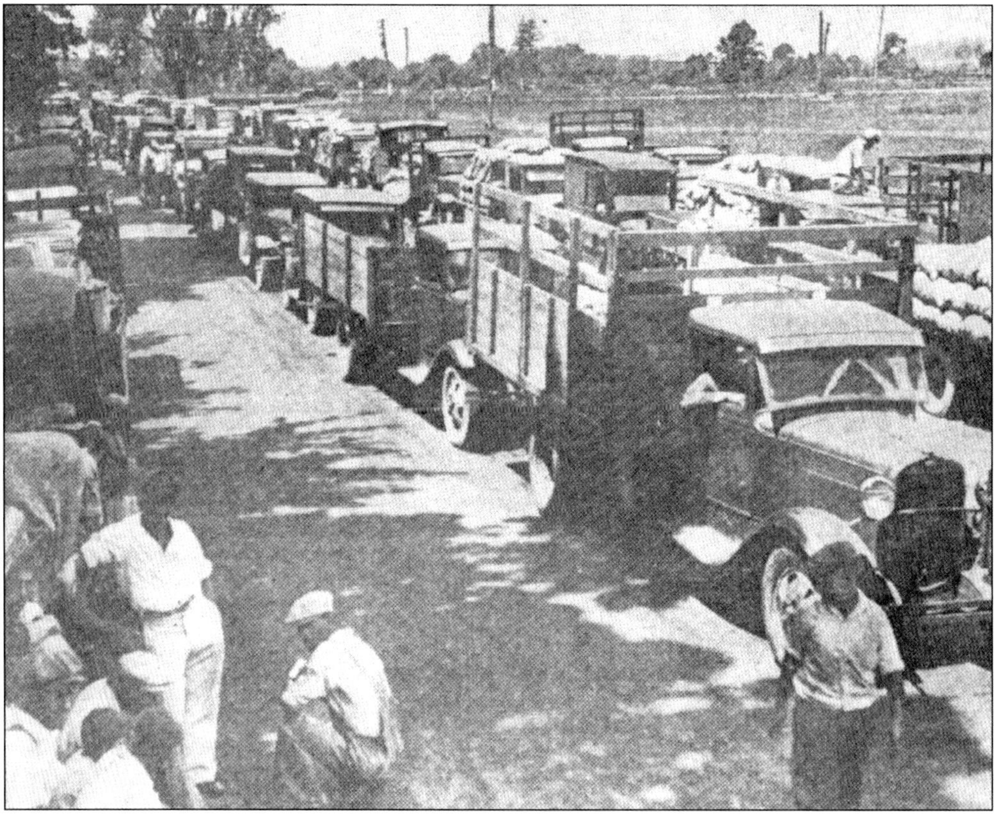

THESE LITTLE TRUCKIES WENT TO MARKET (1935). This is a typical August view of the Tri-County Cooperative Auction Market off Mercer Street as a convoy arrives with loads of farm produce. Incorporated in 1933, it became the most important market of its kind in New Jersey. (Maribelle Taylor and the Trenton *Sunday Times-Advertiser*)

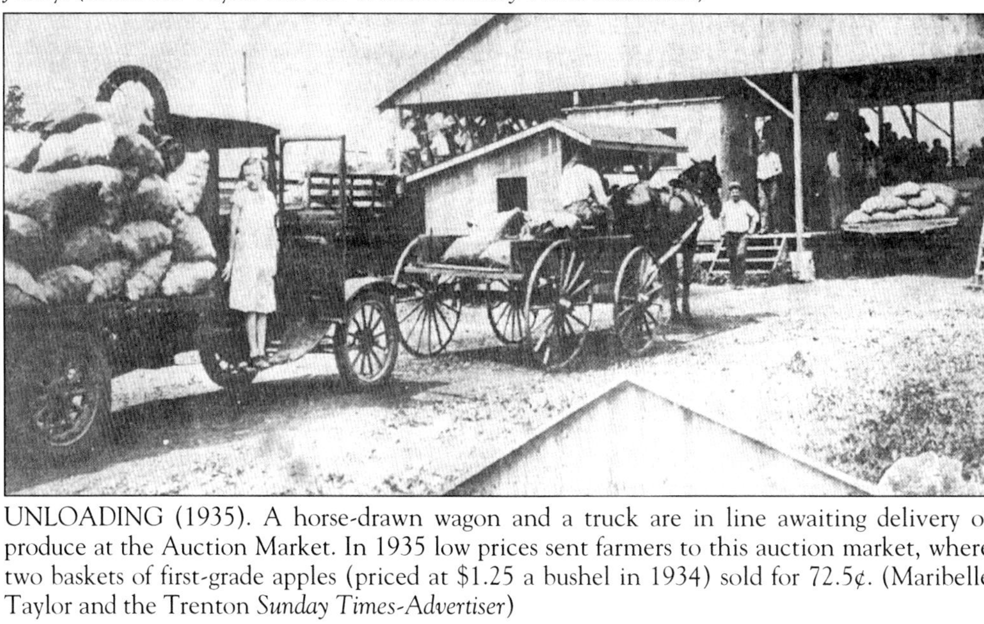

UNLOADING (1935). A horse-drawn wagon and a truck are in line awaiting delivery of produce at the Auction Market. In 1935 low prices sent farmers to this auction market, where two baskets of first-grade apples (priced at $1.25 a bushel in 1934) sold for 72.5¢. (Maribelle Taylor and the Trenton *Sunday Times-Advertiser*)

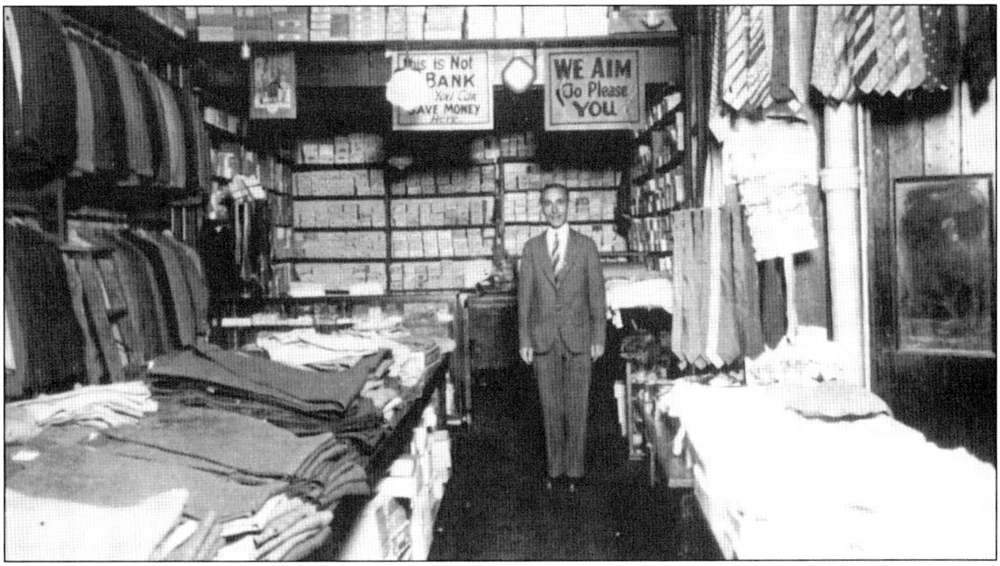

GOLDSTEIN'S CLOTHING STORE (1930s). Suits hang on the left and neckties on the right of this store owned and operated by Philip Goldstein, standing in the rear. Located at 120 Stockton Street where Cricket Converters is situated today, the building was erected in the 1840s and used initially as a tannery. An ice house was at the rear of the property along Rocky Brook. In 1936 Goldstein, who owned the store from 1914 to 1952, was selling wool suits and top coats for $12.50 to $17.50 and Florsheim shoes for $2.98. (David and Helen Goldstein)

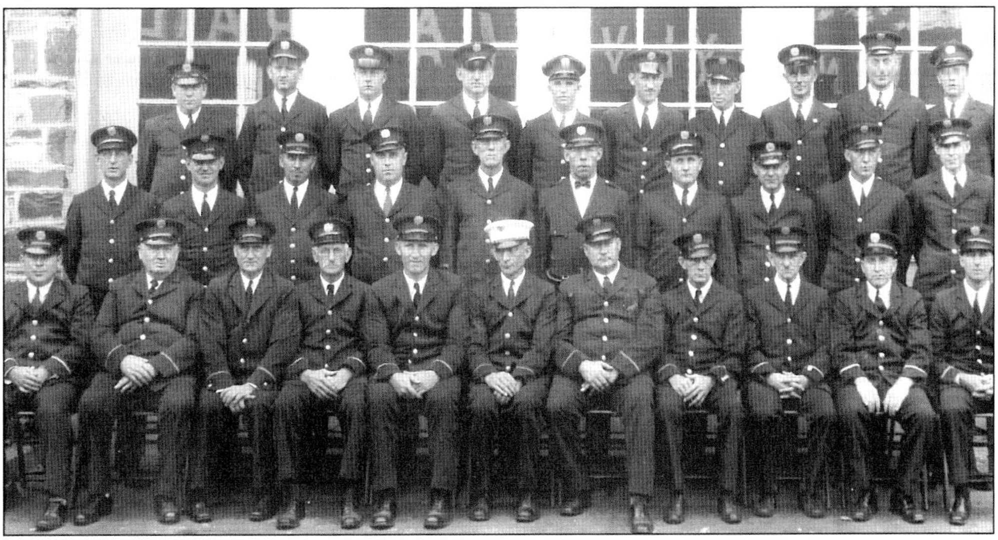

SHARPLY-DRESSED FIREMEN (1935). Firefighters of the Hightstown Engine Company No. 1 are shown in front of the North Main Street firehouse. They are: (front row) Leon Craig, E.F. Tabler, Harry Guidice, James C. Norris, "Baldy" Tabler, Chief Tom Malone, Fred R. Tornquist, Sr., Walter West, V.M. Everingham, Uriah R. Dubell, and Albert Wolfe; (middle row) Willard Norris, Charles Howard, Chester Wolfe, Charles B. Conway, Charles O'Hara, Carlton H. Conover, John Brandt, Fred L. Dey, Clarence E. Conover, and Horace Embley; (back row) Bob Devlin, Russell Crater, Alvin Anderson, Leon Wetherill, Ted Hopkins, Harry Lloyd, Charles Eldridge, Norris Elmer, Ellis Cottrell, and Charles Oldberg. (Hightstown-East Windsor Historical Society)

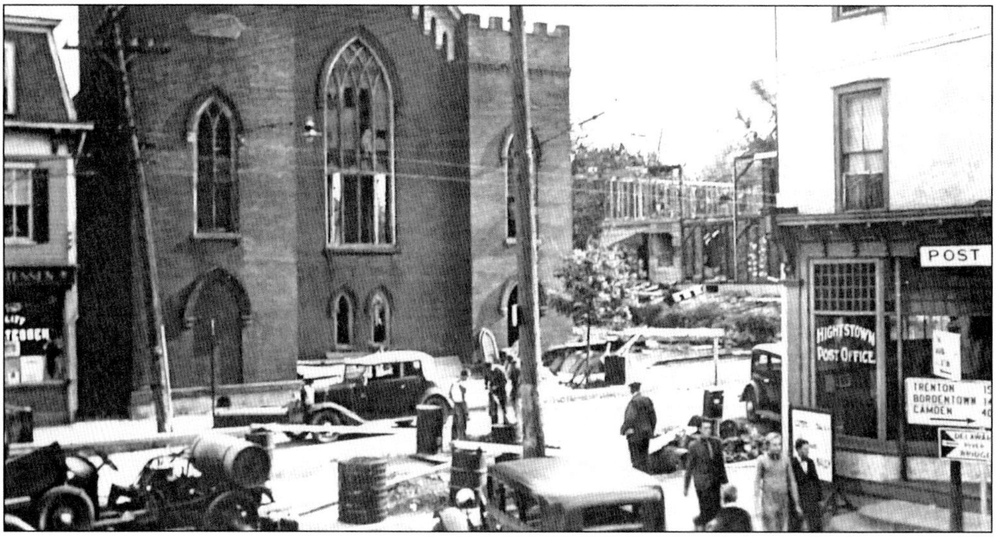

RELIGIOUS LANDMARK RAZED (1936). In the fall of 1936 the Universalist church was demolished to make way for a new post office. Closed in 1918, the church stood at the current location of the driveway belonging to Perritt Labs. In 1834 the First Baptist Church sold their old meetinghouse on this site. The buyer was Charles D. McChesney, a Universalist. The Baptists were under the impression that McChesney was going to use the structure as a barn. Almost immediately he sold it to the Universalist congregation, which renovated and refurnished it as their church, only two doors away from the new First Baptist Church. In the 1835 inaugural service, the Reverend LaFevre stated, "The glory of this latter house shall be greater than that of the former . . ." By the 1870s, Hightstown was one of the only towns in New Jersey with a flourishing Universalist congregation. In 1871, newspaper editor and 1872 presidential candidate Horace Greeley as well as P.T. Barnum attended a dedication for the new church sanctuary. (Hightstown-East Windsor Historical Society)

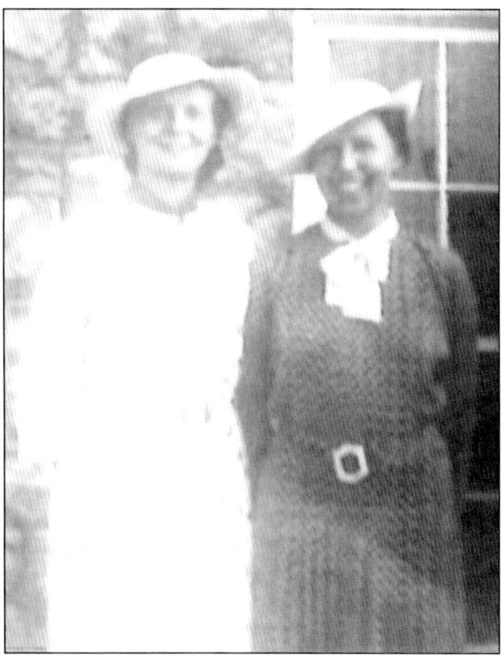

HIGHTSTOWN EDUCATORS (1936). Mrs. Roger (Beatrice) Bentley and Miss Ethel McKnight taught seventh and eighth grade at the Stockton Street School. Ethel and her family moved to Hightstown after her father's death and she attended the Mercer Street School. Later, when she was a student at the Stockton Street School, she recalled "I had to walk. Mr. Hutchinson, who lived next door to us, drove the horse-drawn school wagon, but we lived just inside the two-mile limit. He would go right past us on a rainy day and not give us a ride." Miss McKnight began teaching in 1924 after graduating from the Trenton Normal School. She later received bachelor's and master's degrees from Rutgers University. A district school has been named in her honor. (Janet Field)

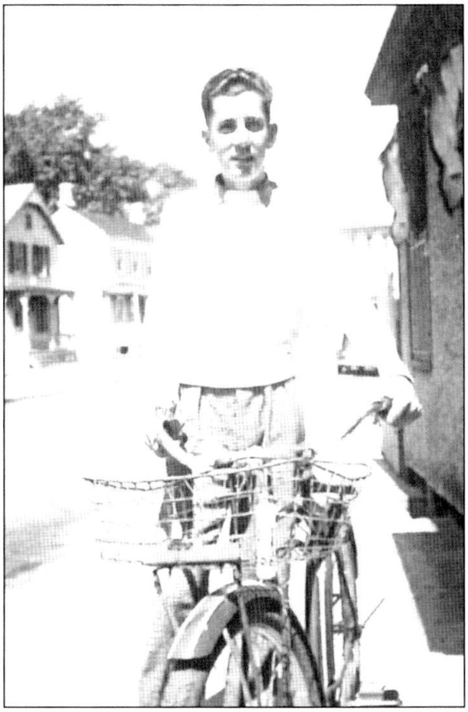

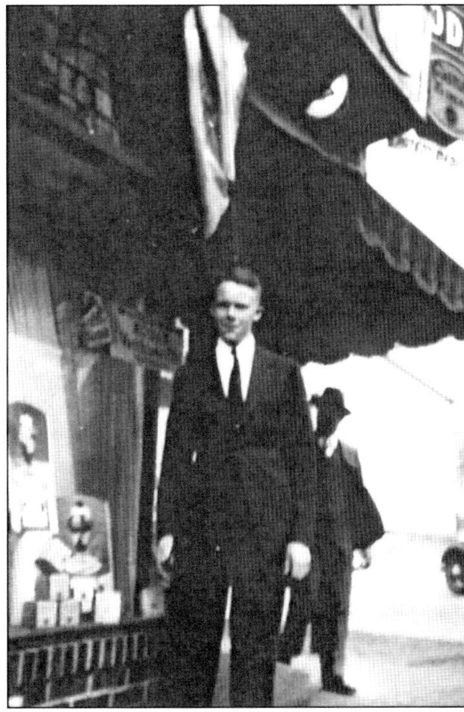

FOUR CONTEMPORARIES (1937). "Doc" Embley ran a soda shop at the corner of Main Street and Rogers Avenue and often took photographs of his customers. Some of them were: (upper left) Fred Tornquist, Jr., with his bike; (upper right) Jerome "Red" Becker, who served later as borough mayor and postmaster; (lower left) Vinton "Snoops" Taylor, and (lower right) Harold "Choppy" Lovett. (Hightstown-East Windsor Historical Society)

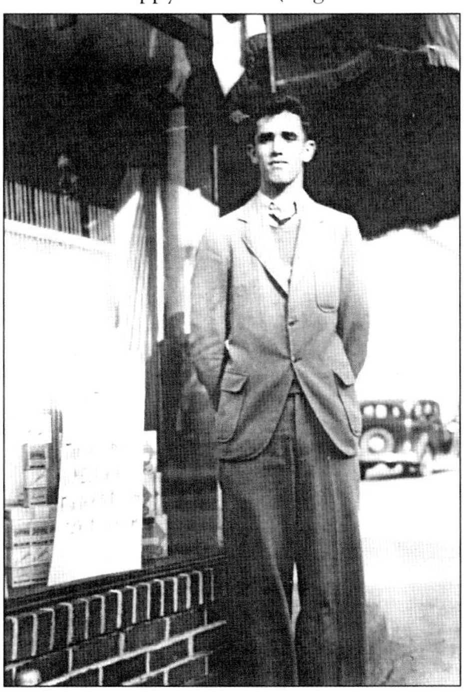

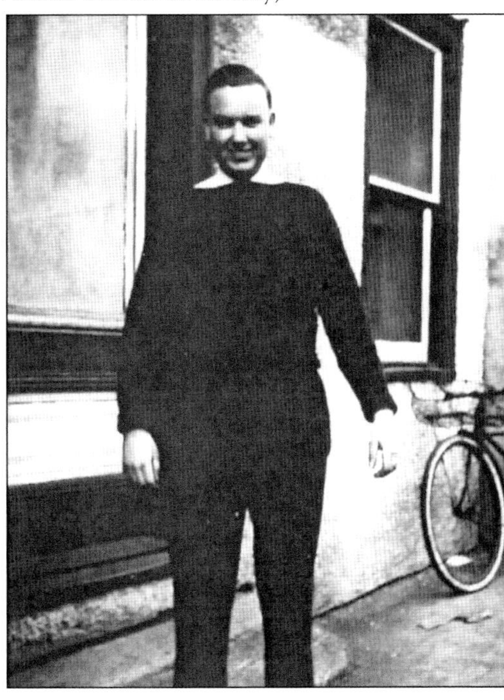

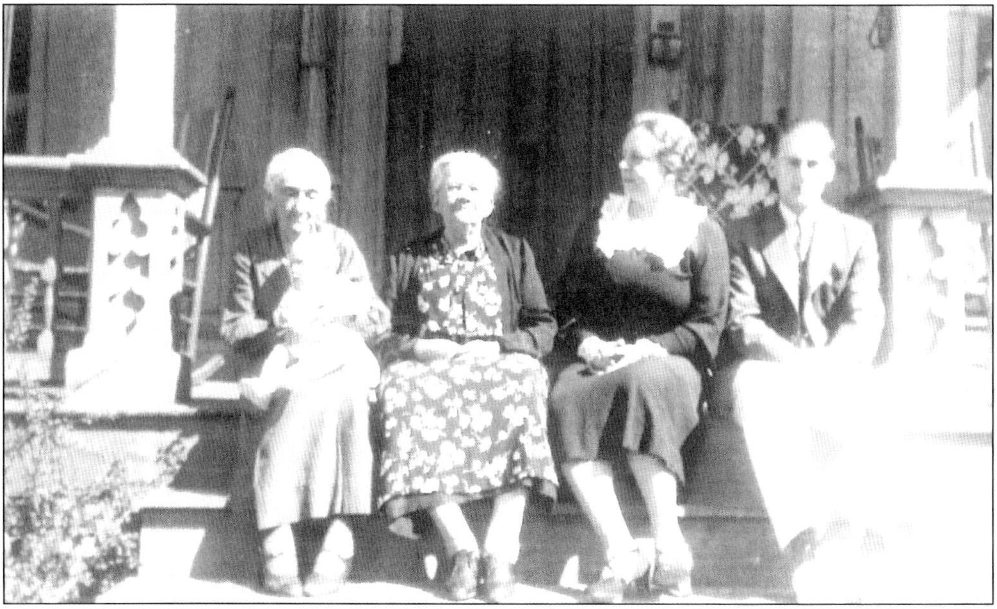

FIVE GENERATIONS (1937). The Robbins home at 171 North Main Street is the location of this September family gathering. Pictured are: great-great-grandmother Emmons (holding baby Clifford "Kip" Robbins), great-grandmother Norris, grandmother Alta Boye, and father Norris Addison Robbins. (Norris Robbins Collection)

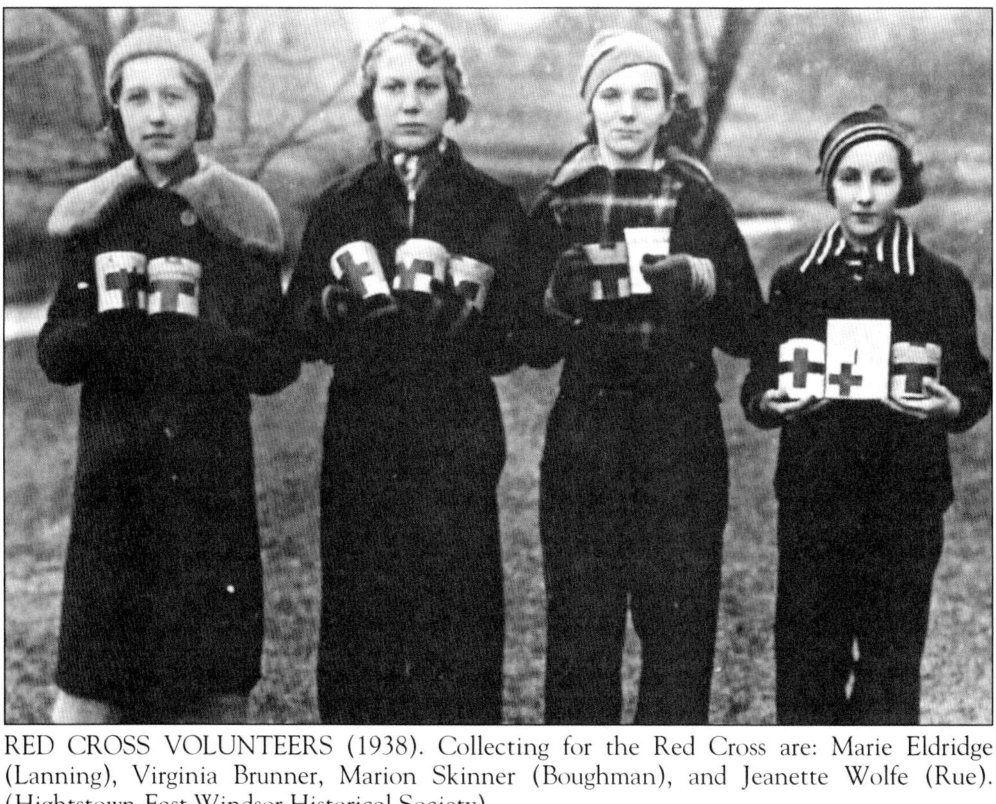

RED CROSS VOLUNTEERS (1938). Collecting for the Red Cross are: Marie Eldridge (Lanning), Virginia Brunner, Marion Skinner (Boughman), and Jeanette Wolfe (Rue). (Hightstown-East Windsor Historical Society)

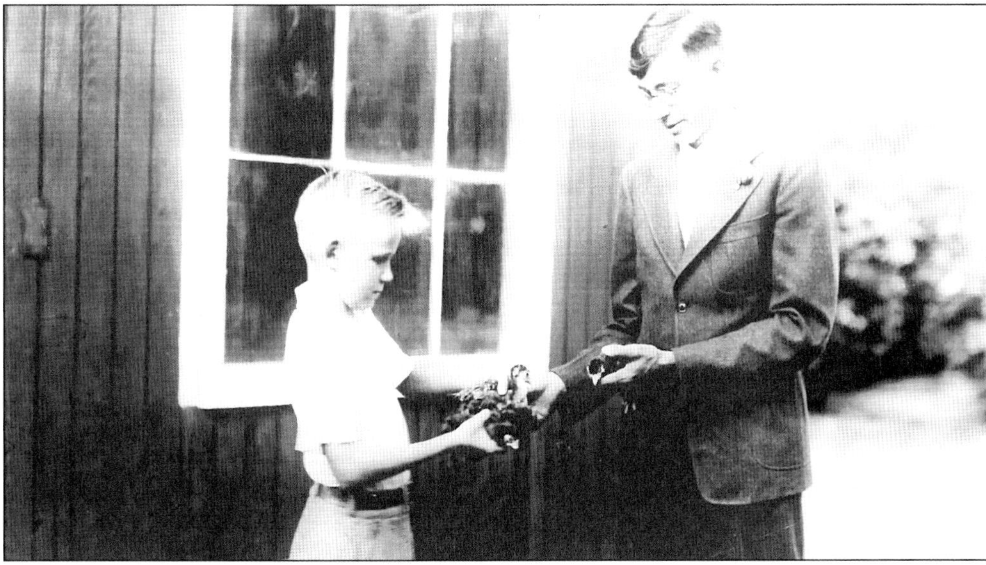

BEGINNING OF A TURKEY FARM (1938). In June, young Dick Lee was given his first turkeys from Frank Okerson, Jr. of Robbinsville to begin a 4-H project. The outgrowth of this project was the Lee Turkey Farm, which is still in operation at present. (The Lee Family)

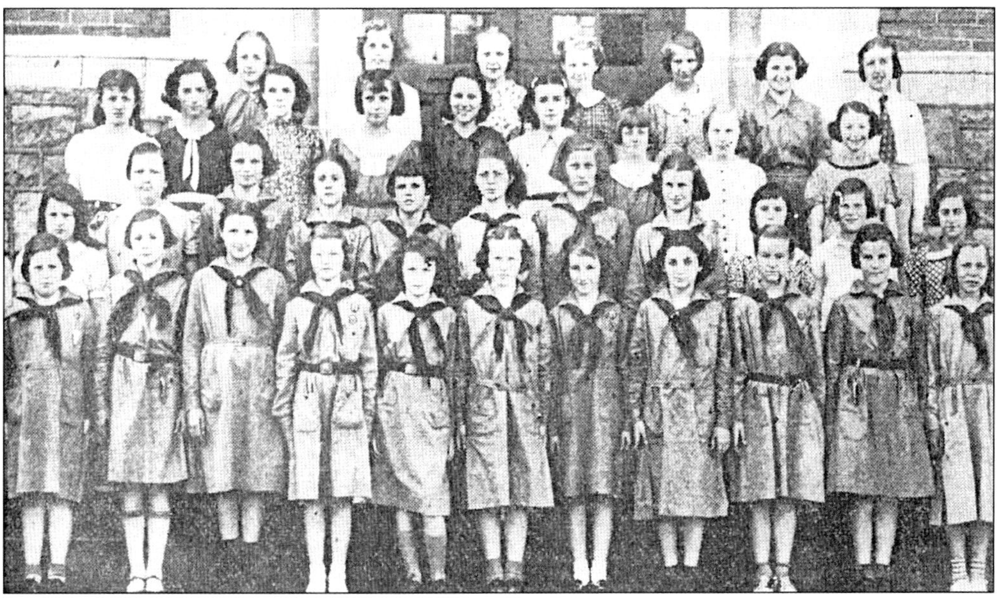

GIRL SCOUT TROOP (c. 1938). These girl scouts under the leadership of schoolteachers Margaret Ragolia and Alice Everett are: (front row) Janet Shivers, Marion Dubell, Josephine Hutchinson, Viola White, Lorraine Carson, Hazel Woodhouse, Jeanette Dixon, Jeanette Wolfe, Avivia Konov, Marion White, Virginia Puglin, and Marie Duphey; (second row) Mae Knosky, Betty Potter, Anna Disborough, Gertrude Bollengier, Betty Peiffer, Jane Hopkins, Shirley Salmonowitz, Marcia Swetland, Gloria Davison, Grace Bradley, Marion Anderson, and Rose Marie Eufemia; (third row) Johanna Damasco, Elsie Dubois, Marion Skinner, Barbara Penrith, Frances Kelty, Winifred Lincoln, Frances Dunphey, Dorothy Bowker, and Josephine Kay; (back row) Barbara Laird, Lois Hopkins, Marion Bowker, Anita Beth Keeler, Caroline Davis, Peggy West, and Helen Eldridge. (Bill and Jeanette Rue)

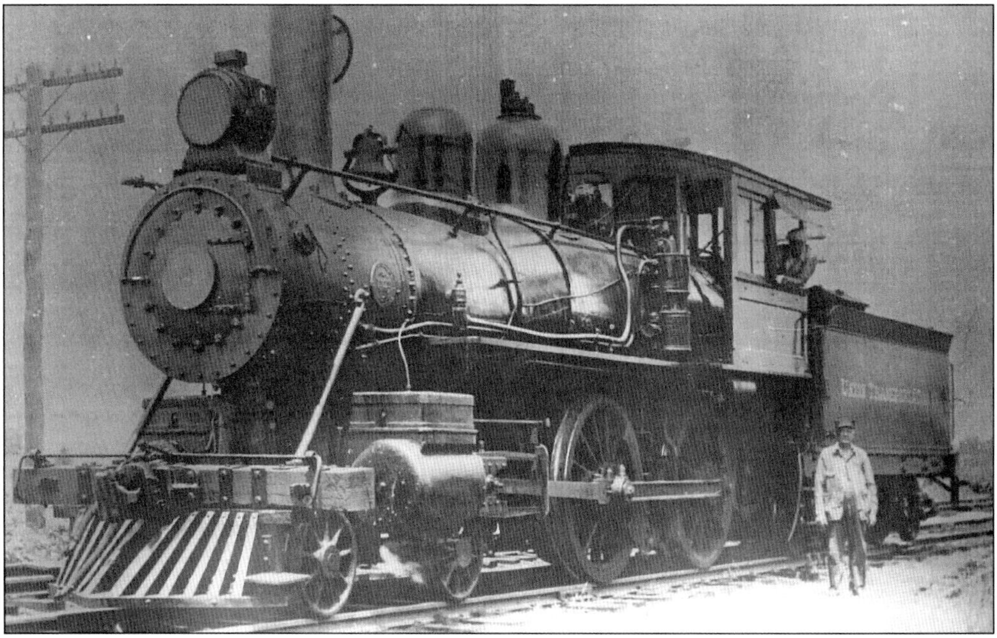

U T ENGINE NUMBER 6 (*c.* 1938). In the 1880s an additional railroad from Pemberton, the Union Transportation Company—familiarly called the U T—met the Camden-Amboy Railroad line at Hightstown. The U T ran through a New Jersey farm belt transporting milk, potatoes, cattle, and produce from Cream Ridge, Sharon, New Egypt, Wrightstown, and other rural areas. Apples from the Lee Farm in East Windsor were often placed aboard U T line cars and hauled to a cider mill and vinegar works in Imlaystown. Engineman Joseph R. Dubell (standing) worked for the U T from 1916 to 1947. Each night he brought the engine to Hightstown and parked it on a siding in back of the Mercer Street School. Oscar Hopkins (in the cab) worked as a conductor and brakeman from 1906 to 1956. In 1907, U T section hands went on strike, demanding $1.55 per day instead of $1.40. (George J. Dubell)

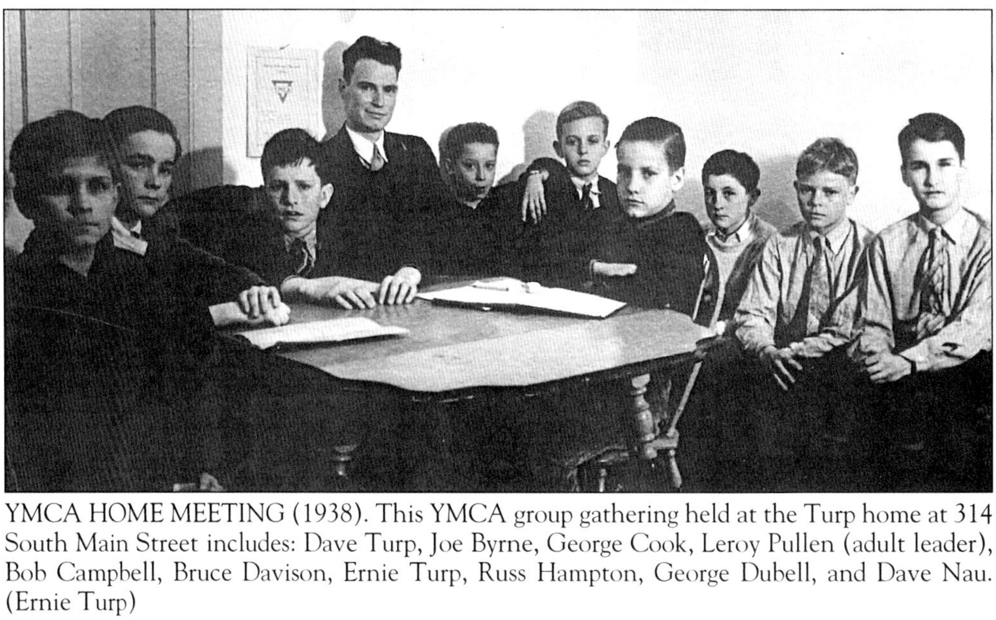

YMCA HOME MEETING (1938). This YMCA group gathering held at the Turp home at 314 South Main Street includes: Dave Turp, Joe Byrne, George Cook, Leroy Pullen (adult leader), Bob Campbell, Bruce Davison, Ernie Turp, Russ Hampton, George Dubell, and Dave Nau. (Ernie Turp)

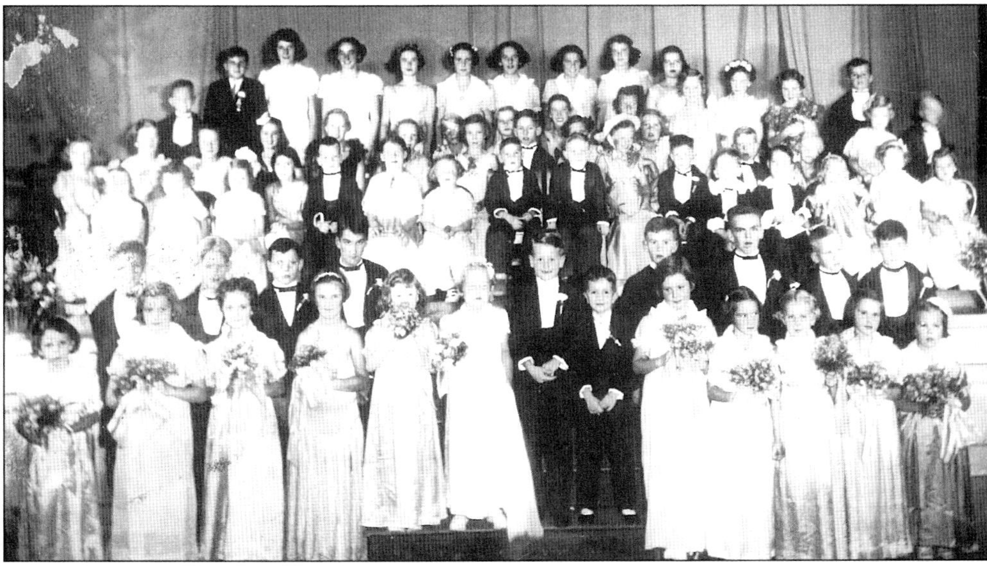

TOM THUMB WEDDING (1938). Some participants in this fall wedding sponsored by the First Presbyterian Church are: (front row) an unidentified bridesmaid; bridesmaids Shirley Appleget (Mohr), Joyce Mount (Schanck), and Margaret Nau; maid of honor Patty Hunt (Scott); bride Betty Lou Matheson (Field); groom Donald Struve; best man Demos Bakoulis; and bridesmaids Mildred Perrine, unknown, Martha Hutchinson, Virginia Turp, and Jean Hutchinson (Esch); (second row) two unidentified groomsmen; groomsmen Milton Hutchinson and David Nau; minister Henry Hunt; and groomsmen Massey Beaulieu, Dick Lee, and unknown. (Pat Scott)

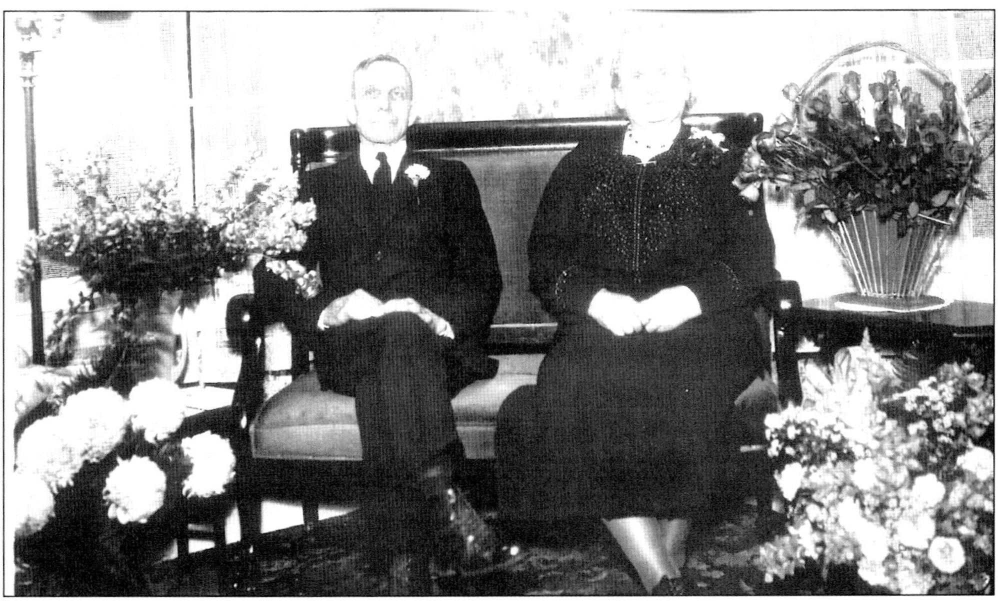

FIFTIETH WEDDING ANNIVERSARY (1938). On December 12, 1888, Samuel Groendyke (1865–1950) and Adelaide Cottrell (1870–?) were married by Dr. O.P. Eaches at the parsonage of the First Baptist Church. At that time Samuel had a farm at 441 Dutch Neck Road. Fifty years later the couple entertained guests at the Cranbury Inn and followed the anniversary celebration with a reception at their home. (Lois Groendyke)

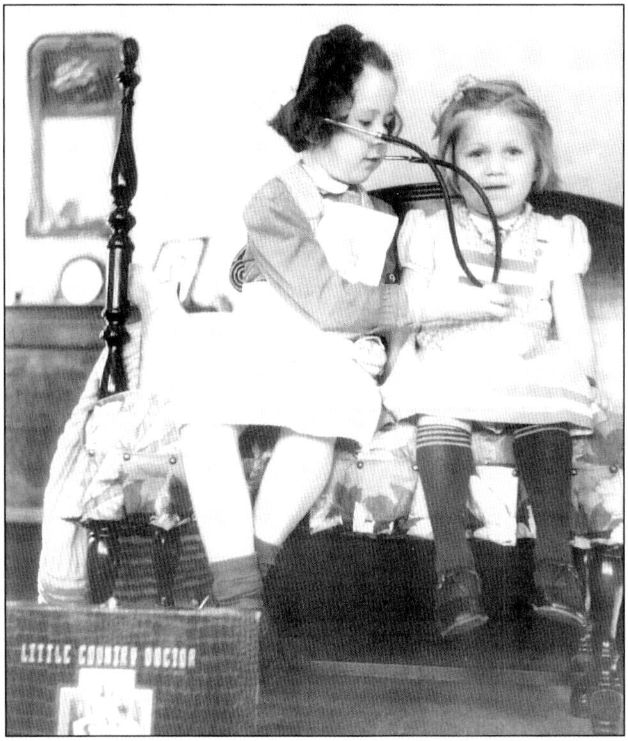

EXAMINED BY "LITTLE COUNTRY DOCTOR" (1938). Good friends Virginia Heyer and Anne Elaine Hancock (Vallaster) play doctor in the Heyer home at 202 Stockton Street. (Elizabeth Silvers)

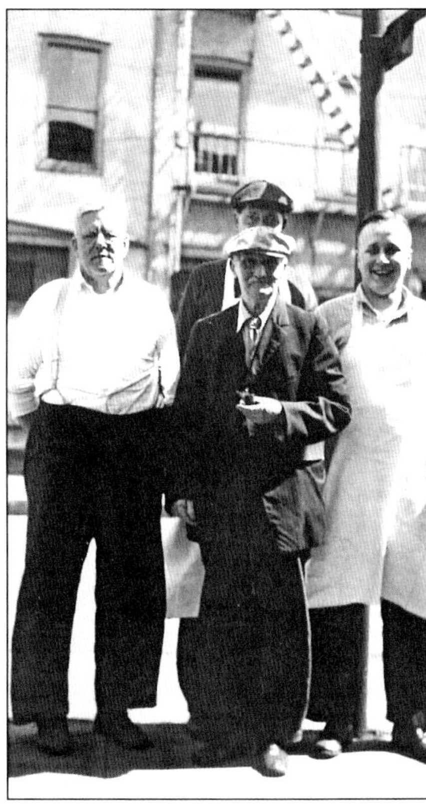

THE BUTCHER, THE BAKER, AND . . . (*c*. 1938). Near their stores on Mercer Street and Rogers Avenue are Benjamin Reed (in front); ? Davison of Ogborn's Oyster House; Alonzo Dey of Dey's Butcher Shop; and Alvin Dey, a grocer. (Hightstown-East Windsor Historical Society)

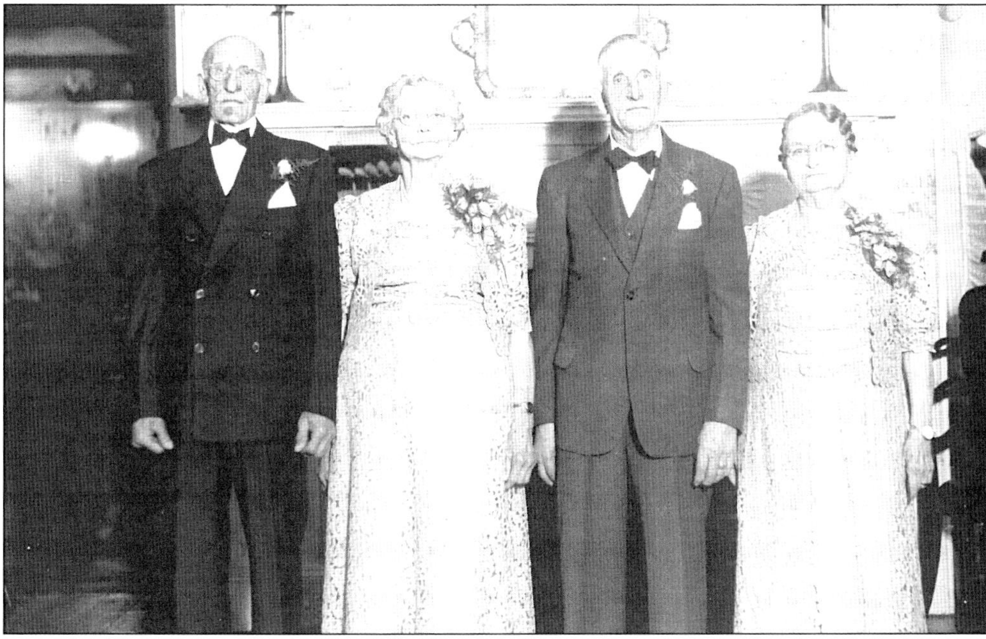

DOUBLE ANNIVERSARY CELEBRATION (1939). Cousins Sarah Bowne and Fanny Mount of East Windsor had a double wedding in 1889 when they married Eugene Roszel and William T. Flock. The Roszels lived on Ancil Davison Road in Cranbury and the Flocks on Flock Road in Hamilton Township. The Cranbury Inn was the location of both couples' 50th anniversary party. Coincidentally, both women died in 1946 at the age of eighty-six. (Lillian Roszel Black)

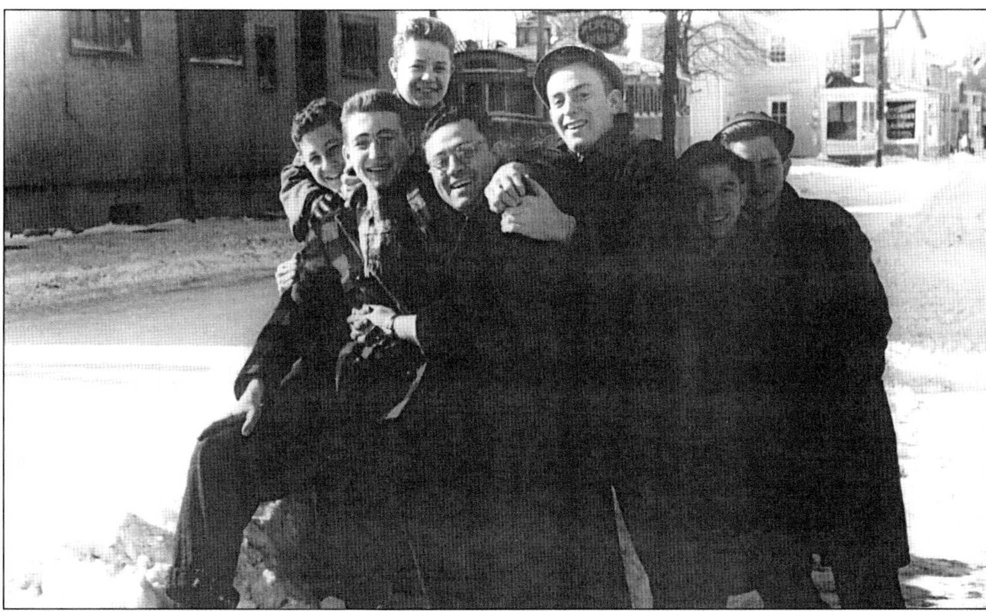

SNOW SHOT (1939). Huddled against a pile of snow with Mercer Street and the Mercer Diner in the background are: William "Bucky" Tabler, Voorhees R. "Spec" Carson, Franklin "Hickle" Blum, Edward Juris, Marvin "Sockie" Chamberlain, Leroy Crawford, and George Cook. (Hightstown-East Windsor Historical Society)

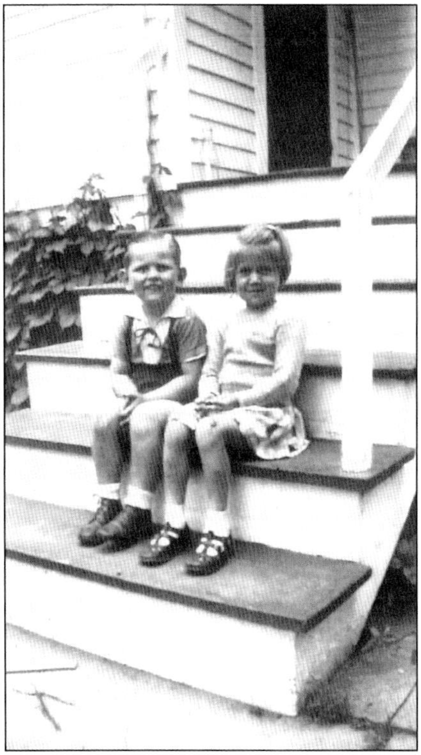

YOUNG NEIGHBORS (*c.* 1939). The back steps of the Underhill home at 401 Stockton Street provide the backdrop for this photograph of Frank Underhill, Jr. and Ann Elaine Hancock (Vallaster). (Elizabeth Silvers)

L.R. WEST ELECTRIC SHOP (1930s). Roy West, ? Berrier, Harold Wyckoff, and an unidentified man fight the morning sun outside Roy's shop at 224 North Main Street. (Hightstown-East Windsor Historical Society)

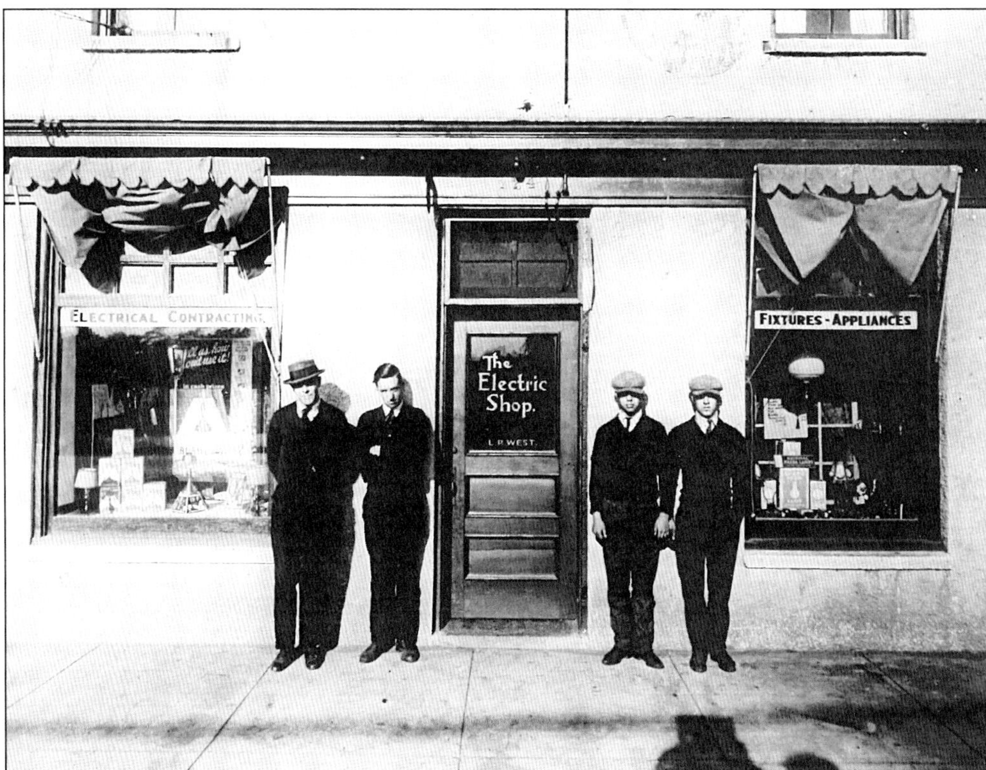

Seven

1940 to 1950

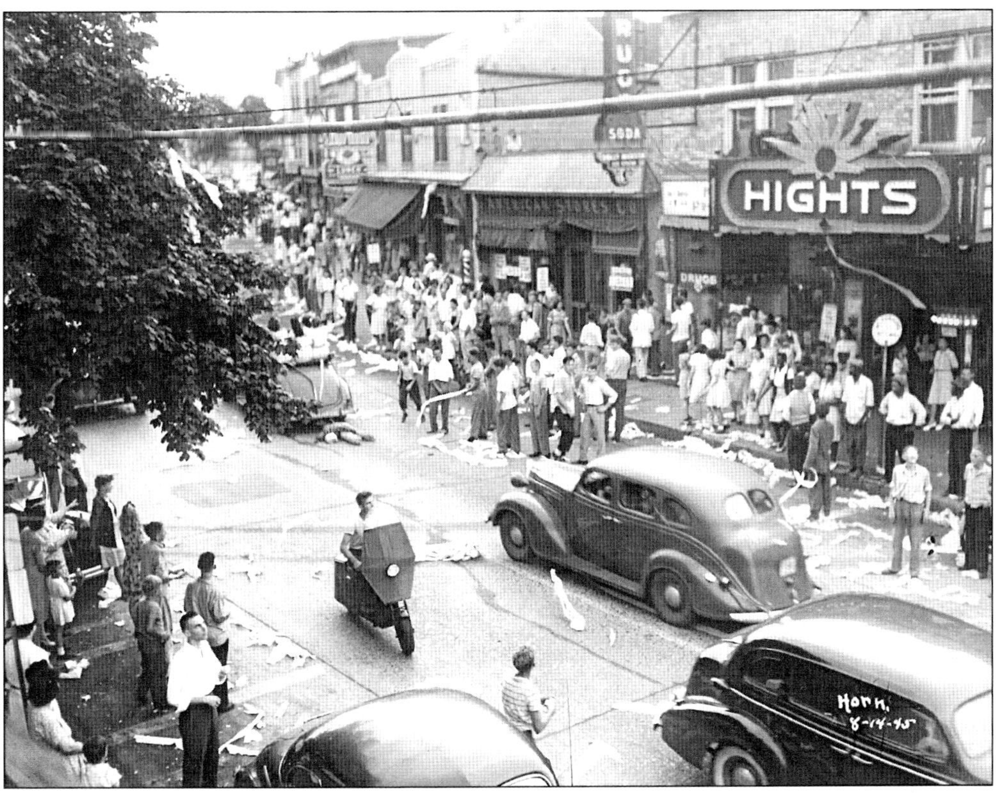

JAPAN'S SURRENDER (1945). Like thousands of communities across the nation, Hightstown held an impromptu celebration on Main Street following the announcement of Japan's surrender by President Harry S Truman on August 14. (Hightstown-East Windsor Historical Society)

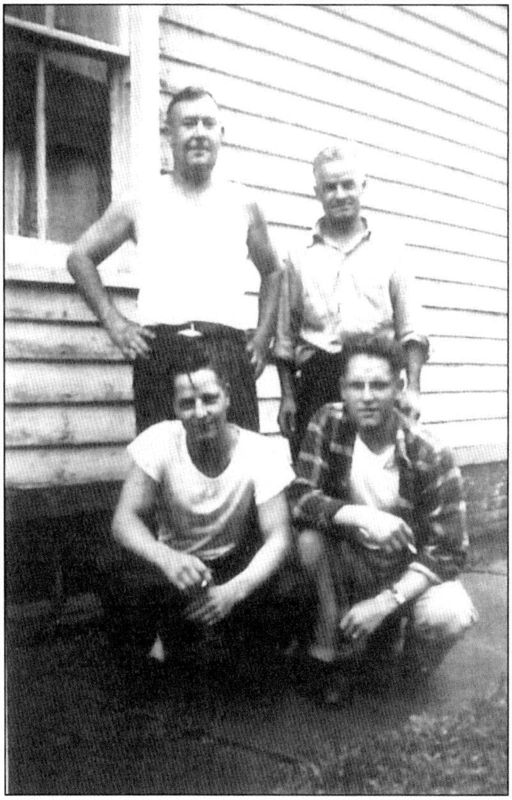

A WORKING QUARTET (1940). Ray and Al Peterson kneel in front of Kip Platt and their father, Ben Peterson. (The Al Peterson Family)

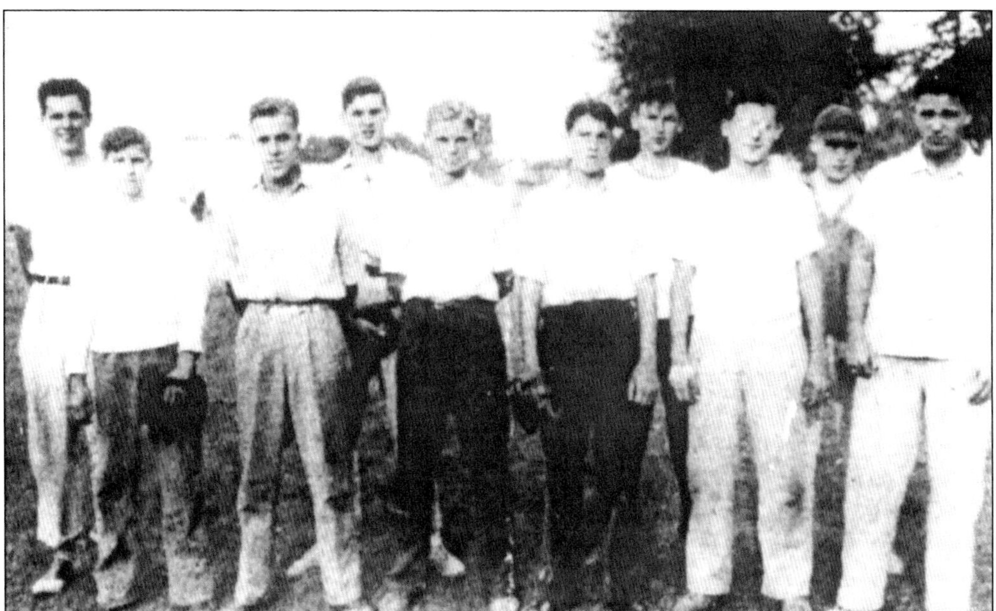

SOUTHENDERS SOFTBALL TEAM (1940). The squad was organized in 1940 and won sixteen titles in twenty-five years of fast-pitch competition. The original group consisted of: Walter Stults, David Turp, Warren Field, Charles S. Stults, Jr., George Dubell, Howard Eldridge, Harry Locke, Ernest Thompson, Willard Davison, and Oscar Hopkins. (Janet Field)

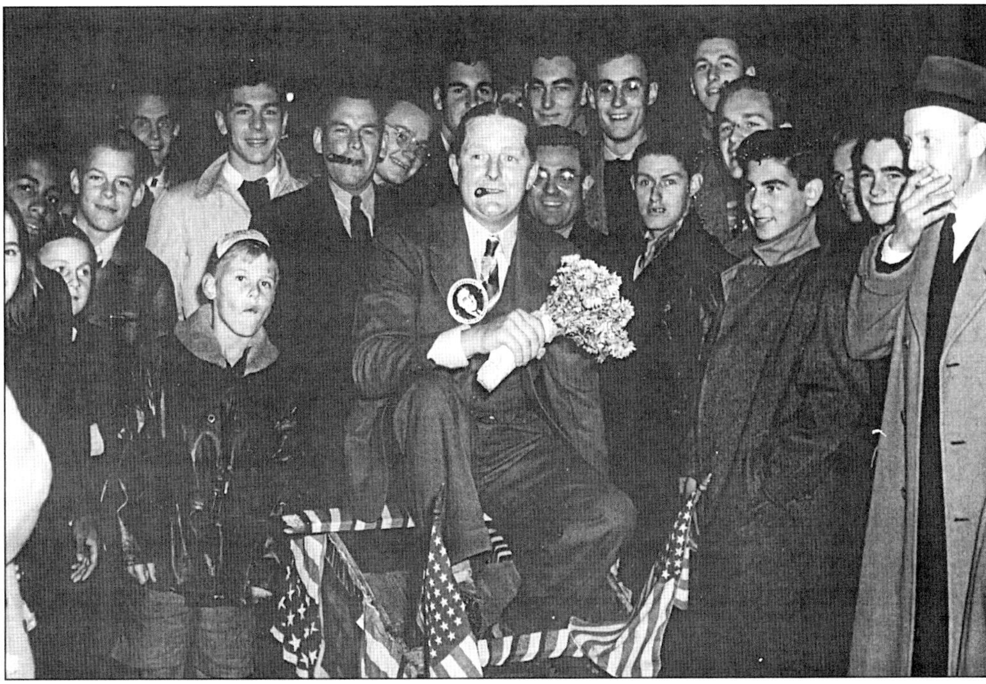

WINNING AN ELECTION BET (1940). Apparently Dick Ewart, a Roosevelt supporter, won an election bet and is being pushed in a wheelbarrow by Ernest Peterson, Jr. In the presidential election on November 5, Franklin D. Roosevelt and Henry A. Wallace defeated Republicans Wendall L. Willkie and Charles L. McNary. F.D.R. was elected for a precedent-setting third term. In front and to the right of Ewart are: Ed Juris, Spike Denelsbeck, Jack McQueen, Joe Byrne, and Lee Hutchinson. (Bill and Jeanette Rue)

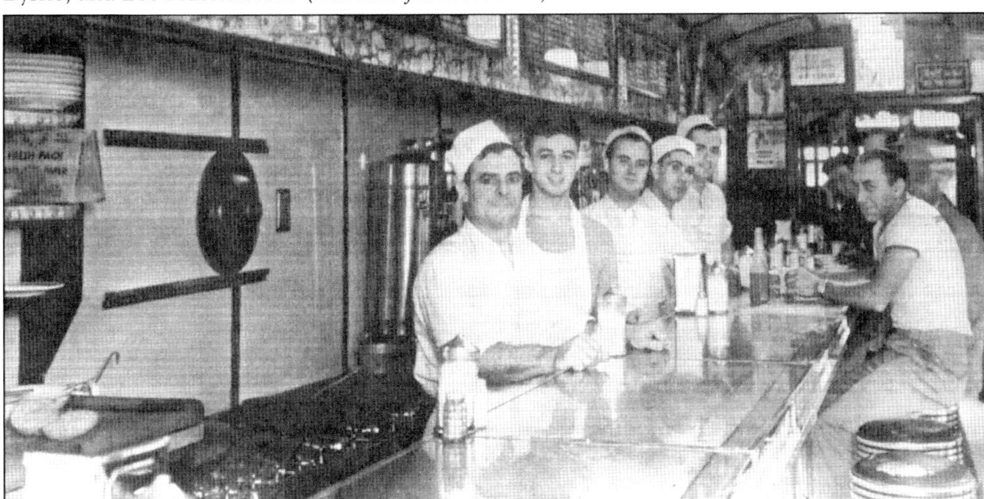

FEATURING THE DINER EMPLOYEES (1941). The third Hightstown Diner on the original location was built in 1941, the year the owner's daughter, Mary Corcodilos, married Nick Mastoris. The new eatery was constructed of modern stainless steel inside and outside. Women waitresses were hired for the first time. Behind the counter are: Chef George Voltis, Tony Corcodilos, Louis Vulgaris, John Psaltis, and Nick Mastoris. The customer in the foreground is Fred Van Pelt. (Tony and Ethel Corcodilos)

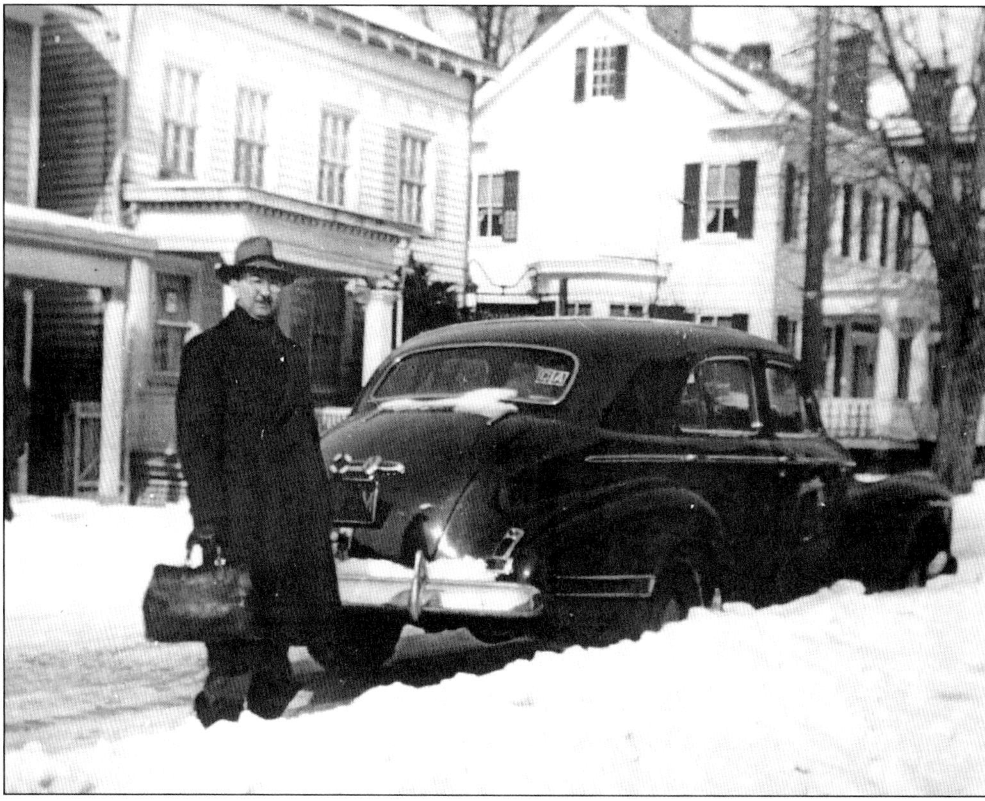

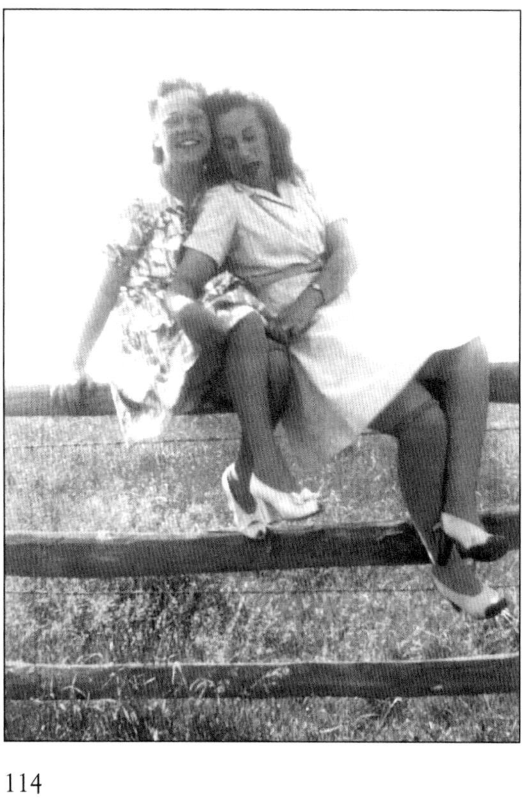

PHYSICIAN'S HOUSE CALL (1942). Dr. Harold C. Cox, Sr. is braving the winter snow on the way to a house call. The white frame house in the right background is the Ely House, currently the headquarters for the Hightstown-East Windsor Historical Society. The two houses at the left have been torn down and the site is currently the entrance and parking area for the borough municipal building. The rear window of Dr. Cox's Buick has both "A" and "C" gas rationing stickers. Beginning in May 1942, gas rationing went into effect in seventeen eastern states. During wartime years, all drivers were issued an "A" and essential personnel received a "C" sticker. (Harold "Skip" Cox)

FENCE SITTERS (*c.* 1943). Judy McGovern (Peterson) and Gloria La Rocco (Lagatutta), wearing spectator shoes and rolled hose stylish in the 1940s, ham it up for the photographer. (The Al Peterson Family)

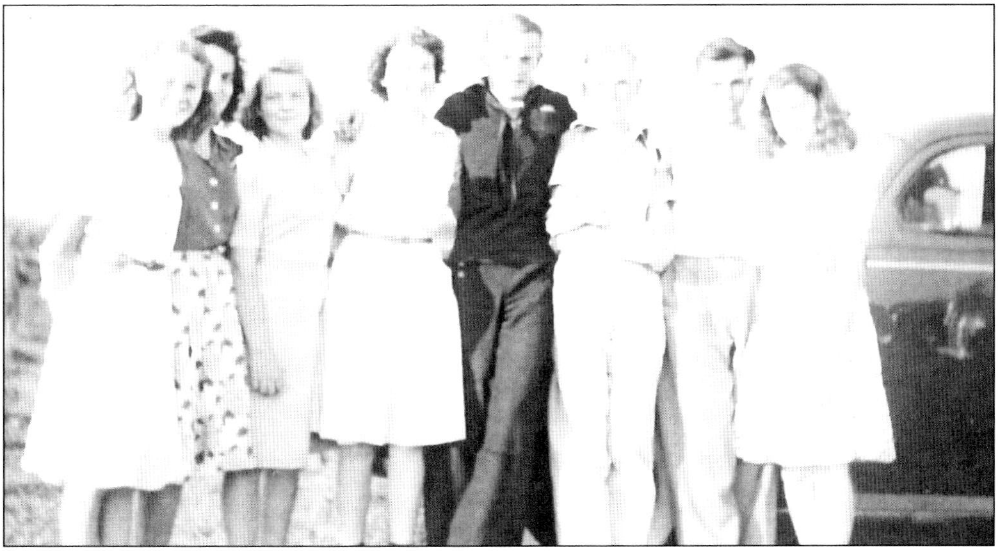

SAILOR ON LEAVE (c. 1943). Frank Stewart, while on leave, poses with some of his friends: Marjorie Lee, Margaret Stewart, Marion Hutchinson (Bowers), Lois Hancock (Groendyke), Dick Lee, Milton Hutchinson, and Jean Hancock (Hutchinson). (Lois Groendyke)

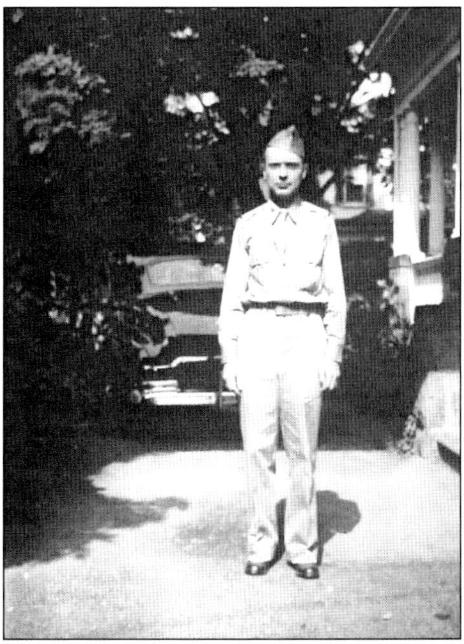

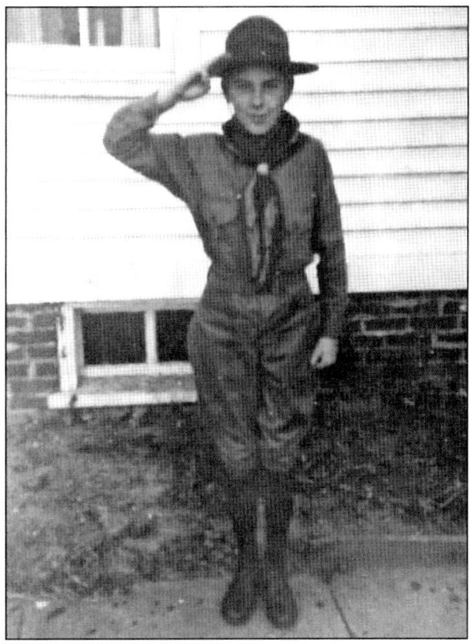

DR. JOHN D. BARLOW (1942). In uniform, Dr. Barlow is shown in front of his 232 Stockton Street home, which also served as his office. He spent four years as an officer in the medical corps of the Army Air Force "patching up wounded flyboys." After graduating from Villanova University and the Georgetown University School of Medicine, he opened his Hightstown office in 1939, retiring in 1980. At that time he was the last general practitioner in Hightstown. Dr. Barlow was a member of the county and state medical associations and was for many years a trustee of St. Anthony of the Padua R.C. Church. (Dr. and Mrs. John D. Barlow)

A SCOUT SALUTE (1942). Robert Hancock of Conover Road renders a snappy salute. His great love was horses and for some time he was employed as a jockey. (Lois Groendyke)

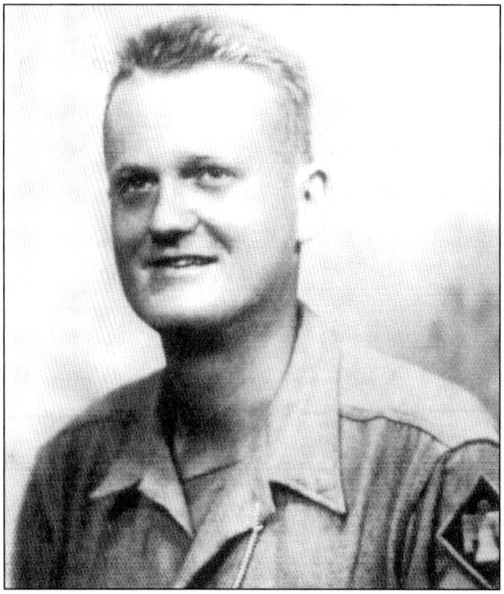

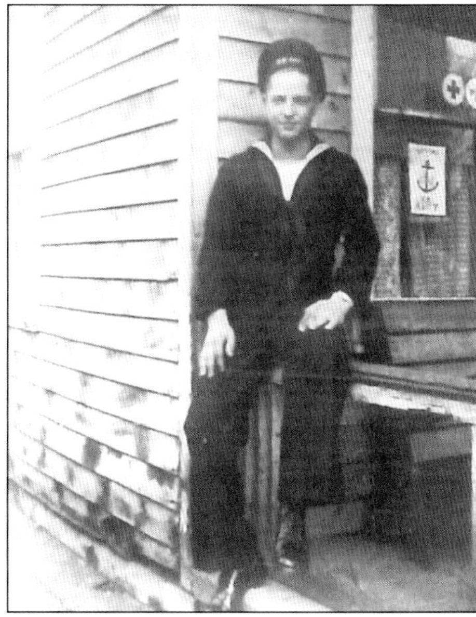

PFC GEORGE FOSTER DENNIS (1940s). Before entering the army, Dennis was managing editor of *The Hightstown Gazette*. In 1942 he graduated magna cum laude from Syracuse University and was elected to the Phi Beta Kappa academic society. Assigned to the "Thunderbird" division, he served as a foot soldier and regimental historian. He was killed in action on September 11, 1944, in southern France. (*The Hightstown Gazette*)

ON LEAVE (*c.* 1943). Raymond Peterson rests on the porch of his home (since razed) at 138 Rogers Avenue. The banner with the anchor in the lower window sash indicates that a resident serves in the navy. (The Al Peterson Family)

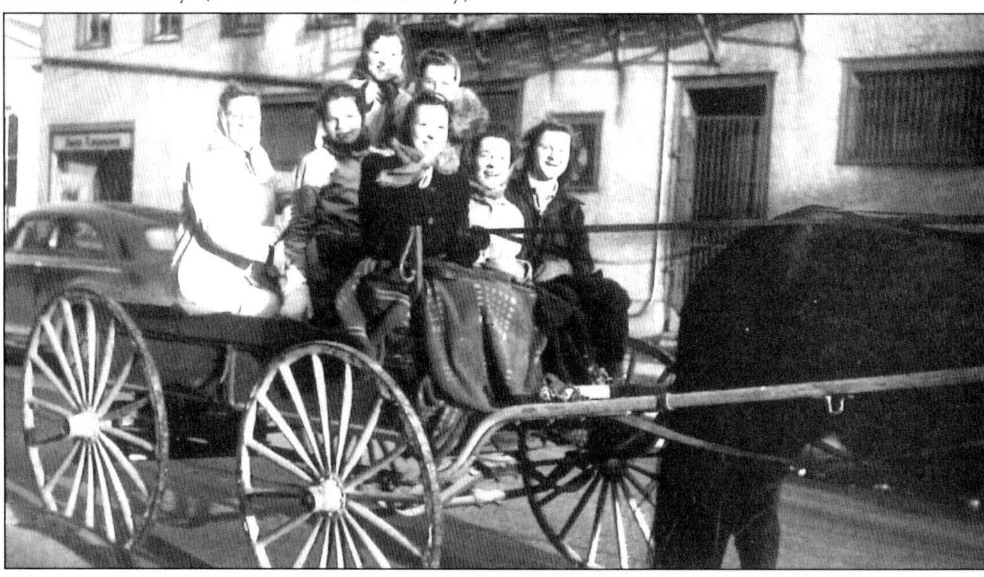

COLLECTING FOR THE WAR EFFORT (1943). Using a horse and wagon that probably belonged to Dick Lanning, these young women are riding along Mercer Street collecting tin. Shown here are: (seated) Barbara Laird (Gravatt), Gertrude Bollenger (May), Esther Crowshaw (Franick), Phyllis Perdoni, and Maribelle Turp (Taylor); (standing) Catherine Grover (Hernwall) and Johanna Damasco (Cappucino). (Maribelle Taylor)

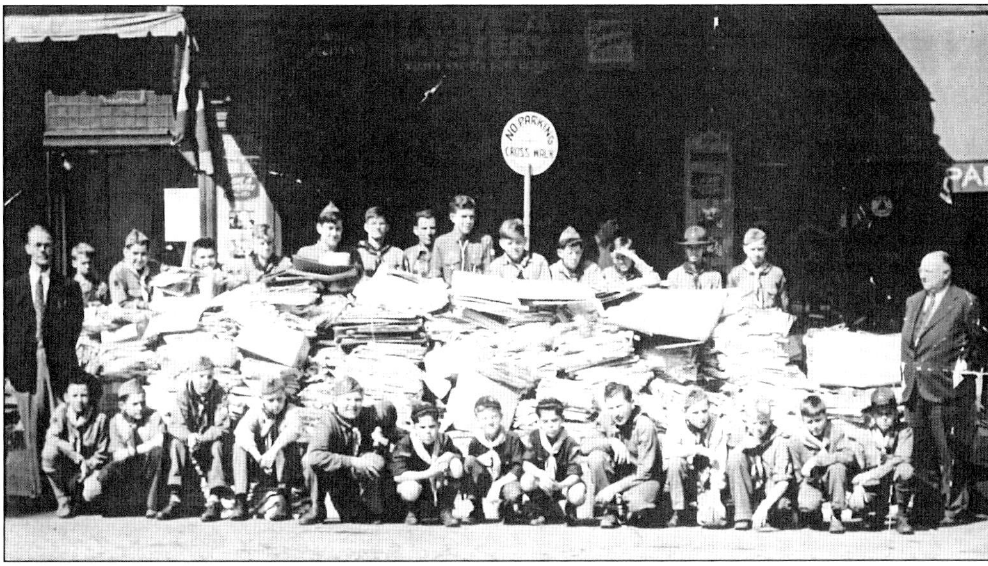

NEWSPAPER DRIVE (1943). Boy Scout Troop 54 and three cub scouts collected newspapers as part of a nationwide effort. Scoutmaster Sanger Robinson is at the left, and Dick Whittey is at the right. Whittey managed the Hights Theater and served on the local board of education. The first four boys in the front row are unidentified, but the others are: (front row) George West, Sidney Barth, Harry Guidice, Harry Barth, Arnold Bogatz, unknown, Robert Dey, William Green, and unknown; (back row) unknown, unknown, Skip Cox, Jack Septak, George Breed, William Homer Thompson, Al Kaplan, George Neighbor, Andrew Jackson Ely, Ray Russo, Leo Sikorski, and two unknown boys. (Harold "Skip" Cox)

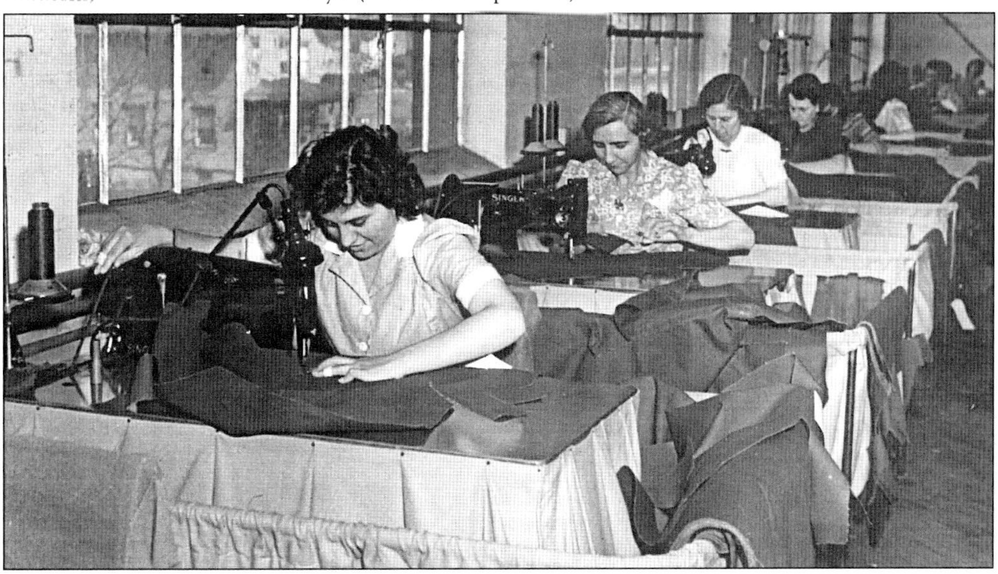

SEWING PARACHUTE PACKS (1944). Beginning in 1942 and throughout World War II, a division of the Hightstown Rug Company made parachutes and parachute packs. During this time the company increased its staff by 25%. Four workers whose faces are identifiable are: Patsy ? (from Jamesburg), Mary Salzer, Margaret Campbell, and Katherine Ziegler (from Cranbury). The house at the corner of Bank and Mechanic Streets can be seen through the factory window. (Hightstown-East Windsor Historical Society)

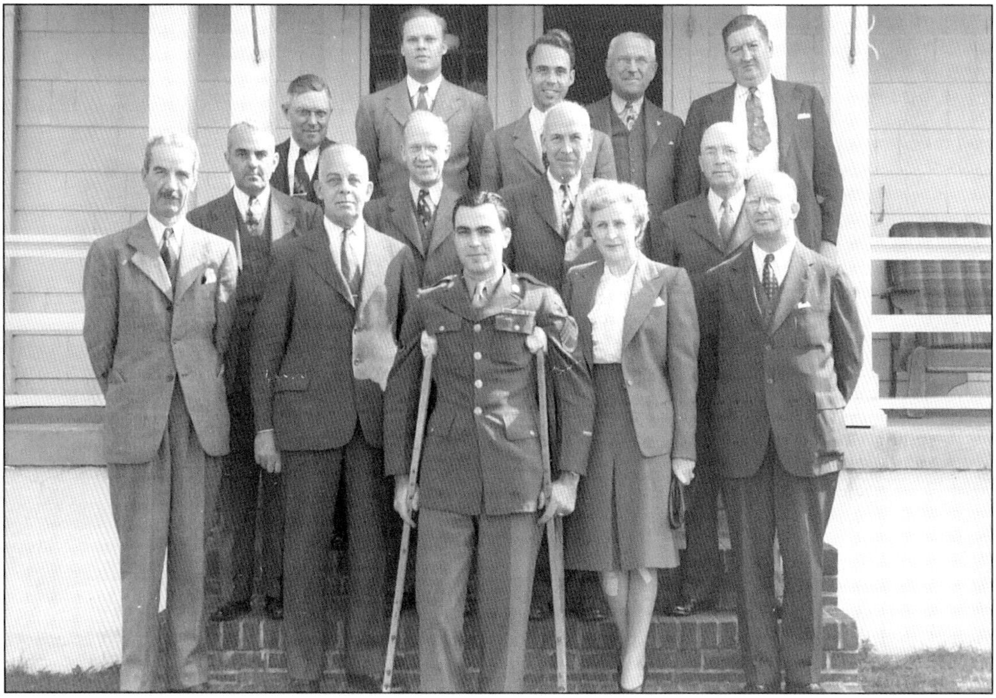

WOUNDED HERO (1944). Sergeant Lewis Swinger, having been wounded in action, returned to Hightstown with a Hightstown Rug Company parachute. Staff gathered outside the Old Hights Inn, where a dinner was given in his honor. They are: (front row) Hugh W. Logan, C. Herbert Davison, Nellie Clendenning (who taught sewing), and Howard C. Davison; (middle row) Clarence Puglin, Emil Abrahamson, Ernest Simpson, and Frederick Branford; (back row) Kenneth Wolcott, Evi Brink, Herbert B. Davison, Ben Elfman, and Samuel Knight. Walcott and Knight managed the parachute division. (Herbert A. Davison)

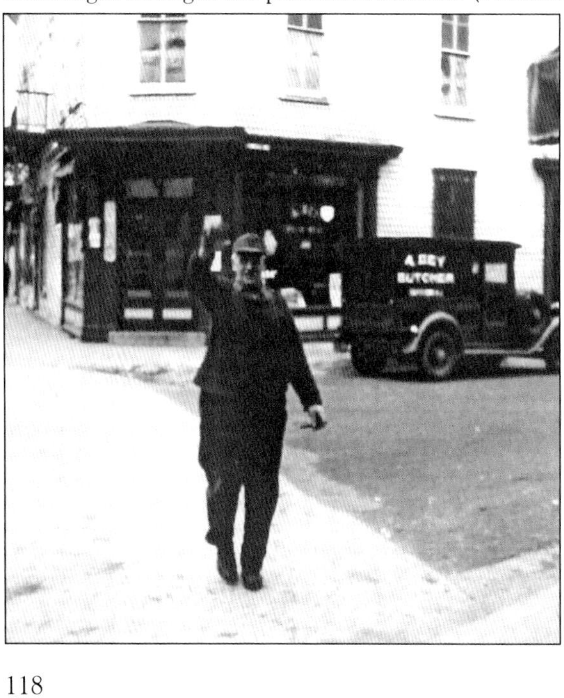

A WAVE FROM THE CORNER OF ROGERS AND MERCER (*c.* 1942). An unidentified man crosses Rogers Avenue. Alonzo Dey's butcher shop and delivery wagon are in the background. Sometime before 1900, Pearce's Dry Goods and Grocery Store occupied this building. Dey's ownership of the market was followed by that of Emil Wolfe and Raymond McNamara. Edward Hutchinson was employed by the three butchers. Jim Johnson recalls "sticking my nose into Dey's butcher shop on the way to the Mercer Street School." He stated that "the lard smelled like bacon as it was boiling off. In November, deer hung in the windows during hunting season, just as hogs and chickens hung there all year." (Hightstown-East Windsor Historical Society)

RUG MILL SETTING DEPARTMENT (*c.* 1943). In this department, employees performed the delicate task of pulling the yarn from the spool prior to weaving. During most years, there were approximately 350 employees and about one-third were women. Annie Conway spent forty-four years working on the setting frame before retiring in 1960. During her first week of employment, she earned apprentice wages of $1.50 per day. In 1945 it was the oldest, largest, and most successful company in town. (Hightstown-East Windsor Historical Society)

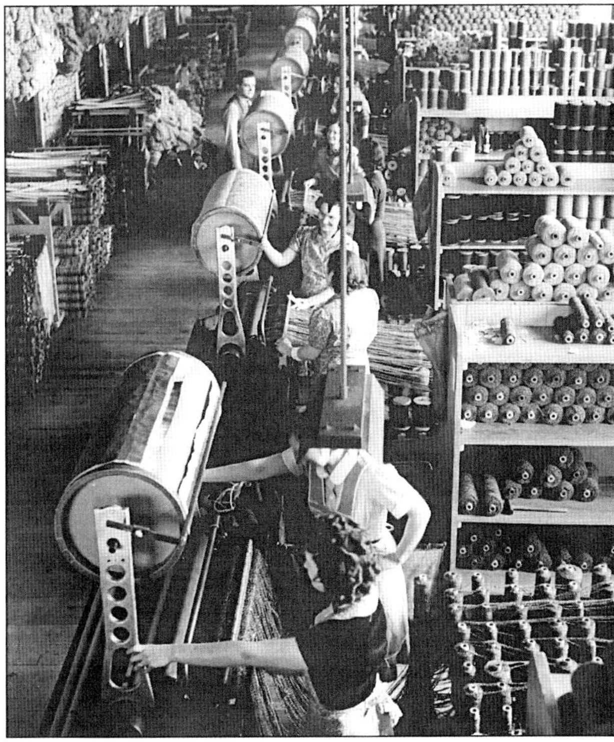

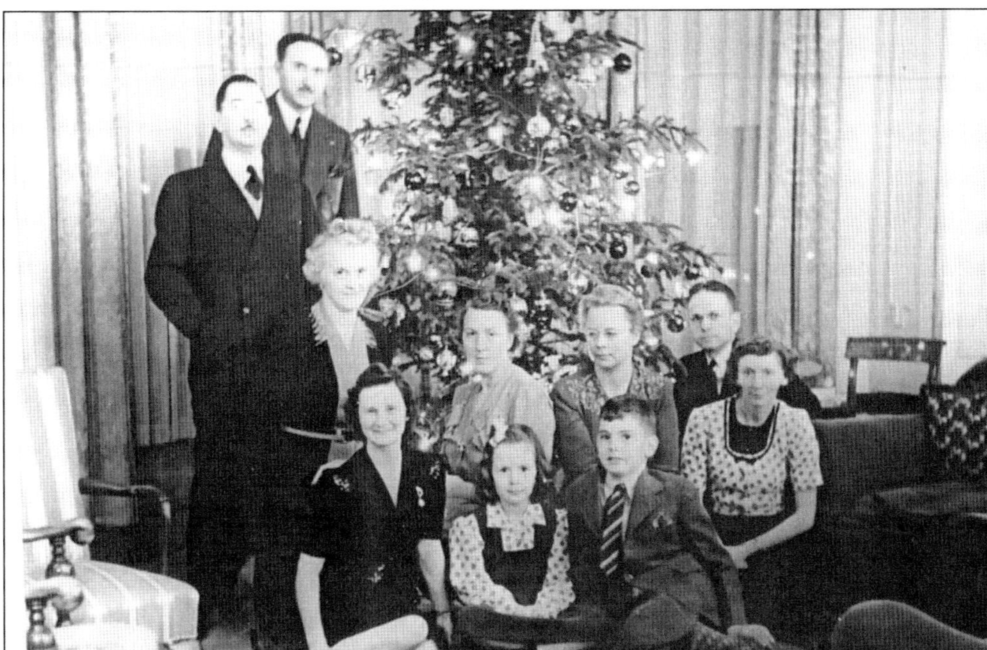

CELEBRATING CHRISTMAS (*c.* 1943). Shown here at the Heyer home at 202 Stockton Street are: (front row) unknown, Cora Virginia Heyer, Skip Cox, and unknown; (second row) Elizabeth Craig Cox, Cora Heyer, Nola Wyckoff Allen, and David Allen; (standing) Dr. Harold C. Cox, Sr. and William S. Heyer. (Harold "Skip" Cox)

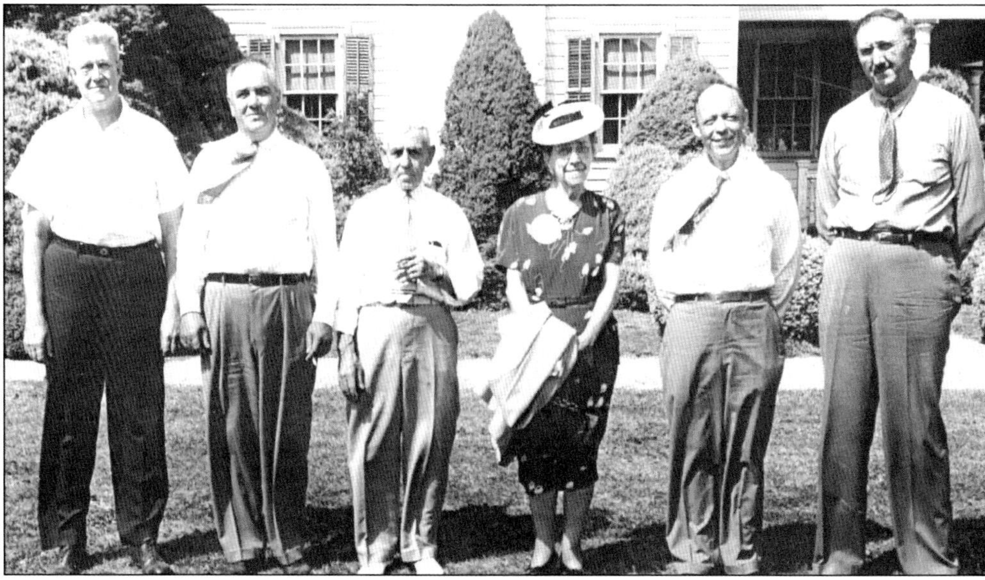

COMMUNITY WORKERS (*c.* 1945). Some of the leaders involved in Hightstown's development during the 1940s were: C. Stanley Stults, Jim Clawson, Charlie Mason, Ella J. Rogers, Joseph Hoch, and William Heyer. (C. Stults Family-Allen & Stults Collection)

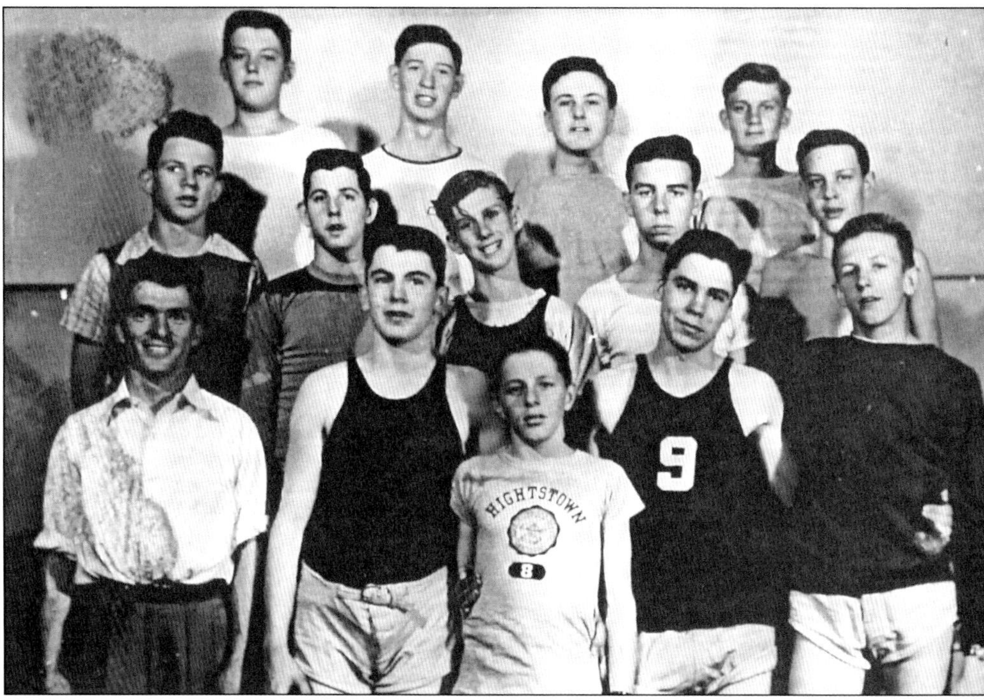

YMCA TEAM (1945). Coach Roy Pullen's teenage basketball squad consisted of: (front row) Ed McColl, Skip Cox, Billy Green, Pete Simonson, and Leo Sikorski; (middle row) John Carduner, Walter Reed, Richard "Torchy" Danser, Robert Bastedo, and Paul Evans; (back row) Andrew Jackson Ely, Dick Ely, Leonard Weinstein, and Jack Septak. Skip Cox remembers that at every meeting one boy was responsible for reading a Bible verse and always looked for the shortest one possible. (Harold "Skip" Cox)

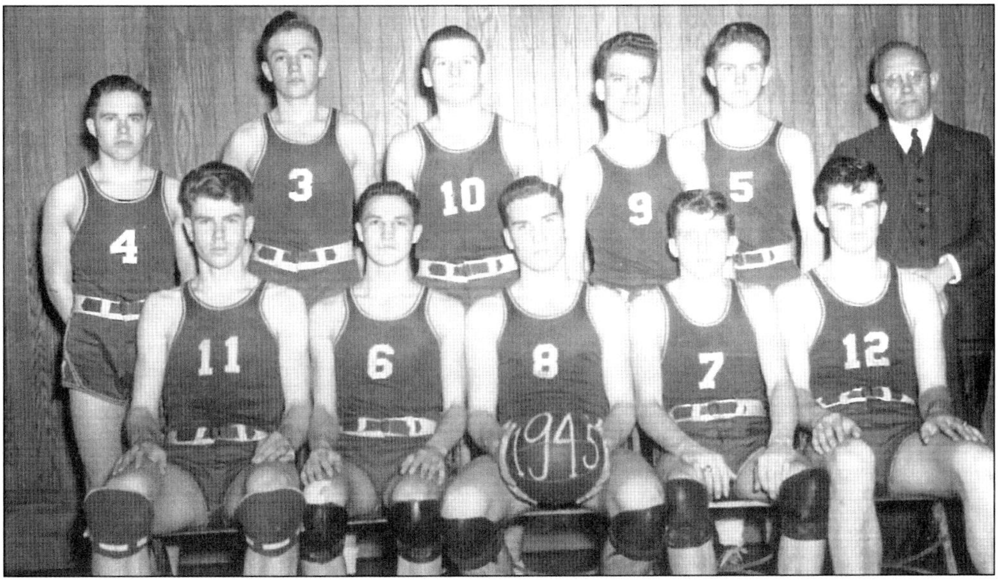

CENTRAL JERSEY CHAMPS (1945). Hightstown High School's 1944–45 basketball team, with a record of 19–3, won the Central Jersey Group I title. They are: (front row) Bill Gauntt, Bob Greczyn, Captain Bert McQueen, Mer Ivins, and Bob Gauntt; (back row) "Bibby" Craig, Art Danser, Stan Sikorski, Russ Beaulieu, F. Broadhurst, and Coach "Bunny" Hunt. (Fred R. Tornquist, Jr.)

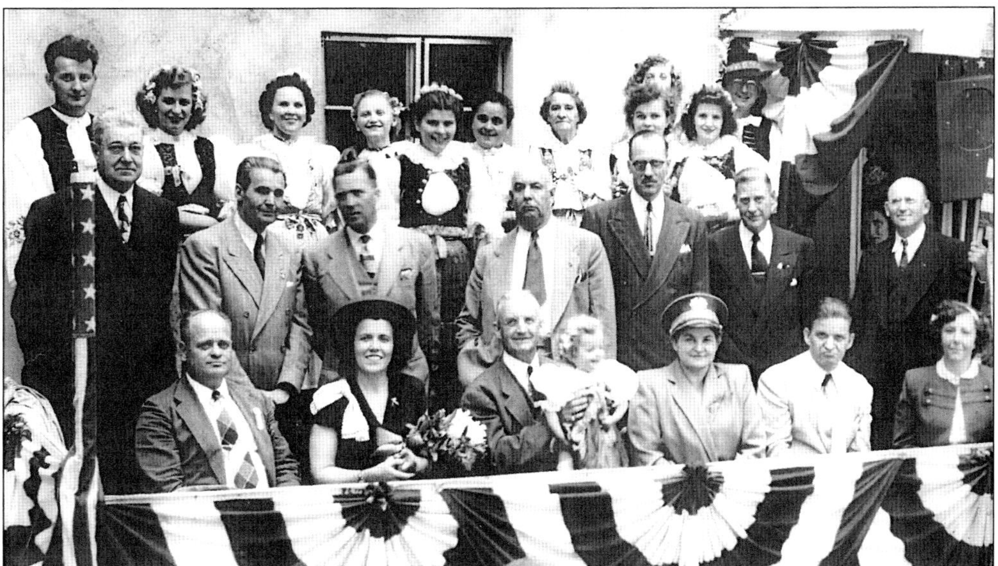

CZECHOSLOVAK GATHERING (*c.* 1946). Assemblyman C. Stanley Stults (at left in the second row) addresses members of the American Czechoslovak Club. Those in native dress and other club officials and guests appear here. They are: (front row) Joe Kokesh, Pauline Galosh Jones, John Meliharek holding his granddaughter Mary Ann, unknown, unknown, and unknown; (middle row) Assemblyman Stults, unknown, unknown, David Lewis, unknown, Bill Mielke, and Martin Stefek; (back row) Steve Hluchy, Betty Valasek, unknown, Anna Vana, unknown, Mary Kovachofsky, Josephine Hustak, unknown, Betty Kavicka Meliharek, Betty Hluchy, and Frank Meliharek. (C. Stults Family-Allen & Stults Collection)

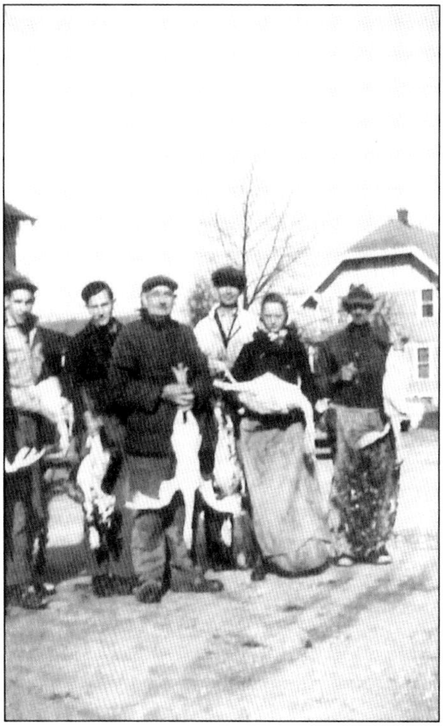

COMPLETED TURKEY PICKING (1946). Homer Staudinger, Richard Anderson, Charles Newman, Levi and Marjorie Lee, and Joe Newman show the results of their turkey picking at the Lee Farm. They used large burlap bags as aprons. Until the late 1940s, chickens and turkeys were sold New York dressed, which means "killed and the feathers plucked." The feet and insides were not touched. Housewives eviscerated the birds after they purchased them. When Dick Lee looked at this photograph recently, he said "If I had turkeys looking like that today, I'd throw them out." (The Lee Family)

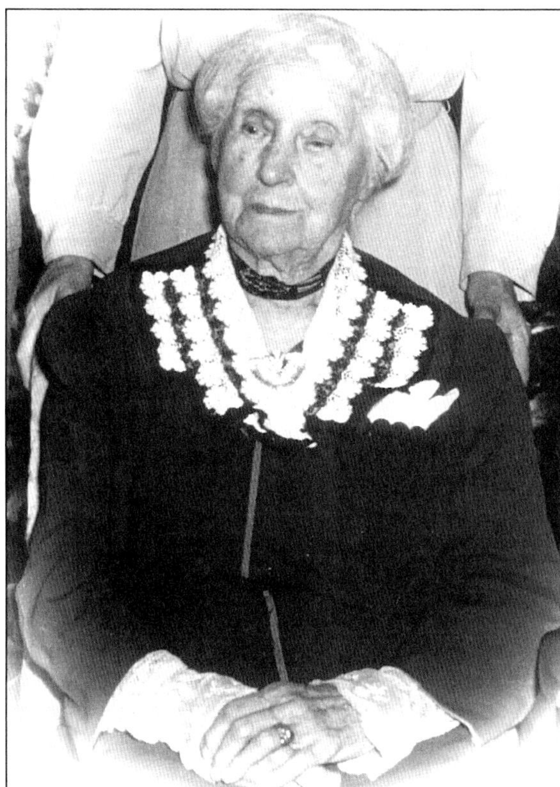

SARAH ANN HOMER THOMPSON (1946). This ninety-eight-year-old lady who was born in Briarly Hill, England, came to the United States in 1907 and settled in Hightstown. The mother of William Homer Thompson, one of the owners of the Hightstown Rug Company, she lived to be 103. (Ernest J. Thompson)

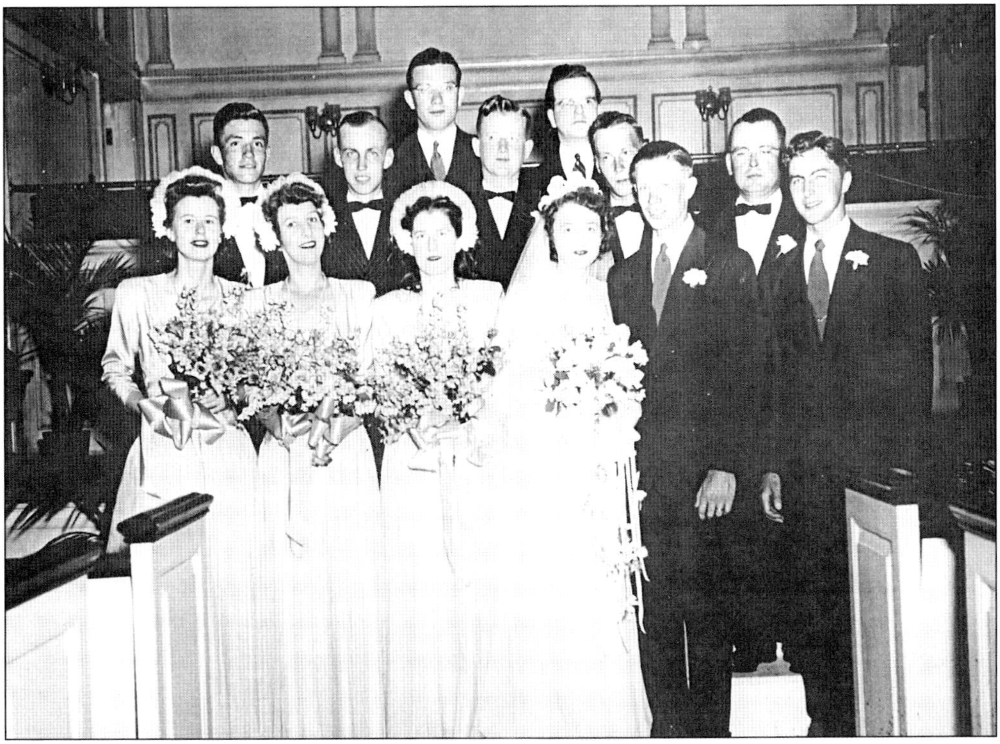

JUNE WEDDING (1947). Lois and Clarence Groendyke's wedding at the First Presbyterian Church had the following participants: (front row) Jean Errickson, Josephine Hutchinson (Coates), Jean Hancock (Hutchinson), and Everett Campbell; (back row) Arthur Danser, Charles Bowers, the Reverend Dave Watermulder, Willis Hancock, the Reverend Stanley Gamebell, and Stanley and Marlin Carson. (Lois Groendyke)

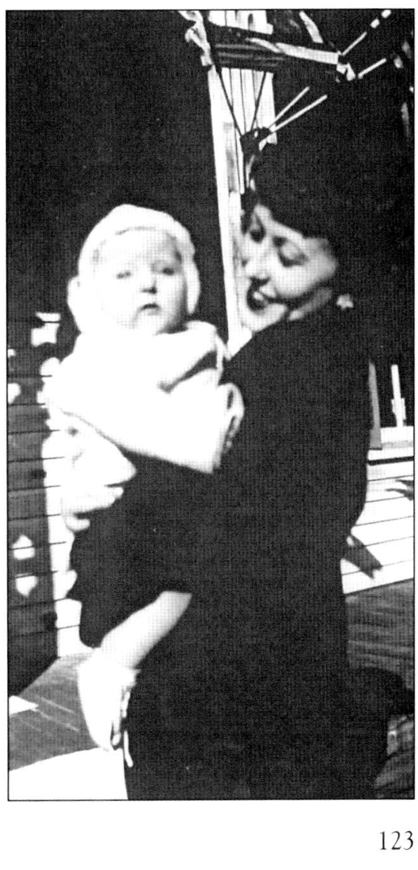

A PROUD, SMILING MOTHER (1945). A. Marie Lanning and her daughter Caroline seem to be enjoying Decoration Day in front of their home at 210 Morrison Avenue. (Cathy Simmons)

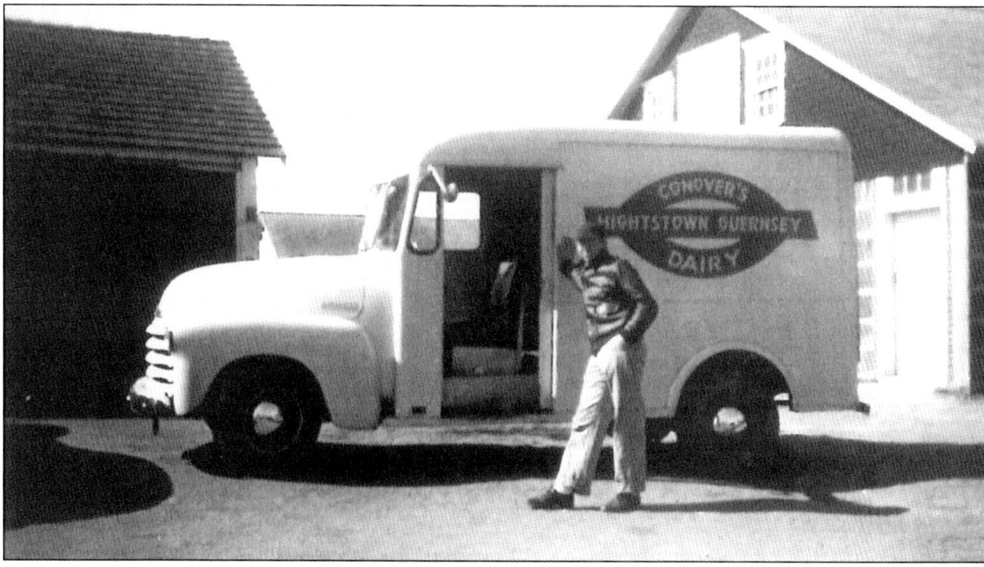

FINISHED MILK DELIVERIES (1948). Clifford H. Conover, son of the founder of Conover's Dairy, leans against the milk delivery truck. (Joan Conover)

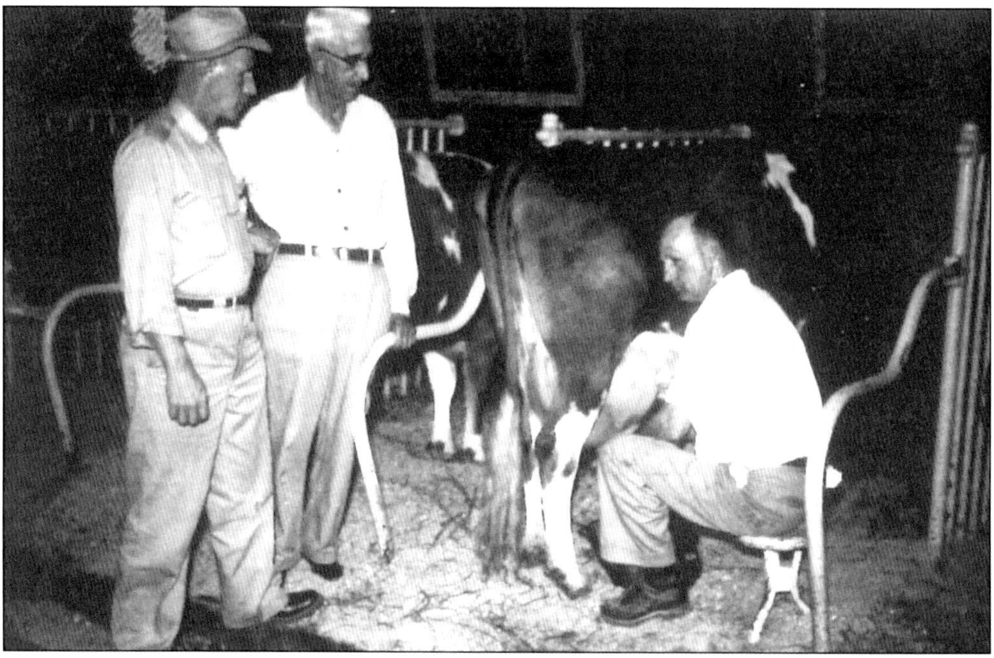

MILKING TIME (1949). Clifford L. Conover (in the center with white hair) and one of the hired hands watch as a cow is being milked at the Conover Dairy Farm. In 1915 at age thirty-one, Clifford purchased a 90-acre farm on Old York Road from James Laird. Eventually, the farm was expanded to about 500 acres through the purchase of adjoining farms. Initially the cash crop was potatoes, but in 1925 Conover purchased sixteen Guernsey cows. The dairy started with two local customers, Dr. Tracy Dawes, DDS, and Dr. George Franklin, MD, who lived on opposite corners of South Street and South Main Street. The number of customers grew rapidly. Milk deliveries were made early each morning, seven days a week, via a Model-T Ford panel truck. The dairy closed in December of 1972. (Joan Conover)

DEY'S DELI (1948). For many years, Alvin Jones Dey (b. 1911) ran this store in the building immediately south of the First Baptist Church. Merchandise on display includes: Mothers Oats, Pablum, Quinlan's Pretzels from Reading, PA, and four kinds of tea—Tetley, White Rose, Salada, and Tenderleaf. (Brenda Dey MacMurray)

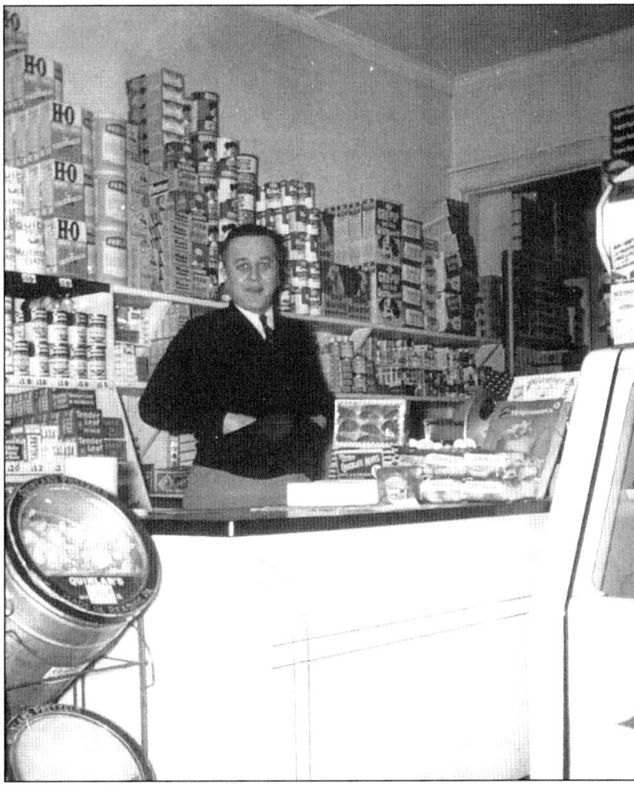

APPREHENSIVE (*c.* 1949). Dr. Harold C. Cox, Sr. treats Lori Liebson of Roosevelt in his office at 208 Stockton Street. (Harold "Skip" Cox)

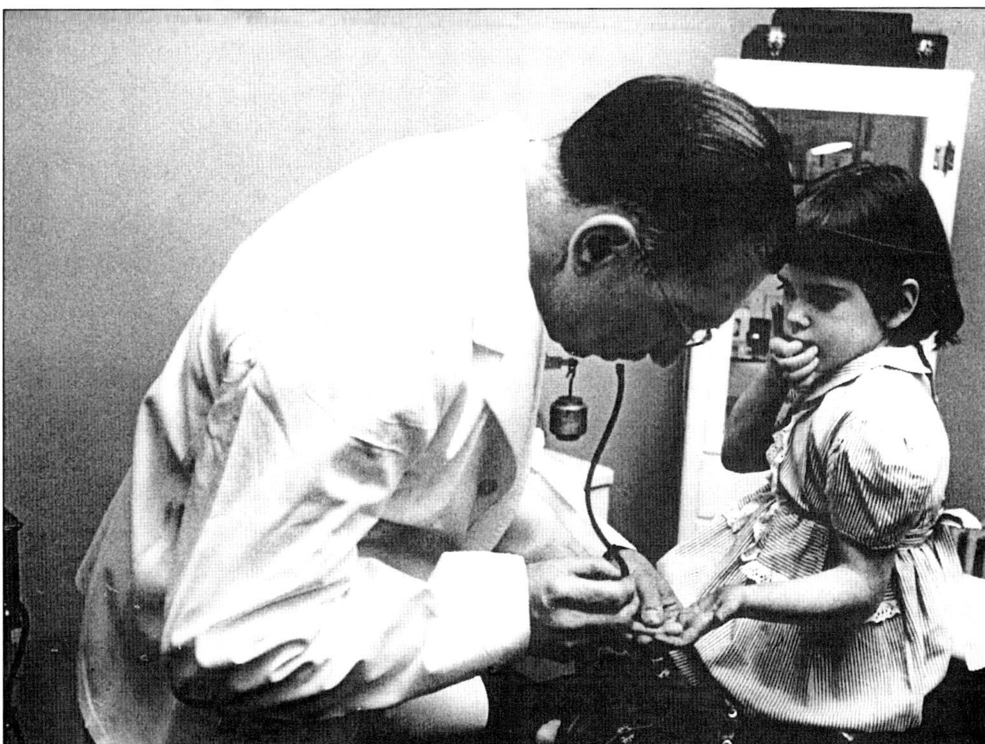

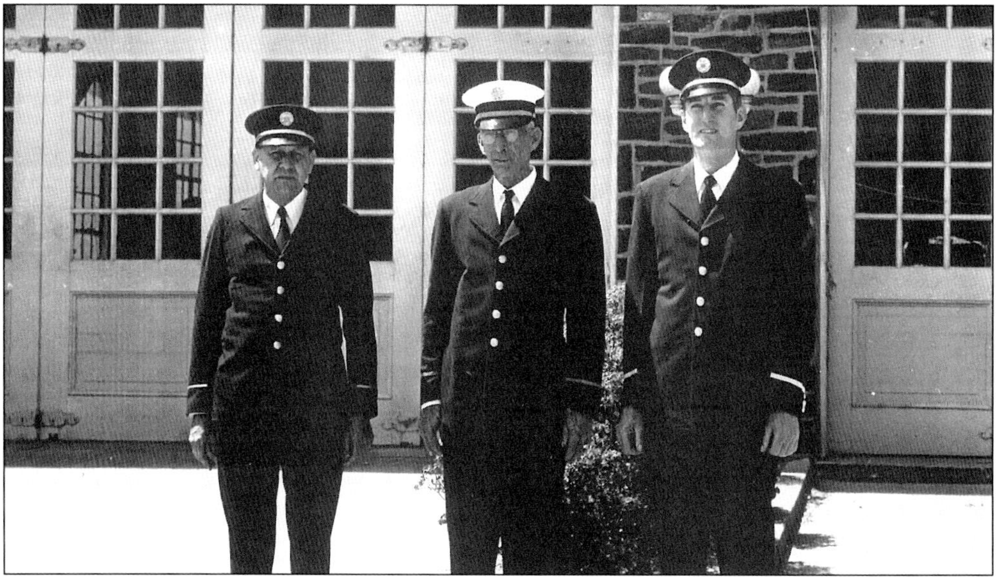

FIRE DEPARTMENT BRASS (1949). In front of the North Main Street firehouse are: Fred Dey (first assistant chief from November 1955 to November 1963), Tom Malone (chief from November 1931 to September 1955), and Fred R. Tornquist, Jr. (second assistant chief from November 1963 to November 1968). (Fred R. Tornquist, Jr.)

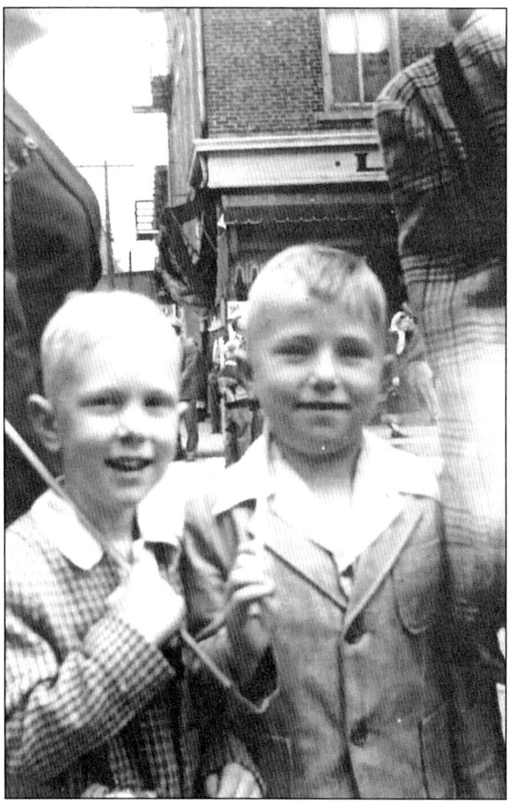

DRESSED FOR THE PARADE (1950). Bob and Bill Hutchinson hold flags over their shoulders as they wait for the Memorial Day parade to pass in front of Luria's Department Store at the corner of Main and Stockton Streets. (Bob Hutchinson)

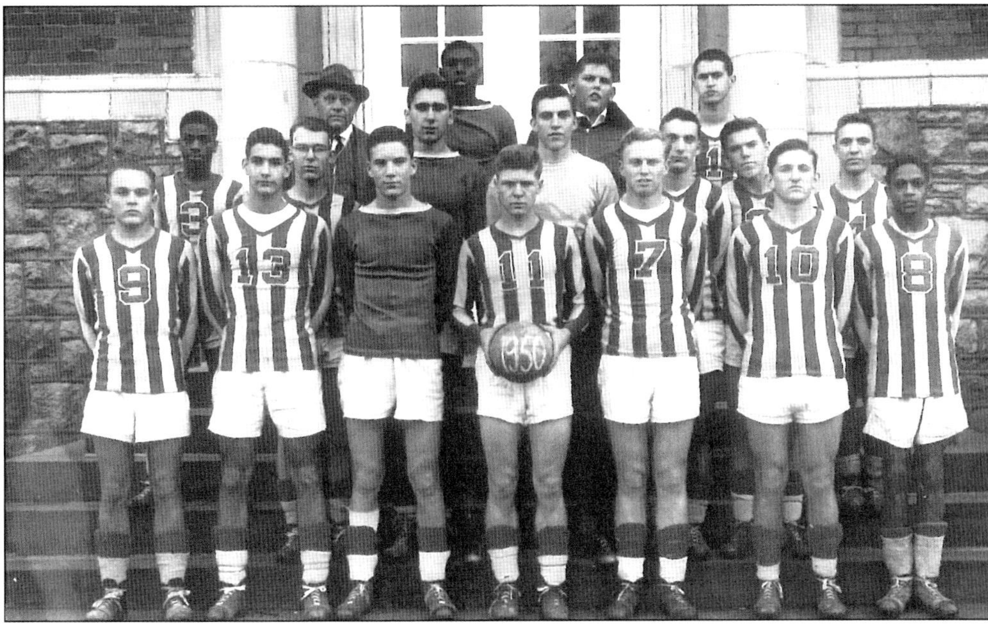

STATE CHAMPIONS (1950). These members of the 1950 Group I New Jersey State Soccer Championship Team, with a 14–1–1 record, include: (front row) Roger Malsbury, Jimmy Russo, John O'Neill, Captain Barry Ivins, Bob Carduner, Bob Lloyd, and Jimmy Muse; (middle row) George Spearman, John Butcher, John Theoharis, Joe Michnisky, Bob Marple, Reggie Ely, and George Deemys; (back row) Coach "Bunny" Hunt, Robert Gunnell, Manager Frank Underhill, and Dave Bunting. (Fred R. Tornquist, Jr.)

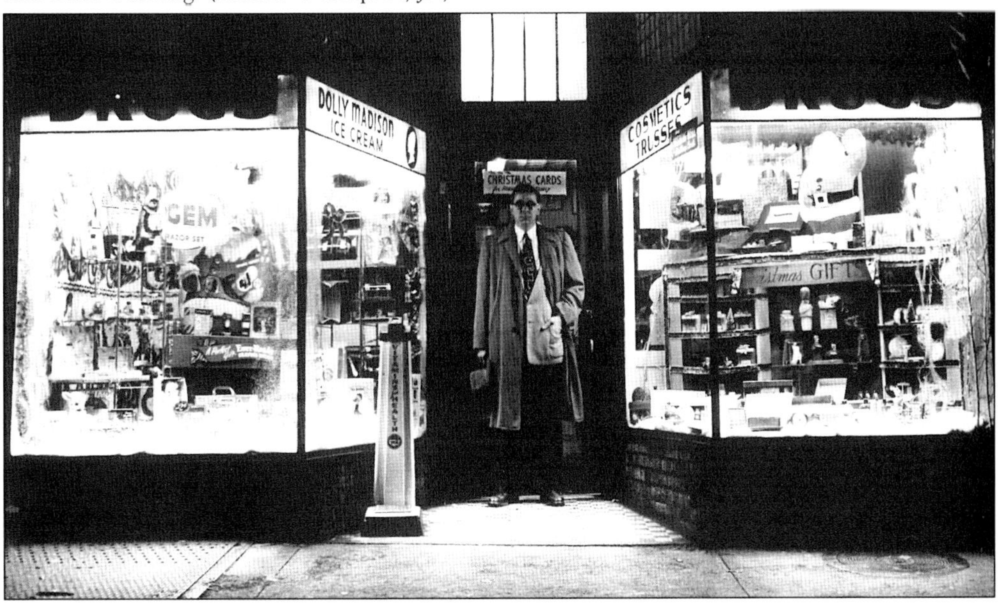

GOLDSTEIN'S (1950). Pharmacist David Goldstein has just closed his Main Street drug store for the evening. For many years, passersby could weigh themselves on the scale conveniently located in the entryway. In 1946, David began working for Mr. Freidman, who owned Hights Pharmacy. Four years later he purchased the drug store and was the proprietor and pharmacist at that location until 1978. (David and Helen Goldstein)

Select Bibliography

Conover, Edna M. "Hightstown—The Past 50 Years." An unpublished paper presented before the Friday Club on January 25, 1946.

Fenity, Leo W. "Portrait of a Country Dairy: Conover's Guernsey Dairy, Inc." Booklet. July 1993.

Geiger, Carl E. *The Peddie School's First Century*. Valley Forge, PA: The Judson Press, 1965.

The Hightstown Gazette (Hightstown, NJ).

Hightstown New Jersey 250th Anniversary 1721–1971. Committee for the 250th Anniversary Celebration, 1971.

Hightstown New Jersey Bicentennial 1721–1921. Official Program. Trenton, NJ: The Smith Press, 1921.

Maxwell, Gertrude. Gertrude Maxwell Papers. Writings and correspondence of Gertrude Applegate Wyckoff Maxwell (1840–1939). Unpublished.

"150th Anniversary of Hightstown Fire Company." Booklet. 1985.

"One Hundredth Anniversary Engine Company, No. l Hightstown, N. J." Booklet. 1935.

Perrine, Calvin H. "Recollections and Inventions." Unpublished manuscript. May 14, 1970.

"Pride in the Past—Planning for the Future, A History of Hightstown and East Windsor Township." Produced by the First National Bank of Hightstown to commemorate its 100th anniversary, September 2, 1970.

The Princeton Recollector (Princeton, NJ).

Rogers, Lloyd W. "Memoirs—An Autobiographical Memoir of Life in Hightstown—1921–1995." Unpublished manuscript.

Rue, Harvey G. "Some Recollections of Hightstown, N. J. Since 1855." An unpublished paper given before the Hightstown Coterie on January 25, 1932.

Stults, (Mrs.) Robert Morrison. "The Romance of 'The Sweetest Story Ever Told,' " *The Etude Music Magazine*, Vol. LV, No. l, pp. 12 and 47. (January 1937).

Sunday Times-Advertiser (Trenton, NJ).

The View of Cranbury (Cranbury, NJ).